# Deconstructing the nation

This book examines the connection between racism and the development of the nation-state in modern France. It raises important questions about the nature of citizenship rights in modern French society and contributes to wider European debates on citizenship. By challenging the myths of the modern French nation, the author opens up the debate on questions of immigration, racism/anti-racism, the nation and citizenship in France to non-French-speaking readers. Until quite recently these matters have largely been ignored by researchers in Britain and the USA. However, European integration has made it essential to look beyond national frontiers. The major part of the analysis concerns the period from the end of the 1960s to the beginning of the 1990s. Yet contemporary developments are placed in a historical context, firstly through a consideration of the construction of the modern question of immigration since the second half of the nineteenth century, and secondly through a survey of political, economic and social developments since 1945. There are analyses of the major debates on nationality in 1987 and the 'headscarf' affair of 1989. Finally, questions of immigration, racism and citizenship are considered within the framework of European integration.

The book will be of interest to all those concerned with questions of immigration, racism/anti-racism and the nation in France. But it also raises wider points which will be of interest to anyone studying racism and state formation.

**Maxim Silverman** lectures in French at the University of Leeds.

## Critical studies in racism and migration
## Edited by Robert Miles
*University of Glasgow*

# Deconstructing the nation

## Immigration, racism and citizenship in modern France

**Maxim Silverman**

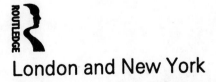

London and New York

First published 1992
by Routledge
11 New Fetter Lane, London EC4P 4EE

Simultaneously published in the USA and Canada
by Routledge
29 West 35th Street, New York, NY 10001

Reprinted 1994

© 1992 Maxim Silverman

Typeset in Baskerville by
Michael Mepham, Frome, Somerset
Printed and bound in Great Britain by
Antony Rowe Ltd, Chippenham, Wiltshire

*British Library Cataloguing in Publication Data*
A catalogue record for this book is available from the British Library

*Library of Congress Cataloging in Publication Data*
A catalog record for this book is available from the Library of Congress

ISBN 0-415-04483-9

# For my parents

# Contents

# Acknowledgements

I wish to thank the following colleagues and friends whose comments and conversation have greatly benefited me in the writing of this book: Etienne Balibar, Zygmunt Bauman, Bryan Cheyette, Colette Guillaumin, Cathie Lloyd, Robert Miles, Véronique de Rudder, John Schwarzmantel, Catherine Wihtol de Wenden. Special thanks to Andrew Rothwell for technical assistance and Robert Miles for his encouragement and help in the production of the manuscript. As always, my greatest debt is to Nina Biehal.

Earlier drafts of the argument expressed here were first published as articles or chapters in Silverman 1988, 1989, 1990a, 1990b, 1991.

All translations of the French are my own except Renan 1990 and Balibar 1991.

# Introduction

In 1989 three female students were excluded from their classes at school in a town near Paris. Their crime was that they refused to remove their Islamic headscarves in class and therefore contravened the secular tradition in French state schools. The affair became a passionate national debate. This debate would have been incomprehensible to outsiders who had not followed events in the years prior to this incident. These were years in which the question of immigration had become politicised and popularised as a problem of non-European immigrants (especially North African) in French society. It would also have been incomprehensible to those who had no knowledge of the secular tradition in France or the development of the modern French republic. They might have wondered how a simple piece of cloth on someone's head could send a whole country into a prolonged frenzy. It would have to be explained that the headscarves were symptoms of a wider crisis in contemporary France. This book attempts to explain the crisis that lies behind the affair of the headscarves.

I will argue that the crisis is above all a national crisis, or rather a crisis of the nation-state. Many of the same aspects of this crisis can be seen in other western democracies today. Yet there are differences and similarities in both the nature and the naming of the crisis. Although questions of migration and racism have been major political issues in a number of countries over the last two decades, the form they have taken has been largely determined by national characteristics and histories. For example, patterns of migration are closely linked to colonial histories; patterns of 'integration' are closely linked to national histories. Governments have often adopted different policies on immigration, and anti-racist movements and movements for human rights have adopted different strategies for struggle.

The prospect of European integration is changing all this. It might be argued (as it is for monetary union, political union and so on) that we do not want uniform practices throughout Europe; that we would prefer to keep our national differences. However, this wish has already been overtaken by events. In recent years governments of the member states of the European Community (EC) have been meeting to harmonise controls of frontiers and to guarantee full rights within the EC only to EC nationals. The future of the eight million or so non-EC nationals resident in EC countries is uncertain. Moreover, racism in Europe affects not only non-EC nationals but minorities of all sorts, irrespective of nationality.

This book is written with European integration very much in mind. In the climate of the construction of the 'new Europe', anti-racist movements and movements for human rights throughout Europe are also thinking differently about rights. As is often the case, it seems easier to harmonise controls than rights. The different national models within which rights have been formulated in the past are barriers to harmonisation today. From the point of view of effective international cooperation between anti-racist movements, it is important that these barriers to understanding be tackled. This book therefore analyses developments in France with a view to breaking down some of the barriers to comprehension.

The problems of understanding and cooperation are considerable, not simply for the mythical outsider who has no knowledge of France at all but even for those who live in neighbouring countries. To a certain extent, the problems are those of different terminology and conceptual framework, although ultimately these differences are determined by historical factors in the formation of nation-states. For example, the major official classification of people in France is in terms of nationality: you are either a national or a foreigner ('étranger'), there being no official and institutional categories to define people once they have French nationality (Dubet 1989b: 24). This is clearly different from the British case where 'ethnic origin' is recognised institutionally (for certain groups) *within* the national community.

This distinction in categorisation poses a real problem for mutual understanding between countries. This is complicated further by the shifting signification of terminology. In France, the official distinction between nationals and foreigners is confused by the popular and political blurring of the terms 'foreigner' and 'immigrant' ('immigré'). Strictly speaking, not all foreigners are immigrants and, conversely, not all immigrants are foreigners. The official category of 'étranger' excludes immigrants who have gained nationality through naturalisation, but includes a considerable number of non-immigrants (for example, children born in France to immigrant parents who have not yet reached the age of majority and with it automatic acquisition of French nationality). In official terms, the important consideration is whether people do or do not have French nationality.

However, these official distinctions between foreigners and immigrants are not always respected. In popular, political and even occasionally official discourse, the category of 'foreigner' can be confused with the term 'immigrant'. In contemporary France, the term 'immigrant' has in turn frequently been used to signify those of non-European origin (or 'appearance'), and specifically North Africans and their children. In other words, a number of distinct categories have become conflated within the term 'immigration' so that what has become known as 'the problem of immigration' can designate specific people, irrespective of their nationality, who are defined as a threat to national unity and national identity.

The term 'immigration' has been used indiscriminately to define vastly different phenomena and groups of people. In fact, 80 per cent of those popularly classified as 'immigrants' have been in France for more than ten years; 23 per cent were born there; 70 per cent of under fifteen-year-olds have never known another country of residence. For those familiar with the British or American experience of institutional recognition of the rights of *communities* rather than simply the rights of *individuals* according to nationality, and the institutionalisation of 'race relations', the use of the word 'immigrant' to define people often born and bred in France might seem baffling. However, the 'race relations' paradigm is equally baffling for many French commentators who regard the institutionalisation of the category of 'race' as a sure way to separate people into distinct communities rather than 'integrate' them, leading to divisions within society according to the recognition of communities rather than cohesion based on individuality, irrespective of origin.

This conception of two distinct models is particularly common in France. As an attempt to depoliticise the headscarf affair, the socialist government of Michel Rocard (1988–91) firmly adopted a policy of 'integration' and created the Council for Integration ('Haut Conseil à l'Intégration') in December 1989. Defining 'integration' at the time of the publication of the first annual report of the Council (February 1991), the President of the Council Marceau Long described it in the following terms:

> There are different conceptions. One is based on the right of ethnic minorities, of communities; this is the concept which has been adopted in the Anglo-Saxon countries but is also prevalent in Europe, notably in Eastern Europe. The other concept is ours, French but also continental, based on individual adhesion.... (Those who talk of communities) are wrong. It's another way of imprisoning people within ghettos rather than affirming their right to opinions as individuals.
>
> (*Libération*, 19 February 1991)

There is clearly a certain amount of truth in this description of the 'two models': the French 'model' founded on the acquisition of rights through individual assimilation within the nation, the British and American 'model' founded on the recognition of differences and special provision for minorities. However, it is misleading when these 'models' are defined in absolutist terms. French history is littered with classifications of groups according to racialised criteria. The continued use today of the term 'French Muslims' ('Français musulmans' or Harkis) to refer to Algerians who fought for France during the Algerian War (1954–62) and who, since their arrival in France during or after the war, have had full French nationality and citizenship status, casts doubt on the individualist and universalist tradition outlined by Marceau Long above. The practice of a number of French local councils of allocating housing or school places according to an ethnic quota system also belies the universalist ideology of French republicanism. More generally, as we have said, although official statistics are based on national criteria (that is, whether one is or is not a French national), the contemporary political and popular discourse of immigration designates specific categories of people according to *racialised* criteria. It is therefore primarily those of North African origin or parentage and blacks from West Africa and the Caribbean who are frequently assumed to be 'the immigrants' (many of whom are in fact French nationals), rather than those of Portuguese, Spanish or Italian origin (many of whom are not French nationals).

On the other hand, the British tradition is not simply one of recognition of differences according to the institutionalisation of the concept of 'race'. Britain also has a powerful tradition of cultural universalism. The Conservative Party election poster of 1983, with the picture of a young black male over the caption 'Labour says he's black. Tories say he's British', makes explicit reference to this tradition (cf. Gilroy 1987: 57–9). The Conservative claim in this poster to colour-free criteria in the definition of nationality is very similar to (and just as misleading as) the familiar republican rhetoric in France used by Marceau Long above, which maintains that French institutions operate only according to individual and 'assimilationist' criteria.

In order to break down barriers to comprehension, there is a need to problematise models which have become stereotyped as polar opposites. The argument in this book will suggest that universalism, assimilation and individualism are not opposites of particularism, difference and collectivity, the former constituting the French model, the latter constituting the Anglo-Saxon model. Instead, these concepts form part of a more complex whole: that of a tension *within* the fabric of western nations. This is not to suggest that there are no substantial national differences in the formulation of questions of migration, racism and rights. But a reappraisal of the conceptual framework of oppositional models might show that, at a deep level of crisis of the western nation-state, the problems are substantially the same.

This book is therefore not a comparative study of different models of immigration and the nation (for example, Britain and France; see Freeman 1979). It makes little reference to the body of research on these issues from the USA, Britain or elsewhere. It is an analysis of the contradictions of the French model and looks specifically at the French discussion of these issues. It will be argued that the French model of the nation and its crisis today are not unique to France but provide a classic picture of the rise and (possible) fall of the older nation-states of the nineteenth century. The psychoanalyst and feminist writer Julia Kristeva has said that 'there is a French national idea which could constitute the *optimal version* of the nation in the contemporary world' (*Le Monde*, 29 March 1991).[1] I think that this is true, providing that this 'version' is seen not as the universalist *as opposed to* the particularist model, but rather as one in which the tension between universalism and particularism is best exemplified. In other words, the French 'version' of the nation is perhaps the clearest manifestation of the contradictions in the formation of all modern nation-states: contradictions which emerge within Enlightenment formulations of the individual and the collectivity.

I will therefore argue that an understanding of the issues of immigration and racism should be grounded in a reappraisal of the contradictions in the modern nation-state. Questions of immigration and racism are not adjuncts to the development of modern nations but a fundamental part of that development. This emphasis means that the argument in this book will not view immigration as separate from (or in opposition to) French society. It does not attempt to fetishise immigration – and therefore dislocate it from the rest of society – through a comprehensive statistical breakdown of numbers of immigrants in France, laws on immigration, rights of immigrants and so on (although aspects of these will be mentioned in the course of the argument).[2] Neither is it an analysis of different 'immigrant' communities in France and their 'interaction' with French society (that is, an analysis of cultural or ethnic relations). It deals not with communities already formed but with the processes by which social relations are historically constructed in terms of communities.

Nor indeed is this book an economic analysis of migration flows and labour patterns. Not that these are considered unimportant matters, and they inevitably figure as well in the course of the argument. However, the framing of the question of immigration exclusively within an economic analysis also tends to dislocate it from the wider contradictions of the national social formation; racism can often be viewed simply as functional within capitalist economies and can consequently be collapsed into considerations of class.[3]

Neither is this book specifically about the rise of the extreme right-wing Front National (FN) in the 1980s. The 'demonisation' of its leader Jean-Marie Le Pen by anti-racist movements during the 1980s failed to locate the complex nature (and causes) of contemporary racism (cf. Taguieff 1991). Racism is a 'total social phenomenon' (Balibar 1991: 75); as such it needs to be situated within the wider social complex.

The discussion in this book therefore seeks to place questions of immigration and racism at the centre of the modern nation-state rather than confine them to the margins. By situating recent developments in France in the context of a historical perspective on the modern nation-state, it attempts to show how questions of immigration and racism highlight the problematic and ambivalent nature of the nation form. The ambivalence of the discourse of nation traverses social relations and runs, like a fault-line, across right- and left-wing politics, and across the state and civil society. It cuts across class affiliations and creates numerous contradictions in the ideologies of parties. At the time of the headscarf affair political opponents often shared the same argument whilst political colleagues fell out; some feminists lined up with political enemies. These contradictions can only be understood within the context of the more profound ideologies of the French republican nation, which do not necessarily respect class, party or any other affiliations.

My discussion of the contradictions and ambivalence of the nation form and the problematic nature of the dichotomy between universalism and particularism will depend to a large extent on a reconsideration of the concepts of 'race', 'nation' and 'culture'. It is therefore necessary to clarify briefly the key terms in this reappraisal. Discussion of the concept of 'race' has traditionally focused on the way it has used a *biological* discourse to distinguish between 'different' populations. On the other hand, discussion of the modern concept of 'nation' has traditionally focused on the way it has used a *cultural* discourse to distinguish between 'different' national communities. Hence a dichotomy has been constructed between concepts of 'race' and 'nation' and, correspondingly, between biological and cultural characteristics. This has also led to the firm distinction, by some theorists, between concepts of racism and nationalism (for example, Anderson 1983: 136).

However, the differences between the concepts of 'race' and 'nation', between racism and nationalism, and between biological and cultural definitions of communities are not necessarily so clear-cut. As a number of British commentators on the so-called 'new racism' have shown (Barker 1981; Centre for Contemporary Cultural Studies 1982), the discourse of cultural absolutism and difference to define the nation (that is, an essentialist definition of the national community in which differences are fixed and naturalised) can act in a racist manner to subordinate and exclude others in a similar way to the discourse of biological determinism and hierarchy. Yet the term 'new racism' to define contemporary expressions of racism based on cultural absolutism rather than biological hierarchy might be misleading (cf. Miles 1989), since cultural definitions of the nation have for long had the potential to act in this way. This is especially true in the French case where a biological discourse of 'race' has always been less prominent in discourses of exclusion than a cultural discourse of 'nation'. Indeed, sometimes it is not at all easy to locate precisely the frontier between biological and cultural characteristics; phenotypical features, intellectual ability, cultural characteristics and biological determinism can be articulated in the classification of groups.

The argument in this book will consider not the differences between concepts of 'race' and 'nation' and between racism and nationalism but rather the articulations between them in the development of the modern nation-state. The idea of a common and trans-historical culture defining the French nation has been a powerful means of racialising the 'French people'. I shall use the term racialisation to refer to the process by which social relations are conceived as structured according to common biological and/or cultural absolutist characteristics. In which case, it can be applied to a discourse of 'nation' which employs a fixed concept of cultural difference as well as to the overt discourse of 'race'. In other words, cultural difference can become racialised when that difference is conceived in immutable and essentialist terms. In modern French history, the cultural-absolutist concept of the national community has been as responsible for the conception of a natural, organic, homogeneous and exclusive collectivity as any discourse based overtly on the concept of 'race'. It is precisely the ambivalence of the culturalist concept of the nation which lies at the heart of racism in France (see Chapter 1).

In my definition, the term racialisation assumes that the concepts of 'race' and 'nation' are social and imagined constructs; that is, they are historically situated and historically variable concepts for the definition of social groups. Racialised classifications of people can be both a means of domination and exclusion of social groups (in which case racism can be the effect of racialisation) and a means of struggle and resistance by groups against domination and exclusion. Examples of the use of a racialised discourse for the mobilisation and empowerment of discriminated groups are anti-colonial struggles (Fanon 1952; Memmi 1985) and civil rights movements (Black Power in the USA in the 1960s). In France, the racialisation of politics in the 1970s and 1980s was, similarly, a means of both exclusion of and resistance by certain minority groups.

Although I will be using the concept of racialisation to refer principally to the contemporary period in France, this should not imply that French society was not racialised before. As I have mentioned above, the central argument in this book sets out to show the continual presence of an ambivalent discourse of culture in the formation of the modern French nation-state; its effect has been both to preach inclusion according to universalist criteria and to practise exclusion through racialising the French community and its Other. However, this discourse is historically variable. My argument here considers the way in which the contemporary racialisation of the issue of immigration articulates a number of diverse elements in the post-colonial era.

The major part of the analysis therefore concerns the contemporary period, from the end of the 1960s to the present day (Chapters 3, 4 and 5). Yet, throughout the text, contemporary developments are placed in a historical context, especially through a consideration of the construction of the modern question of immigration since the second half of the nineteenth century (Chapter 1), and through a survey of political, economic and social developments since 1945 (Chapter 2). Finally, I situate the questions of immigration, racism and citizenship within the framework of European integration (Chapter 6).

If the French sociological tradition on questions of immigration and racism has lacked a detailed class analysis, then perhaps the British discussion has tended to overlook the importance of the nation (cf. Allen and Macey 1990). This book considers the relationship (or articulation) between immigration, and concepts of 'race' and 'nation' in the development of modern France. The crisis of the nation today in France has much to teach us about the crisis of the nation form in general, and the problems of democracy and citizenship in the 1990s.

# Chapter 1

# Immigration and the nation-state

> People like to say: revolution is beautiful, it is only the terror
> arising from it which is evil. But this is not true. The evil is
> already present in the beautiful, hell is already contained in the
> dream of paradise and if we wish to understand the essence of
> hell we must examine the essence of the paradise from which it
> originated.
>
> (Kundera 1983: 234)

## THE QUESTION OF IMMIGRATION

Immigration is a fundamental feature of the formation of modern
France. Of the major western countries only North America and
Canada have experienced a more profound immigration than
France. Three large waves of immigration have occurred over the
last hundred years: the end of the nineteenth century saw an influx
of Belgians and Italians, the 1920s saw the arrival of Poles, Czechs
and Slavs, and the post-war period has seen an immigration from
North and West Africa as well as a large Portuguese immigration
in the 1960s. In the 1930s, the number of immigrants in France
as a proportion of the total population was roughly the same as
today – about 7.5 per cent of the total population. One in every
four French nationals has a parent or grandparent who is/was not
French.

Only recently have these facts been brought to light. Until the
1970s immigration had been a marginal interest for researchers.
School history books did not teach the importance of immigration
in the development of modern France (Gaspard and Servan-
Schreiber 1985: 185). Immigration was not deemed worthy of
serious consideration, either in terms of its effect on society or as

a phenomenon in its own right. Periodically, politicians and planners had debated questions of immigration (for example, at the end of the nineteenth century, during the 1930s and immediately after the Second World War). Yet these issues were confined, in the main, to articles and documents of a specialist nature, written either by demographers or economic planners. Only two major scientific studies of immigration had appeared before the 1960s (Mauco 1932; Girard and Stoetzel 1953). Historians had largely failed to reflect on these issues in their discussion of the modern history of France.

The contemporary interest in questions of immigration roughly corresponds to the change in immigration policy at the end of the 1960s. With the introduction of the first measures of immigration control in the modern period and moves towards a social policy of integration of immigrants came a wave of research projects on the question of immigration. If, formerly, immigration had been confined, in the main, to the specialised fields of demographic and technocratic planning, it was now at the intersection of a far more diverse disciplinary interest: that of sociology, geography, history, psychology, ethnology, economics, law and others. At the same time, immigration became the subject of a number of official reports which reflected the wider historical, social, psychological and ethnological approaches to immigration along with the economic and demographic perspectives. By the early 1980s most official publications on immigrants in France discussed – if only briefly – the history of immigration in France (see, for example, INSEE 1983: 6–7; Secrétariat d'Etat Chargé des Immigrés 1983: 5), and had sections on aspects of culture and social problems.

The change from an economic to a social/cultural perspective on immigration parallels the change in focus from immigrants as a simple labour force ('les travailleurs immigrés' or 'la main-d'oeuvre étrangère') to immigrants as social actors or victims, from the 'first' to 'the second generation' ('la seconde génération' or 'les jeunes issus de l'immigration'), from immigrants as single men on temporary work and residence permits ('une immigration temporaire') to families settled in France ('une immigration sédentarisée'). In the 1980s 'les jeunes' became the major symbol of the new focus on the 'problems' of installation and integration. Both official reports and research at large reflected (or constructed?) this new perspective on immigration. In the 1980s there were official studies on the problems of immigrant youth in French society (Marangé and Lebon 1982), delinquency and identity crises of immigrant youth (Malewska-Peyre 1982), immigrant youth in the schools (Berque 1985) and so on.

It is important to consider why the issue of immigration should have passed swiftly from the margins to the centre of political debate and theoretical and empirical research. The switch in focus and terminology outlined above is symptomatic of this shift. This will be considered further in later chapters. However, for the moment let us consider not why immigration has become politicised and analysed differently over the last twenty years but rather how immigration has been treated during this time of change.

I do not intend to survey the mass of recent research on immigration in France (for three extensive surveys of this nature, see Sayad 1984a; Clavairolle 1987; Dubet 1989a). However, it is useful to outline the broad framework within which the question of immigration has been approached in recent years. In the most recent of the surveys mentioned above entitled *Immigrations: qu'en Savons-nous?*, the sociologist François Dubet situates immigration at the centre of three major social processes: the first is *integration*, by which Dubet means the functional role played by immigrants in France ('the place to which they are assigned, basically their "function" within a wider setting'); the second is *assimilation*, by which he means mechanisms of cultural identification ('the cultural dimensions of the process of immigration and the cultural and social differences established between immigrant groups and those who welcome them'; the third is that of *national identification*, and questions of *citizenship* and *political participation*. Dubet suggests that these three processes – which he reduces schematically to economic, cultural and political/sociological processes – provide the major theoretical perspectives governing research on immigration in the social sciences (Dubet 1989a: 7).

One might argue with the terminology employed by Dubet (for example, the distinction he makes between integration and assimilation). Yet his survey is a good description of the conceptual framework within which immigration in France has become circumscribed. He points out that studies on immigration are invariably a mixture of these three approaches rather than confined to any one approach. As I noted in the introduction, there are considerable differences between the French and the British conceptual frameworks for the analysis of questions of immigration. Not only is there no substantial tradition of class-based analysis in France, but there is significantly a complete absence of the 'race relations' perspective developed in Britain (cf. Banton 1967; Rex 1983). These differences are largely determined by the respective national and colonial histories of the two countries.

The French conceptual framework (defining official approaches and sociological research) is heavily dependent on the distinction between French nationals and foreigners (rather than that between 'ethnic minorities' and the majority), and on questions of culture rather than the concept of 'race'. Yet to suggest that all French research falls into the dualistic pattern of the 'French/foreigners' approach (often collapsed into a dichotomy between the French and 'immigrants') would be as erroneous as to suggest that all British research is of the problematic 'race relations' variety. Misunderstandings between the two countries are often a result of just such stereotyping. Recently in France, there have been as many critiques of the dualism of the 'French/immigrants' approach as there have of the 'race relations' approach in Britain. We will return to this issue later in this chapter.

However, in both countries dualism often has the tendency to slip back into the analysis, despite the conscious warnings against the resulting stereotyping and essentialising of communities. For example, in his comments on the work he is surveying, Dubet suggests that neither French society, on the one hand, nor immigrants, on the other, should be considered, respectively, as unified groups defined by clearly circumscribed and homogeneous cultures (Dubet 1989a: 48). Nor should immigrants be seen simply as passive victims of processes of economic, cultural and political exclusion for they are actively engaged as actors in the evolution and transformation of these processes (Dubet 1989a: 7). These are both important rectifications to some of those studies which situate the relationship between 'host society' and immigrants in simplistic dualistic terms of domination/subordination.

Yet this welcome call for a more nuanced approach to the question of immigration is at times contradicted by the type of dualism (even essentialism) that he is warning against. Dubet states:

It is important to say that immigrants are torn between two cultural and social worlds, that they wish (as is only normal) to

enter into the new world without losing their identity, to trans-
form themselves whilst remaining faithful to themselves.

(1989a: 59)

It is difficult to see what 'their identity' was before becoming split,
or what is meant by 'whilst remaining faithful to themselves'. These
expressions reinforce the dualism of the two groups ('two cultural
and social worlds') and seem to imply an essentialist concept of
identity. There have been numerous analyses of the identity crises
of children born in France of immigrant parents according to their
position 'between two cultures' or 'between two worlds' (see for
example UNESCO 1983), frequently presented in terms of a
dichotomy between the 'traditional' culture of home and family
and the 'modern' world of school and French social life.

Furthermore, although aware of the ethnocentric connotations
of the concepts of assimilation and integration, Dubet seems to
accept their analytical validity more or less unquestioningly. However, the dichotomy described above and many of the terms (like
assimilation and integration) used to construct such dichotomies
are not unproblematic. Immigration is not simply the point of
intersection of two cultural communities but rather the point of
intersection of fundamental aspects of the national/social (and
international) complex of France today.

This not only implies questioning the dichotomy between the
French and immigrants. It also means questioning other binary
oppositions related to the whole debate which obscure the full
complexity of social relations today. For example, when the question of immigration became a major political issue in the early
1980s, it was not infrequently framed in terms of a 'for or against'
perspective, or, more generally, in terms of the polarised opposites
of racism and anti-racism. A number of books demonstrated the
importance of immigration in the development of the French
economy, French society and the French nation (see Ben Jelloun
1984; Cordeiro 1984; Stasi 1984; Gaspard and Servan-Schreiber
1985). Others saw in the recent migration flows from North Africa
a fundamental break with previous patterns of immigration to
France (mainly European), in order to demonstrate the threat
posed by immigration to the French economy, French society and
the French nation (see Griotteray 1984; Le Gallou 1985). Analysis
of immigration – and political and public opinion at large –

appeared to become polarised between the 'for' and 'against' approaches, and 'immigration' became a party political football.

However, although the debate was constructed as a struggle between opposites, the two tendencies were more like doubles in which one was a mirror image of the other. So intolerance is opposed by tolerance, an exclusive community is opposed by an inclusive community, a false equality is opposed by a true equality, and so on. Racism became reduced to a question of intolerance (the remedy for which would therefore be more tolerance) or irrationality (the remedy for which would be more rationality) or exclusion based on origins (the remedy for which would be a greater degree of assimilation or integration) and so on.

Immigration can represent both the liberal republic and the threat to the liberal republic; it is the embodiment of France's capacity for assimilation and proof of a break-down in assimilation; it is the embodiment of pluralism and proof of the impossibility of pluralism. It has become the ambivalent site of struggle over apparently polarised models of republican France. In the 1970s, there were major debates linking immigration with questions of modernisation of the economy and questions of social security. Immigration was represented as both the embodiment of modernisation and progress – without which the post-war economic reconstruction of France could not have taken place (Cordeiro 1984) – and the reason for the slow rate of modernisation, since North African immigrants were commonly associated with a backward, peasant and pre-industrial society; it was both of benefit to the social security system (Le Pors 1976) and a drain on it (Icart 1976). This 'for' and 'against' paradigm was already apparent at the beginning of the 1970s. As Pierre and Paulette Calame pointed out, 'for some the foreign worker is a bottomless pit for social welfare, for others a source of perpetual benefit for France' (1972: 54). Immigrants were seen in purely functional terms: they made the economy and the welfare state work either more effectively or less effectively. Their status as a *separate* labour force or presence in the welfare system was accepted more or less without question. As the historian René Galissot has remarked, 'even if the devalorisation of immigrants is challenged they are still considered in the same light; even when repatriation is opposed, immigration is still seen as a phenomenon that must be managed more efficiently' (1985a: 62).

'Pro-immigrant' anti-racism invariably followed the consensus agenda on immigration and merely took the opposite view. So, whether it was the economy or social security, the fertility of immigrant couples or the delinquency of immigrant youth, or the 'problem' of illegal immigration ('immigration clandestine'), the terms of reference were the same; all that separated the two 'sides' was their 'for' or 'against' posture. Anti-racism became trapped in the argument around the legitimacy or illegitimacy of immigration (Sayad 1986). Pierre-André Taguieff has noted that 'anti-racism has too often settled for a simple inversion: for the catastrophe vision of immigration it has simply substituted the vision of immigration as a "chance for France"' (Taguieff 1989: 98). The response to a pseudo-scientific demographic survey in 1985 published in *Figaro-Magazine* (October 26) entitled 'Will we still be French in thirty years?' – which 'proved' that there would be nearly thirteen million non-European foreigners in France by the year 2015 – closely followed the pattern outlined by Taguieff: the Minister for Social Affairs, Georgina Dufoix, published shortly afterwards a counter-dossier criticising the scientific validity of these demographic projections yet implicitly accepted the logic of 'the numbers game' in the discussion of immigration.

Hence discussion of immigration was frequently trapped within the binary oppositions of inclusion and exclusion, assimilation (or integration) and repatriation, or entangled within the ambivalent concept of cultural difference. Anti-racism moved from the negative images of the 1970s (immigrant as victim) to the positive images of the early 1980s (immigrant as success or as social actor). Rarely were voices heard which challenged the dualist framing of the debate around immigration and attempted to situate immigration within the more complex totality of the modern national/social formation (however, see the excellent analyses of Abdelmalek Sayad).

Although still beset by some of the same problems of definition and approach, the question of immigration in the mid-1980s also became the site of a wide-ranging and passionate debate about the French nation-state, national identity and issues of citizenship. This body of research would fall under the third of Dubet's categories, that of political and sociological processes. A number of the texts mentioned above also deal with aspects of these questions. Yet others extended the debate significantly to engage in a reappraisal of the history and structures of the French nation. If not entirely absent from the British debate on immigration and racism (see, for example, Gilroy 1987; Miles 1987a, 1987b), the 'national question' has nevertheless been only peripheral to these discussions. The recent work that has been done on the nation (see Nairn 1977; Anderson 1983; Gellner 1983; Samuel 1989; Hobsbawm 1990) has not, on the whole, emerged from considerations of immigration.

In France, on the other hand, the rediscovery of the importance of immigration in the making of modern France has highlighted aspects of republican France which have for long gone unquestioned. The historian Gérard Noiriel (1988a) maintains that it is precisely the model of the nation upon which republican France is founded that has led to the historical amnesia concerning the role of immigration in the development of French society. He suggests that the ideas of assimilation, uniformity and universality of the French model of the nation – 'la République une et indivisible' – have been crucial in masking ethnic, regional and other differences. The historiography of France has traditionally emphasised the homogeneity of the nation rather than its differences. This was very different to the national historiography of that other great country of immigration, the United States of America. The idea of the 'melting pot' acknowledges the importance of an amalgamation of different groups in the formation of the nation.

Recent studies of the nation and its historiography have been an important contextualisation of questions of immigration. By pointing up the centralising and assimilationist tendencies of the French nation-state, they have explained how the dichotomy between the French and immigrants came about: the juridical and political structures established during the nineteenth century institutionalised the distinction between the national and the non-national and did not recognise any sub-divisions of these categories. Furthermore, this contextualisation of questions of immigration implies that immigration as such should not be the object of study but rather the French nation-state which has framed the question of immigration in a particular way (cf. Oriol et al. 1985). Noiriel (1988b: 6) puts it like this: 'instead of seeing immigration as a phenomenon which is exterior to "our" history, we should see it as a problem which is an internal constitutive part of that history'.

It is not a question of providing an 'alternative' history of France alongside a 'traditional' history; it is more a question of re-evaluating national history from within, that is, questioning the assumptions and determinations upon which national historiography is founded. This approach questions the 'common-sense' notion of the unity and homogeneity of the nation and of what Raphael Samuel has termed, in relation to Britain, the notion of 'continuous national history' (Samuel 1989). 'France' and 'immigration', 'the French' and 'immigrants' are not opposites but part of a more complex whole.

However, the reappraisal of the formation of the nation and national historiography is itself not unproblematic. Here too myth is not absent (though could it be otherwise since historiography and myth are partners in the construction of the past?). In a number of works on the nation written in the 1980s the homogenising and unifying force of that brand of revolutionary French republicanism known as Jacobinism is stripped away to reveal a plural and diverse France underneath. In his ambitious but unfinished history of France, Fernand Braudel devotes a long section to the diversity of France (1986: 27–107). He quotes Yves Florenne (p. 30) who challenges the famous Jacobin slogan 'la France une et indivisible' by suggesting that France is 'one and divisible' (*Le Monde*, 9 April 1981).[1] Hervé le Bras and Emmanuel Todd (1981) also talk of the diversity of France which has survived the unifying process of industrialisation (p. 7). Bruno Etienne (1989) highlights the pluralism of France in order to challenge the concept of a monolithic French history, culture and identity.

The other side to this approach is that which sees Jacobinism as destructive of all differences in its construction of a unified and centralised nation-state (Weber 1976; Coulon 1979). In a sense, these approaches are two sides of the same coin. They are both critiques of the centralising ethos of Jacobinism from a more pluralist perspective. These studies have all challenged the myth of the historical unity of the French nation-state. Yet this type of historiography of the nation tends to be based on a dichotomy between a centralising and assimilationist Jacobinism, on the one hand, and the existence of minorities, on the other, as if these are separate and autonomous entities. In other words, analysis of the nation of this sort often objectifies the state and minorities and posits an opposition between them. It seems to me that there are problems with this approach:

(i) it rests on the assumption that the identity and culture of minorities *precede* the act of nation-building and are demolished by, or persist in spite of, the drive for uniformity instituted through the state. Yet just as 'nations as a natural, God-given way of classifying men, as an inherent though long-delayed political destiny, are a myth' (Gellner 1983: 48–9), so too should it be recognised that the inherent destiny of minorities is also a myth. Their 'essence' and 'roots' are as dependent on a retrospective unity as are those of the nation. The frontiers (both geographical and metaphorical) defining the nation-state and minorities are produced at the same time and by the *same* process.

(ii) it rests on the assumption that assimilation (of the centralising state) and difference (ethnic, regional and so on) are opposites, even that they represent two distinct models of the nation.[2] The fact that they are frequently seen as opposites is the cause of many problems today.

Assimilation and difference have been constructed as polar opposites; however, the reality might be more complex. Furthermore, this dualist historiography of the nation has very clear repercussions for the question of immigration today, since contemporary policy and debate on immigration are trapped in the paradigm of assimilation and difference. This dichotomy needs to be thoroughly reappraised in a way that goes far beyond questioning the opposition between 'the French' and 'immigrants'. At the heart of the modern project of nation-building is not the opposition between but the ambivalence of assimilation and difference. This process becomes clearer if, instead of accepting too quickly the 'two models' theory of the nation, we question the frontiers between them.

## THE TWO MODELS OF THE NATION

In France the Revolution is commonly seen as the triumph of a new concept of the nation. Armed with the enlightenment concepts of reason, will and individualism, the Revolution established the nation as a voluntary association or contract between free individuals. This concept of the nation triumphed over the other major model for the formation of modern nations, that of the concept of a predetermined community bound by blood and heredity. The dichotomy between what one might call the contractual and the ethnic models of the nation is often presented as an opposition between the *universalist* ideas of the French Enlightenment and the *particularist* ideas of German romanticism (whose raison d'être is not reason but emotion, not individualism but the

concept of the 'volk', not contracts but origins). Hence the opposition between the two models is often constructed as an opposition
between the French and German concepts of the nation.

This dichotomy is at the heart of Ernest Renan's famous lecture
at the Sorbonne in 1882 entitled 'What is a nation?'. The importance of this text in theories and discussions of the nation (not
simply in France) cannot be overestimated. Renan's description of
the two models has often been accepted unquestioningly, no
matter what one's position on his preference for the contractual
model ('a daily plebiscite' in his much-quoted words). Yet the
ambiguities of Renan's text are a key to the confusion surrounding
paradigms of the nation.

In fact Renan proposes to clarify matters, which he says remain
confused, by distinguishing between 'race' and nation. 'In what
ways does the principle of nationality differ from that of races?' he
asks (1990: 12). He then eliminates 'race', religion, language and
geographical frontiers as suitable criteria for the foundation and
legitimising of nations; nations are formed, instead, through the
association of individuals who voluntarily affirm their shared and
common past and future. Yet if his conclusion is firmly on the side
of the contract and human will, his imagery speaks a very different
language. He talks of the eighteenth century as a return to the
spirit of antiquity in the way in which the words 'fatherland' and
'citizen' recovered their former meaning;[3] he compares this process with the attempt to 'restore to its original identity a body from
which one had removed the brain and the heart' (1990: 13); he
calls the nation 'a soul, a spiritual principle' (1990: 19); he talks of
ancestors, of the heroic past of glory, sacrifice and suffering, of the
past in the present and determining the future ('we are what you
were; we will be what you are') (1990: 19). This is not the imagery
of the rational Enlightenment; it is the imagery of romanticism.

One problem here is the notion of a dichotomy between rationalism and romanticism in the first place. In fact, the division is far
more problematic. An analysis of Renan's lecture shows that his
concept of the nation is informed by ideas of the spirit and
tradition. Much of the imagery he uses is in keeping with that of
the so-called Germanist tradition. It is true that Renan's imagery
is not that of a biologistic essentialism but it often seems to verge
on a cultural essentialism or absolutism. It is precisely Renan's
rejection of biologism and his thorough critique of the notion of
the pure race that have led commentators to classify his theory of

the nation as the opposite of the 'racial' theory of the nation. Yet cultural absolutism can also be grounds for racist exclusion. As I have already suggested, in the history of modern France the tradition of biological racism has probably been less prominent than that of a national/cultural racism (or perhaps, more appropriately, a cultural/racist nationalism).

This is not to suggest that culture is a euphemism for the concept of 'race' or that Renan's theory of the nation is implicitly based on racist criteria. It is to suggest, instead, that the concept of culture in Renan's text is highly ambivalent. It is true, as Alain Finkielkraut points out, that Renan rejects the particularist, 'volksgeist' concept of culture when he invokes 'the spirit of Goethe' and says 'before French culture, German culture, Italian culture there is human culture' (Finkielkraut 1987: 46). Yet it is also true that his reference to the nation as 'a spiritual principle' invokes the counter-revolutionary discourse informed by the romanticism of Herder. 'Culture' slides easily, almost imperceptibly, between an essentialist and voluntarist perspective, a fact which Finkielkraut's dualist approach to the 'two models' never broaches.[4] When, at the turn of the century, the racist nationalist Maurice Barrès proceeded to appropriate Renan's discourse on the amputation of Alsace-Lorraine by Germany (1870), but from an essentialist rather than the contractual perspective on the nation, Finkielkraut interprets this as a reversal of Renan's views. Yet, far from being a reversal, the position of Barrès is deeply informed by aspects (especially the metaphorical aspects) of Renan's discourse on the nation. It is these very aspects which underpin the national racism of the anti-Dreyfusards, Action Française and even Vichy.[5] It is of little surprise that Maurice Barrès could claim that Renan was an ancestor of Action Française and that Renan can easily be mobilised in support of today's national racism (see Griotteray 1984: 130).

Prior to his 'conversion' to the contractual theory of the nation, Renan had indeed held views based explicitly on racist theories. He argued that the two noblest races were the Semitic and Aryan races but the former was inferior as it was associated with religion and the past, whilst the latter was associated with scientific and artistic genius and the future (Poliakov 1977: 15–16). Renan had also annotated Gobineau's famous L'Inégalité des Races Humaines (1853) and been inspired by it (Sternhell 1977: 120). Yet even then Renan's 'Semites' (just as Gobineau's 'working and rural populations') – both of whom were characterised as specific 'races' – were defined 'not so much according to physical characteristics, as we now believe, but according to common social characteristics which distinguished them from other groups' (Guillaumin 1972: 261). Cultural and social traits were therefore the major determinants of differences of 'race' in the development of theories of 'race' in the middle of the nineteenth century.

In fact, Renan's thought, like that of many others, was marked by conflicting traditions of the time, which Martin Thom has referred to as those of ethnographic Indo-Europeanism, on the one hand, and a rationalist 'classicism', on the other (Thom 1990). There are traces of both of these discourses in the 1882 lecture. This is perhaps the reason for the ambivalence of the term culture in defining the nation. This ambivalence could be found in both the anti-Jacobinism of Renan and the Jacobinism of the Left. The Left's refusal of the notion of 'race' was as problematic as that of Renan. As Pierre Guiral has remarked:

> Jacobinism leads naturally to an affirmation of superiority, not according to ethnic characteristics but because the French people as a group is the bearer of a message that Napoleon called the noble idea of civilisation. It is therefore an idea of superiority and of an ineluctable superiority.
>
> (1977: 37)

Any cursory consideration of representations of the French nation over the last hundred years is bound to stumble across the metaphors of 'the soul', 'glory', 'the fatherland' and others which underpin Renan's concept of the nation. These are the familiar consensus images of the French nation, a common discourse which traverses Right and Left, republicans and anti-republicans. The fact that they can function as consensus metaphors must be partly the result of the distinction made by Renan between cultural definitions of the nation and cultural/somatic classifications of 'races'. This construction of a dichotomy between the theory of 'race' (considered unacceptable) and the project of a common, organic, trans-historical national community (considered highly desirable) obscures the problematic areas of proximity in definitions of the two types of community. Anti-racism has frequently shared a similar discourse (or even the same discourse) as racism yet maintains its distance simply by cloaking itself in cultural nationalism as opposed to biological racism. It was not only de

Gaulle who had 'a certain idea of France': the Left were often more enthusiastic about the nobility and purity of French identity. It was a racialisation and 'essentialisation' of France which, as René Galissot notes, was based on 'a series of distinctions: religious, cultural, those of origins... rarely explicitly racial' (1987: 23).

This ambiguity between nationalism and racism is fundamental for an understanding of the treatment of the question of immigration. In the first major study of immigration in France, Georges Mauco (1932) uses Renan's distinction between 'race' and nation to distinguish between the 'purity of the race' and the 'purity of the nation'. Talking of the wave of immigration between the wars, he suggests that if the 'race' is not threatened by the new immigrants – because, following Renan's logic, the purity of the 'race' is a myth – it is possible that the nation *is* threatened (1932: 556). Quoting Renan to reinforce the notion of the spiritual nature of the nation – 'a nation is a soul, a spiritual principle' (1932: 557) – he continues: 'The influence of foreigners from the intellectual point of view, although not clearly discernible, manifests itself especially as the opposite of reason, care, and a sense of balance and finesse which characterises the French people' (1932: 558). This passage continues in the same vein, suggesting that the superiority of the French compared with foreigners lies not in any crude biological difference but in cultural and intellectual differences.

The influence of Renan is also evident in the discussion of the naturalisation of foreigners in France at the same time: 'Whether one likes it or not, these new Frenchmen will not have the same memories, the same past as us. In a few years' time what will be the state of the soul of the French nation?' (Charlotte Salmon-Ricci quoted in Schor 1985: 530). Anti-immigrant and anti-semitic nationalism between the wars was, of course, widespread (see Schor 1985). Statements of the kind noted above are not racist if one maintains Renan's distinction between 'race' and nation – and between racism and xenophobia. Yet if these distinctions are seen as problematic, and racism and nationalism are perceived as profoundly articulated in the modern nation-state, then the above statements cannot be categorised so simply. I would suggest that, contrary to Renan's claim that it is necessary to distinguish between 'race' and nation to avoid confusion, it is precisely the distinction itself which is the cause of the confusion. Benedict Anderson (1983: 136) is surely wrong when he maintains that racism and nationalism have separate histories and natures (cf. Gilroy 1987: 44–5; Miles 1987b). Even if it is true that their origins and early history were different, this does not preclude their profound and complex articulation during the nineteenth century (in the same way – and at the same time – as the convergence of the nation, the state and citizenship, which also have different origins and early history). I would maintain that racism in France over the last hundred years is, at heart, a classic case of national racism, that is, a racism which is deeply embedded in the structures (institutions/ideologies) of the nation-state (cf. Balibar in Balibar and Wallerstein 1988). The divorce between the concept of 'race' and nation, and between ethnic and contractual models of the nation, has made it more difficult to locate this racism at the heart of everyday, common-sense nationalism. This confusion is compounded by the assumption – made by Renan but widely accepted – that racism is a matter simply of biology and origins and not of culture.

An example of the problem today can be seen in a recent article by Dominique Schnapper (1988), director of studies at the prestigious Ecole Pratique des Hautes Etudes en Sciences Sociales and a member of the Commission of Nationality in 1987. Schnapper reappraises Renan's 1882 lecture with a view to formulating an approach to the nation relevant to today's society. In highlighting the simplistic nature of the classic opposition between the ethnic (German) and contractual (French) models of the nation, she too points to the parts of Renan's text where he talks of ancestors and a shared heritage. However, because Renan rejects the ethnic transmission of this cultural heritage – 'for Renan, the heritage was intellectual and moral, not biological' (1988: 92) – Schnapper accepts his notion of the trans-historical community more or less uncritically. Considering that the 'new' racism of the contemporary period is based, first and foremost, on cultural differentialism and not biologism (although we have already questioned how new this form of racism is in France), Schnapper's approach in this article (typified by the title 'The nation as community of culture') actually compounds a national/racist discourse, although this is clearly not its intention (cf. Schnapper 1991).

The distinction between the two models of the nation is highly problematic. The tension between the two models (if indeed they can be categorised as two distinct models) is located not simply between countries (for example, France and Germany in the past, France and the USA or Britain today) but within them, not simply between texts but within them. This tension is part of what Zygmunt Bauman (1991) has called the ambivalence of modernity: a tension born from within the dichotomy, from the inevitable contingency which no amount of neat classification and ordering will efface. Alongside the claim for the 'open' nation, constituted through the voluntary association of individuals, is the 'closed' nation, constituted by the predetermined nature of the community; alongside the claims for universalism are a multitude of particularisms; alongside assimilation there is always difference.

This tension is at the heart of the construction of the modern nation and the dichotomy between nationals and foreigners. However, there is little or no mention of this ambivalence in those texts written in the 1980s on the nation and identity to which I referred above (Le Bras and Todd 1981; Braudel 1986; and others). Jacobinism is often presented as a monolithic destroyer of pluralism and differences; or, on the other hand, pluralism and differences make up the patterning of France despite the monolithic state apparatus of Jacobin republicanism. In both these interpretations, the universalism of Jacobinism is presented *in opposition to* the particularism of regional, cultural, ethnic and other minorities; assimilation is counterposed to difference. This conceptualisation reinforces the notion of a dichotomy between distinct forms of organisation, instead of reappraising the dichotomy itself.

A reappraisal of this nature clearly involves something other than challenging the concepts of universalism and assimilation from a pluralist perspective. The anti- and post-colonial discourses of difference and diversity, and the anti-state discourses of the 1960s showed the concepts of universalism and assimilation to be dependent on particularist, ethnocentric ideas of superior and inferior cultures. Yet the suggestion that universalism is also a particularism only goes so far in reappraising the fundamental paradigms within which our thinking on these matters is structured. It is not a question of aligning universalism *alongside* other particularist forms in a relativist or pluralist perspective; as I suggested above, it is rather a question of seeing both as part of a more complex whole which is modernity. Universalism and particularism, assimilation and difference are products of a single anthropological project in the modern era, namely the enlightenment concept of 'Man' (*sic*) and the community.

In exploring this terrain, Etienne Balibar has proposed that the very constitution of 'universalist' ideas is one and the same as the construction of the notion of 'race':

> It is a question of the 'internal liaison' which was established between the notions of Mankind, the Human species, of the cultural progress of Mankind, and of the anthropological 'prejudices' concerning races or the natural bases of slavery. It is a question of the very notion of race, whose modern meaning dates from the Enlightenment – that great blossoming of universalism – and affects its development in return: not in a tangential way, external to its 'essence', but intrinsically.
>
> (1989: 11)

Balibar's approach leads him to conceive of racism not as an element in or adjunct to the development of modern nation-states but an essential part of their constitution:

> There is no clear line of 'demarcation' between universalism and racism. It is not possible to define two separate entities, one of which includes all ideas which are (potentially) universalist, whilst the other includes all ideas which are (potentially) racist. I would express this in a Hegelian terminology: universalism and racism are determined opposites, which means precisely that each one affects the other 'from within'.
>
> (1989: 13–14)

I believe that these comments are an important correction to thinking today which is founded on misleading binary oppositions. This is not simply a philosophical point. It is at the heart of the problematic nature of all discussion of 'race' and nation today for it implies that racism is not an external evil which periodically plagues the body politic; it is an integral part of the very constitution of modern nation-states. This reformulation of racism is especially important in understanding the difficulties of anti-racist strategy. For if it is true that, far from being opposites, racism and anti-racism share a more fundamental conceptual framework, then anti-racism itself is clearly in need of being rethought (cf. Taguieff 1988a; 1991; *Mots* 1989). Concepts of racism have reached a worrying impasse (see especially Chapter 4). Nevertheless, from this impasse there are signs of the possible emergence of a different challenge to exclusion constructed around citizenship rights (see Chapter 5).

The question of immigration in contemporary France concerns

the profound and complex articulation of concepts of 'race', nation, culture and citizens' rights which I mentioned above. The fact that, as I suggested, their origins and early history were not the same is a useful reminder that it is only at a certain moment in time and at a certain conjuncture that they became articulated. I believe that it is important to locate this historical convergence of practices and terms, for only then does it become possible to reformulate concepts of the individual, the community and rights in the new historical context of today. The next section therefore discusses this convergence and the birth of the modern dichotomy between nationals and foreigners.

## THE 'NATIONALISATION' OF FRANCE

The ambivalence around inclusion and exclusion is at the heart of the formation of the modern French nation.[6] For, at the time of the Revolution, the new concept of universal human rights was constructed within the *particularist* framework of the nation. In other words, Rousseau's 'Man' (does 'he' ever exist in 'his' universalist, natural and pre-social form? ) was immediately contradicted by his 'citizen', since the Declaration of the Rights of Man and the Citizen of 26 August 1789 clearly limits the universality of citizenship by making it dependent on nationality (article 3) (Bruschi 1987: 26). The republican ideal – founded on the liberal conception of the free individual inherited from the philosophers of the Enlightenment – was therefore hijacked by the nation and was quickly incorporated within a distinction between nationals (citizens) and non-nationals (non-citizens). This tension between the universalism of the Enlightenment concept of Man, and the particularist framework of the nation within which 'he' was to be situated, is central to the history of the modern French nation. This contradiction appears even more marked when one remembers that it was precisely the break with privilege and particular interests and the creation of a common good that were central to the Revolutionary ideal. By defining the common good within the exclusive framework of the nation, the Revolution crystallised the tension between universalism and particularism of the Enlightenment.

Yet if it was the period of the Revolution which established the nation as the guarantor of the common good, it was not then that the distinctions between the national and the foreigner (as we know them today) were constructed. As Hobsbawm points out:

> We cannot...read into the revolutionary 'nation' anything like the later nationalist programme of establishing nation-states for bodies defined in terms of the criteria so hotly debated by the nineteenth century theorists, such as ethnicity, common language, territory and common historical memories.
>
> (1990: 20)

Renan's discussion of the nation in 1882 according to the issues mentioned by Hobsbawm would have been inconceivable in the Revolutionary period. The 'nationalisation' of the citizen and French society was therefore not introduced in complete form with the removal of the monarchy in 1789; instead, it was a discontinuous historical process. The discrepancy between nationals and foreigners established at the time of the Revolution remained more conceptual than actual. It was not particularly marked in the immediate aftermath of 1789 (Bruschi 1987: 28; Benot 1989: 40) or even throughout the first half of the nineteenth century (Noiriel 1990: 9). The concept of the foreigner remained a very ill-defined one compared to subsequent representations, whilst access to citizenship for those of foreign origin was a fairly simple procedure. The word 'immigrant' hardly appeared at all in documents of the time (Noiriel 1988a: 78). National frontiers remained as ill-defined as under the Ancien Regime, whilst social rights were scarce for nationals and foreigners alike.

It was not until the second half of the nineteenth century – and more specifically the first decades of the Third Republic (1870–1940) – that French society became nationalised (Weber 1976).[7] This process was due to the convergence of a number of important developments. Firstly, this was the time both of rapid industrialisation in France (later than in Britain) and of profound demographic crisis (Mauco 1932: 17–18). Industrialisation demanded a hugely increased labour force which could not be provided by national manpower; hence the recourse to foreign labour and the origins of immigration in the modern era. From the very beginning, immigration was therefore defined according to economic and demographic criteria. This is the classic framing of immigration in France over the last hundred years – and the cause of numerous contradictions.[8]

Yet if industrialisation and demographic crisis were the major 'pull' factors for immigrant labour, immigration in its modern sense is, first and foremost, a product of the state. People crossed frontiers in the first half of the century and there were foreigners in France;[9] yet it was only through the institutional framework of the developing state that the concepts of frontiers and foreigners were crystallised in the way we know them today (Lochak 1988: 76–7; Hobsbawm 1990: 91). Indeed, the census – this system of statistical classification of the population and the 'territoire' – was itself a sign of the new role of the state in defining social relations. It was only with the development of the modern apparatus of the state in the second half of the century that the idea of the natural frontier separating one population from another became widespread (Nordman 1986: 51–2). Christian Bruschi also talks of the role of the state under the Third Republic in specifically defining the areas of 'le territoire' and 'la population', and says that it was only in 1874 that the term 'nationality' acquired the sense it has today (Bruschi 1989: 263–4).

It was during the early years of the Third Republic that the state became instrumental in laying down all the ground rules for social relations in the modern era: that is, regulating relations between capital and labour by channelling possible class conflict into a consensus relationship on industrial relations (hence reducing the revolutionary potential of the proletariat) whilst, at the same time, guaranteeing certain rights for workers as protection against the harshness of the free market; introducing measures on social welfare; constructing the new sphere of the 'social' according to national criteria (Balibar 1988: 228–9). This was a highly ambiguous process: society was democratised but, at the same time, social relations became subject to a far greater degree of surveillance and control through the institutions of the expanding state. The development of free, national education is a good example of this ambiguity: it was both a means of freedom and enlightenment but also developed a disciplinary ethos born from the idea of 'dangerous youth' (Perrot 1989: 20–1).

This profound institutionalisation of social relations transformed the hazy distinction between nationals and non-nationals into a clear division between them. The state and the nation, whose origins and history were *not* the same, then became inextricably intertwined. As Lochak points out, the state became the 'juridical personification of the nation' (Lochak 1988: 78). It is through the power of the national state (or rather the state-hegemonised nation) that foreigners were no longer 'those who are born outside the frontiers of the state but, in a much more profound way, those who do not belong to the *body* of the nation' (Lochak 1988: 78). The construction of 'the national' and 'the foreigner' was part of the same historical process (Sayad 1984b).

The demarcation of two separate identities was, at the same time, the construction of inequalities between them. There were some fifty 'propositions de loi' relating to immigrants between 1883–1914 (Mauco 1932: 59–60). Noiriel outlines a number of these measures which produced juridically, administratively and ideologically the new concept of 'the foreigner'. The first census to provide statistics on the numbers of foreigners in France was in 1851; the 1880s saw an important debate in parliament on the possibility of imposing a tax on foreigners in order to protect the jobs of French workers; the same decade saw the introduction of proposals to codify immigrants according to their employment status and oblige them to declare their residence at the town hall (1888); the first discussions around codifying the identity of foreigners took place at the same time (and were eventually to result in the identity card for immigrants in 1917); the law of 1890 against accidents at work protected only nationals and caused an enormous outcry in Belgium; the first real Code of Nationality was introduced by the law of 1889 (Noiriel 1988a: 71–116).[10]

However, another major aspect of the process of nationalisation of French society, and one less frequently discussed in this context, is the development of colonialism under the Third Republic (see Balibar 1984, 1988). Colonialism established a 'space of migration' between the 'metropole' and the colonised countries (and vice versa) which was a classic channel for the mobilisation of foreign labour (Talha 1985). At the same time as 'internationalising the economic system' (Talha 1985: 98), colonialism established, as we know, political, juridical and cultural structures which institutionalised the distinction between nationals and 'natives' ('indigènes'), or citizens and subjects.

The institutionalisation of definitions of the national and the foreigner therefore took place within a 'domestic' and international context (at home *and abroad*) during the first decades of the Third Republic. There are clearly important connections between national and international developments of the time, just as there are between the economic, political, social and ideological configurations. For example, it was at this time that the modern popular ideas of French identity and the homogeneity and continuity of the French nation were constructed and disseminated (Citron 1985, 1990), particularly via the history books of the nascent, secularised education system (Citron 1988: 18–19).[11] There is little doubt that Jules Ferry, the major force behind free and secular education in France, saw a clear link between the civilising missions of education and of colonialism. In 1883 he extended the law on public education to Algerians in the name of the 'duty of the superior races to civilise the inferior races', a duty which conferred on the 'superior races a right with regard to the inferior races' (quoted in Siblot 1989: 63). His racist approach to education was legitimised in the following terms: 'Can you deny that there is more justice, more material and moral order, more equity, more social virtue in North Africa since the French conquest?' (quoted in Colonna 1975: 70–1).

In fact, the duty to civilise 'the inferior races' was not pursued particularly systematically. For example, only a tiny proportion of 'natives' in Algeria attended French schools. Assimilation was never intended for whole populations – and, in any case, was a highly ambivalent process even for that handful who did 'assimilate'. It is true that assimilation in the colonial context was a juridical process (concerning those who demanded full citizen rather than subject status), and was therefore different from the political concept of assimilation of foreigners in France (see Bruschi 1987: 44). Nevertheless, the requirements of cultural conformity were more or less identical in both forms of assimilation and it is here that the most profound contradictions of the modern national state are to be found.

One of the contradictions defining the position of immigrants in France comes from the tension between the demographic and economic arguments for immigration (mentioned above). The idea of 'making Frenchmen from foreigners' was a significant argument behind the liberal terms for naturalisation in the law of 1889. Yet, on the other hand, immigrants were also seen as temporary workers filling a gap in the labour market. The ideas of the permanency of immigrants through settlement in France, which underlay the demographic perspective, were therefore in constant conflict with those of the temporary nature of immigrants which was central to the contract-labour perspective. Thus immigration was, from the very beginning, the site of the contradictory forces of inclusion in and exclusion from the nation.

Yet, as suggested above, the major ambivalence comes through the link forged between a uniform culture, on the one hand, and membership of the national/political community on the other. The idea of (cultural) assimilation was eventually made a requirement for naturalisation.[12] But when the concept of culture was itself not immune to racialised definitions of 'us' and 'them', then nationality and citizenship could change swiftly from a gift open to all who settled in France to a possession of the chosen few. For immigrants aiming at naturalisation, the unity forged between national/political affiliation and cultural conformity was always likely to result in the former being refused, or begrudged, for failure to fulfil the latter. The slogan of the 'paper Frenchmen' ('Français de papier') coined by Action Française to describe naturalised French men and women – and of course Jews – (and echoed by today's New Right) is a result of the essentialist cultural definition of the nation.

It is clear in Renan's text that the culturalist definition of the nation is dependent on both a *retrospective* and *prospective* vision; that is, the idea of the nation as a cultural community progressing through time, linking past, present and future (cf. Anderson 1983). It is a deep, trans-historical and organicist concept of the community. This retrospective and prospective homogenisation of France was established at this time through the development of the state mentioned above. One might add, as part of this process, the construction of a retrospective social geography, giving a demographic and geographical unity and homogeneity to France from pre-Revolutionary times. In his discussion of the history of the term 'natural frontier', Daniel Nordman notes:

> The expression is extremely rare, right up until the end of the eighteenth century....However, it is frequently used in the second half of the nineteenth century and in the twentieth century, employed retroactively by historians in their studies of the Ancien Régime and the Revolution.
>
> (1986: 51–2)

This trans-historical and organic-culturalist concept of the national community – and let us not forget that it is the *national* community which is to supersede all other forms of identification in the modern era – is at the heart of the ambivalence of assimilation. For assimilation maintains that there is both an initial difference which must be obliterated ('you must be like us') and an initial difference which can never be obliterated ('you can never be like us'). The foreign body can never be fully assimilated: there will always be a trace of that otherness – that other history – which needed assimilating in the first place.

Assimilation contains a double-bind at its very core; for the community which the outsider is required to join is, at all times, just as ready to reject this figure on the grounds of ethnic, national or cultural difference. The ambivalence of assimilation and difference is a product of the modern national state. If it is true that the group *par excellence* which has suffered the full rigour of the illusion of assimilation is the Jews (Bauman 1991), it is no less true that the same procedure has been applied to other immigrants as well. By making membership of the political and national community dependent on cultural conformity, the national state created a national racism *at the same time as* a 'liberal' republicanism; they are part of the same process. Zygmunt Bauman suggests that the numerous contradictions underlying the fragile unity between the political and the cultural would eventually bring about the ultimate failure of the whole modern project (Bauman 1991). Certainly these contradictions are crucial today to the crisis of and struggle over the relationship between political structures and forms of social/cultural organisation.

## THE NATION-STATE TODAY: PROBLEMS OF INTERPRETATION

As stated above, my discussion of immigration and racism in contemporary France is situated in the context of the development and consolidation of the modern nation-state. However, it is relevant today to ask ourselves whether this framing of the question of immigration is now in crisis, or even coming to an end. Or, to put it another way, is the current obsession with immigration in France itself indicative of a crisis in the structures of the nation-state? Have we already passed into a new paradigm for the consideration of immigration: that is, one in which Europe has displaced the nation-state as the major political and administrative organisation within which immigration is constructed? The so-called post-colonial order, which has seen the creation of new alliances and formations between European nations, might have already introduced a very different determining paradigm for immigration. How, then, are individuals and communities to be defined if the fundamental structures within which they have been situated in the modern period are in the process of disintegration (or at least transformation)?

These are open questions to which there are no easy answers. However, there are perhaps some preliminary statements that can be made. Any discussion of new paradigms needs to be careful lest it loses sight completely of historical determinations. For example, the term 'the post-colonial era' can suggest a clean break with the colonial era and obscure the relevance of the colonial legacy today. Etienne Balibar maintains that the suggestion that decolonisation closed a chapter in French history and allowed France to open new avenues of development and communication (notably in the context of Europe) perpetuates a myth and is the source of a common misunderstanding of the structures of contemporary France. 'In fact it is the opposite which is largely true: contemporary France has been formed through and by colonisation' (Balibar 1984: 1741).

It is not simply a question of a colonial mentality which has persisted in the post-colonial era – especially with the immigration of former colonised peoples and the repatriation of over a million 'pieds noirs' (the European settlers in Algeria) at the end of the Franco–Algerian war in 1962. It is more fundamentally a question of the juridical structures of the French state which were largely formed in the context of management of the colonies abroad and immigrants at home, and which are still the source of modern forms of exclusion today. Balibar sees colonialism as a fundamental determinant of contemporary racism: 'Racism in France is essentially colonial, not in terms of a "leftover" from the past but in terms of the continuing production of contemporary relations' (1984: 1745). Of course, this contextualisation of contemporary racism fails to account for new forms of anti-semitism. Nevertheless, it is true that the political, social and ideological complex in France is still largely structured according to state institutions established during the high period of national hegemony and colonial expansion a century and more ago, even if today these are in crisis and being struggled over.

On the other hand, if it is true that the phenomenon of immigration over the last hundred years has been inextricably linked to the triumph of the nationalisation of society, industrialisation and colonialism, then any cursory glance at the world today will tell us that there has been a major evolution since the classic period of their hegemony. This does not necessarily imply the demise of the nation-state as such. But it does imply the transformation of the western nation-state in the contemporary world. The link between the nation and the state has become visibly dislocated and the gap is likely to grow even more. The globalisation of capital and culture, traversing nation-states, is increasingly making the rhetoric of sovereignty, independence and so on look hollow. Migration of people and goods has exposed the inherent instability of the alliance between the nation and the state; an alliance built on shaky foundations ever since the former was constructed according to the retrospective illusion of unity and continuity, whilst the latter was always prey to economic and other forces which did not respect national frontiers. The added presence of the concept of cultural uniformity in this shaky alliance was perhaps always a recipe for disaster. The articulation of nation, state and culture was therefore always a problematic unity and the cause of numerous tensions in the modern period. The dislocation of these elements today, the breakdown in blood and soil definitions of the community and the reformulation of the notion of citizenship are all factors in the contemporary crisis of the nation-state.

It is therefore relevant to ask whether this crisis coincides with the end of the classic phase of modern immigration into Western Europe or whether it coincides with a shift to a renewed immigration from the South to the North and, in the context of the end of the Cold War, from the East to the West. And if the struggle has shifted from the frontiers of the nation-state to those of Europe, it is now a question of establishing who is to be included and who is to be excluded and what criteria will be used to define the internal and external frontiers of the new order.

These questions are clearly of great significance today. For example, for anti-racist movements and movements for equal rights, an understanding of present changes is fundamental for strategy. For, without this understanding, opponents of racism will be fighting old battles with outdated weapons no longer suited to contemporary struggles. Worse still, they can find themselves using the very discourse – that of cultural difference – which now forms the basis of the new national/European racism of the New Right.

One has the feeling that the situation today is pregnant with possibility. On the one hand, there is the genuine case for a new ordering of social relations which breaks with monolithic constructions of the community (nation, 'race', patriarchy) inherited from the past. On the other hand, there are also clear signs of a different 'new order' constituted by new structures of exclusion, violence and racism. Today's post-colonial order is radically different from the old nationalist/colonialist order; yet we are still experiencing the full consequences of the demise of colonialism. At present the new order is not at all clear; it is being struggled over and consequently remains open-ended.

# Chapter 2

# Post-war immigration in France

This chapter traces the broad outlines of migration flows to France, official policy and political debate on immigration and aspects of racism and anti-racism in the post-war period. It does not attempt an exhaustive coverage of these areas (see, for example, Wihtol de Wenden 1988a). It is intended to provide the general political context for the following chapters.

It is important to underline one of the major problems with any such survey. As already argued, 'immigration' cannot be analysed simply through statistical evidence concerning migration flows, on the one hand, and social and economic 'integration' of immigrant communities in France, on the other. This statistical evidence is based on nationality and not on ethnic or other criteria. It therefore recognises only the divide between nationals and foreigners. Yet the sociological, political and ideological realities of what goes under the name 'immigration' today go far beyond the national/foreigner divide. Racism does not stop, as do the statistics, with the acquisition of French nationality. People from the French overseas departments (French Guinea, Guadeloupe, Martinique and Réunion) are not foreigners; neither are the 'French Muslims' (Harkis) who fought for France in the Algerian war of independence and were largely repatriated to France with the 'pieds noirs' after 1962; neither are those of Algerian parents who were born in Algeria before 1962 (that is whilst Algeria was still French territory); nor those born in France of foreign parents who have acquired automatic French nationality at the age of eighteen. However, although they do not appear *statistically* as foreigners they are frequently classified *popularly* as immigrants due to the contemporary racialised association between immigration, those of North African origin and blacks.[1] On the other hand, white non-French Europeans resident in France (especially from Portugal, Italy and Spain) do form part of the statistical evidence on foreigners in France yet are less likely to suffer the stigma attached to immigration today.

During the last twenty years, numbers have become a highly politicised and controversial issue in the debate around immigration. Although this has often been recognised by demographers themselves (see Lebon 1988: 27; Le Bras 1988a: 40), the statistical fetishisation of 'immigration' has nevertheless increased over the years. Frequently, in official documents, polemical debate and the media, the problematic nature of the use of statistics is not discussed. Official figures have been used to give credence to racist arguments (see *Le Figaro Magazine*, 26 October 1985). Numbers have frequently been used in opinion polls on immigration to ask leading (or misleading) questions.[2] Furthermore, even the official figures themselves vary depending on whether it is the census figure which is quoted (which may not include all foreigners in France) or that of the Ministry of the Interior (which counts residence permits, some of which belong to foreigners who are no longer in the country; see Le Moigne 1986: 12). The census figure is usually about 500,000 lower than that of the Ministry of the Interior. Confusion also exists around the nationality of those in mixed marriages (Dubet 1989a: 56). For these reasons the following discussion uses statistics sparingly.

## 1945–55: THE STATE, DEMOGRAPHY AND THE ECONOMY

In the immediate post-war period there was a broad consensus amongst demographers, economists and politicians that the reconstruction of France would necessitate a substantial increase in foreign labour. The major reason for this was the demographic crisis. After the war France had a population not only less dense but also far less well-endowed with young males than neighbouring countries. The country had been in a similar position after the devastation of the First World War and had then received more than one million immigrants in five years (between 1921–6).

However, in 1945 it was decided that the recruitment and placing of immigrants should be carried out by the state rather than left to the employers, as had been the case in the previous post-war period. The National Immigration Office (ONI) was therefore established by the ordonnance of 2 November 1945. Its purpose was to oversee an immigration policy. Pierre Bideberry, a former director of the ONI, described its objectives as follows:

– to avoid all unfair competition in work and salaries with the national labour force; – to protect the national community through an effective selection process based on considerations of health, employment and moral conduct; – to protect the immigrants against diverse forms of exploitation and to avoid the abuses of which they had been victims in the past; – to guarantee as far as possible a distribution of foreigners in France.

(1969: 19)

Noteworthy in this statement are the links made between immigration and economic, ethnic and national considerations. The introduction of foreigners into France would be a carefully monitored build-up of a new work-force, operating principally according to the criteria of ethnic and cultural 'balance', assimilation and national cohesion (cf. Wihtol de Wenden 1988a: 85; Perotti 1985: 13).

However, the demographic, economic and national arguments did not sit easily together. The demographic argument, favouring a huge immigration into the country (estimated at five million for the reconstruction of France), was at odds with arguments linking immigration both to specific areas of employment and to a restrictive concept of the cohesive nation-state. Regarding the first of these restrictions, Gary Freeman notes that

the requirement that each entrant possess a work permit from the Ministry of Labor meant that immigration which did take place under the auspices of ONI would necessarily be tied to the domestic employment scene and not to long-range demographic considerations.

(Freeman 1979: 71)

The wider demographic perspective, which envisaged a mass, permanent immigration, was therefore not adopted by the economic planners at the newly created General Commission for the Plan nor by those at the Ministry of Labour (under whose auspices the ONI was placed) who saw immigration as a temporary phenomenon responding to conjunctural requirements and not in competition with the domestic work-force. The contradiction between the economic and demographic arguments for immigration in 1945 is underlined by Carliene Kennedy-Brenner (1979: 30) in her analysis of post-war immigration in France for the Organisation for Economic Cooperation and Development (OECD/OCDE). Protection of the national interest was also important in the argument that ethnic proximity was essential for easy assimilation of immigrants into France. Yet the discourse of 'assimilability' and 'adaptability' was itself at odds with the dominant economic argument favouring short-term immigration to fulfil specific needs. In theory, it excluded most non-European immigrants and virtually reduced possible sources of immigrant labour to Italy, West Germany and Spain. A conflict of official interests and considerations in post-war France therefore subjected immigration to contradictory discourses: the views of demographers at the newly formed Ministry of Population (established through the decree of 24 December 1945) were contradicted by those formulating the first economic plan, whilst neither of these perspectives was necessarily in line with the imperative of assimilability.

Yet state policy on immigration was over-determined by more practical considerations as well. The fact that the ONI received its funding not from the state but from payments made by employers hiring foreign workers made it cheaper for employers to recruit directly rather than through the ONI. Furthermore, employers could recruit foreign workers far more quickly if they ignored the official procedures. For employers wishing to engage foreign workers, the official mechanism consisted first of all of establishing a work contract defining conditions of work and housing; next submitting the contract to the departmental service of employment and labour which then passed on the request to the Ministry of Labour. If approved, the request was only then submitted to the ONI. The ONI would then send it to one of their overseas offices to make the necessary arrangements for selection of appropriate candidates according to medical and professional criteria and according to age (Kennedy-Brenner 1979: 23). Although the aim of this procedure was to guarantee a monitored immigration according to specific manpower needs defined by the Ministry of Labour, in practice employers often chose to recruit directly. Ironically, the bureaucracy of the official procedure reduced the chances of an immediate immigration responding to economic demand. Direct recruitment proved far more effective in this respect. However, this clearly made a mockery of a state-controlled immigration policy.

In fact, the attempt to organise a controlled increase in immigration after the war proved to be a failure. Instead of a massive immigration to aid in the economic reconstruction of the country, the number of foreigners in France actually declined over the next ten years, falling from 1,743,000 (4.2 per cent of the population) in 1946 to 1,553,000 million (3.6 per cent of the population) in 1954. Ironically, the only substantial increase in this period was in Algerian immigration which was not regulated by the ONI because of the status of Algerians as French subjects with the right of entry and stay in France (Wihtol de Wenden 1988a: 108–9). Free movement between Algeria and France, instituted by the law of 20 September 1947, was repealed only in 1964 when the Franco–Algerian agreement was established to limit the numbers of Algerians admitted into France. Between 1946–55 Algerian immigration far outstripped the total number of immigrants recruited through the ONI. A population of 20,000 in 1946 had increased to 210,000 in 1954. This represented an average increase of 32.5 per cent each year compared to an average increase in the total immigrant population of barely 1.3 per cent annually in the same period.

The procedure of controlled recruitment of immigrants through the ONI was soon outflanked and bypassed by more diverse and unorganised processes of immigration. The lack of any regime concerning Algerian immigration also applied to the overseas departments of Guinea, Guadeloupe, Martinique and Réunion (though, as we have seen, since they were integral parts of the French state their populations were also not legally immigrants at all but French nationals). The French ex-colonies in West Africa (including Mali, Mauritania and Senegal) benefited from a fairly liberal immigration regime. Elsewhere a number of bilateral agreements (with Italy in 1946 and 1951, West Germany in 1950, Greece in 1954) specified particular numbers allowed to enter the country and requirements for entry. The variety of procedures of entry into the country militated against the possibility of controlled immigration through a single agency of the state.

However, the most striking example of the failure of the ONI to regulate the level of immigration was the return to the unfettered and exploitative practices of the 1920s. Allowing the market to be the real arbiter of immigration relocated effective control in the hands of the employers. This was undoubtedly reinforced through the system of regularisation whereby immigrants who had entered the country outside the jurisdiction of the ONI could legalise their position merely by proof of an offer of work. This procedure was to become the major mode of immigration into France in the 1960s until measures were taken to regain control through the ONI in 1968.

The heterogeneous nature of immigration, the failure of the ONI and the minimal prominence given to the topic in official circles make it impossible to talk of a coherent state policy on immigration in the immediate post-war period. Immigration was seen primarily in economic terms. The demographic and national arguments, as well as the argument supporting state-controlled immigration, soon gave way to an acceptance, even an encouragement, of a market-led approach for economic ends. Official endorsement of this position (or rather absence of position) can be seen in the report of the Employment Commission of the Third Plan (1953): 'Recourse to immigrant labour should be considered not as a palliative which would resolve periods of temporary crisis, but as a continuous approach, indispensable for the realisation of the needs of the Third Plan' (quoted in Ministère des Affaires Sociales et de la Solidarité Nationale 1986: 10). The immediate post-war paradox of a notional policy of state control coupled with a tacit official acceptance of the fact that immigration should respond to the forces of supply and demand was to be a constant feature of policy on immigration until the late 1960s. It defines the major parameters within which official discourse on immigration was situated in this period.

## 1955–68: THE BOOM YEARS

The rate of immigration began to accelerate rapidly only from the mid-1950s. In the 1960s the average number of people entering France each year was well over 100,000. There were three times as many entries between 1955–65 as the preceding decade. According to the statistics provided by the Ministry of the Interior, between 1955–65 the number of immigrants in France rose from 1,574,000 at the end of 1955 to 2,323,000 at the end of 1965.

Although this period saw a significant increase in numbers entering France, the migration flow was haphazard and became progressively more diversified. Between 1955–61 the main sources of immigration were still the southern European countries, Italy and Spain. In 1959 the largest immigrant population was the Italians. However, between 1960–5 the Italians were outstripped first by the Spaniards, then by the Portuguese. Bilateral agreements with Spain (1961) and Portugal (1963) ensured this shift in European sources of immigrant labour. There was a large rise in Portuguese immigration during the 1960s. From an estimated 20,000 at the time of the 1954 census, rising only to 50,000 by 1962 (according to the census of that year), the number of Portuguese immigrants had reached 213,000 by the end of 1965 (according to the statistics of the Ministry of the Interior) and 758,000 by the census of 1975.

However, another transformation in the migration flows to France was also taking place at this time. Europe was no longer the single source of foreign workers, for emigration from former African colonies and the French-speaking West African states provided a new source of mass immigration to France (which does not imply, however, that there were not immigrants from Africa before this period). Although Algerian immigration, which had been considerable after 1945, diminished during the Algerian war, the numbers increased again with the Evian agreement in 1962 which marked the end of the war and Algerian independence. The agreement maintained the principle of free circulation between the two countries. Between 1962–5 a total of 111,000 Algerians entered France, compared to the average of 11,000 per year during the Algerian war. This upsurge led to the Franco–Algerian agreement of 10 April 1964 by which numbers would be limited and reviewed trimestrally in consideration of the economic situation in both countries.

In 1963 bilateral agreements were also signed with Morocco, Tunisia, Mali and Mauritania and in 1964 with Senegal. These agreements gave an important boost to the numbers of nationals from each country allowed entry into France. The number of 67,000 Moroccan workers who entered France between 1962–6 made their proportional increase the highest of the three North African countries. If we consider also the bilateral agreements signed with Yugoslavia and Turkey in 1965, it is clear how diverse the migration flows to France became during this period of economic expansion and reconstruction.

Coupled with the diversity of the migration flows was a parallel diversification of the methods of recruitment of foreign workers. The proliferation of bilateral agreements was just one of the ways in which the recruitment of foreign workers was effected outside the channel of the ONI. Yet a more significant bypassing of the ONI was constituted by those entering either on a tourist visa or, as we have said, clandestinely and subsequently being 'regularised' on proof of an offer of work. This was the period often classified as that of 'spontaneous' or 'uncontrolled' immigration ('l'immigration spontanée' or 'l'immigration sauvage'), that is, a flow of immigrants into the country responding to economic demand (although these terms also have other ideological connotations which will be considered further on). In 1965 the numbers who entered through the official channel of the ONI had fallen to 21 per cent (79 per cent 'regularised') and in 1968 this figure fell further to 18 per cent (82 per cent 'regularised'). Between 1965–70 roughly 65 per cent of entries were legalised *a posteriori* rather than through the official channel of the ONI.

However, as we have remarked, this situation was not a source of regret. On the contrary, politicians and economic planners conceived of immigration as a necessary, structural element in a programme of economic reconstruction, and consequently allowed the law of supply and demand to dictate the migration flow. Georges Pompidou declared in 1963 that 'immigration is a means of creating a certain flexibility in the labour market and avoiding social tension' (statement of 3 September, quoted in Perotti 1985: 17), whilst in 1966 Jean-Marcel Jeanneney, the Minister of Social Affairs, actually endorsed the practice of illegal immigration: 'Illegal immigration itself is not without a certain value, for were we to pursue a policy of strict enforcement of the rules and international agreements governing this area, we would perhaps lack the manpower we need' (quoted in Ministère des Affaires Sociales et de la Solidarité Nationale 1986: 10).

The need for a new labour force to perform the necessary tasks in the reconstruction of industry took precedence over all other economic considerations. Since it was impossible to satisfy this demand for labour from France alone, foreign workers were seen as indispensable to economic prosperity. Moreover, it was often a question of preferring immigrant to French workers. The majority of tasks that needed performing called for a very specific type of labour force, one that would, above all, be mobile, have no particular skills or qualifications and could easily be made redundant if need be. These were precisely the qualities that the immigrant possessed in abundance (Perotti 1985: 8). Michel Massenet, director of the Population and Migrations section at the Ministry of Labour (1962–8), noted the advantages of young Algerian immigrants who had 'the 'merit' of being mobile and taking positions where the use of French labour would risk inflexibility; for example, in terms of increases in salary and redundancies in the event of restructuring' (quoted in Cordeiro 1984: 41). As we shall see, only a few years later Massenet was putting forward a very different view of Algerian immigration. Yet in the first half of the 1960s official statements on immigration largely stressed the importance of a cheap, unqualified foreign labour force for the new economic demands of the country. In the 'economic planning perspective on immigration' adopted by French officials (Freeman 1979: 117), immigrants were envisaged simply as a mobile and malleable work-force. Apparently they did not have the same needs as other human beings, since their primary function was to serve a specific economic purpose in France.

During the 1960s employers eagerly welcomed the new work-force. They were able to entice potential immigrants to France (especially from North Africa), recruit at will from the pool of labour around the factory gates and pay low wages with little worry about state interference. They were legally obliged to give official notification of the employment of foreign workers but many did not do so, preferring instead to exploit the precarious nature of a foreign worker's illegal existence in the country. Often unaware of the procedure of regularisation whereby they could legalise their situation, many foreign workers therefore had no choice but to live as illegals ('clandestins') in France.

Largely unregulated by the state, immigration was once again in the hands of the employers. Although industry benefited the most (especially the steel and automobile industries and the building trade) agriculture also welcomed a seasonal immigrant work-force to replace those who had forsaken the land in order to work in the towns. Throughout this period, the political parties of the Left and the trade unions had little influence on the employment of foreign workers and their conditions of work. In any case, the principal protagonists, the Communist Party and the largest trade union the CGT, had an ambivalent attitude towards immigrants: slogans of solidarity with immigrant workers from North Africa (July 1955, June 1959 and November 1961) were offset by demands for a protection of 'national interests' (Wihtol de Wenden 1988a: 120–1).[3]

Unprotected by the state, virtually absent from political debate and largely disregarded by the unions, immigrants were considered a peripheral presence in French society. The following years saw a progressive politicisation of the phenomenon of immigration and a movement (in the national consciousness) from the periphery to the centre (Freeman 1979; Wihtol de Wenden 1988a). Yet, during this period, immigration was confined largely to the technocratic and demographic discourse of economic planners, linked to the manpower needs of an expanding economy, and it was left largely to the employers to fill the institutional void concerning all other aspects of the process of migration.

Consequently, immigrants were marginalised and excluded from full participation in French society. Economically they frequently performed the dirtiest and most menial tasks; legally they were disadvantaged as they were not French citizens and therefore did not have the same rights as the French; socially and geographically they were confined to areas on the outskirts of major cities. The shanty towns ('bidonvilles') were indicative of the appalling conditions in which many lived and of their marginalised presence in France.

However, the crisis in housing for immigrants was sufficiently severe to provoke some official response to their social conditions. The SONACOTRA, established in 1956 for the construction of hostels and family lodgings for Algerian immigrants, was expanded in 1962 to be responsible for the reception and housing of all immigrants. The Social Action Fund (FAS), initially created in 1958 to aid Algerian workers in France, was also reformed in 1964–6 to cover the needs of all immigrant workers. And in 1966 a national commission was established, endowed with financial resources, to consider the problems of immigrant housing (CNLI). These measures hardly constituted a social policy on immigration. However, they do mark the first tentative steps towards a recognition of the social dimension of immigration. The way this dimension was interpreted was to be crucial in the change in discourse and the formulation of policy on immigration at the end of the 1960s.

## 1968–74: A 'NEW' IMMIGRATION POLICY

The period 1968–74 was crucial in terms of the different ways in which immigration came to be perceived in official circles. From

having been considered a peripheral and temporary phenomenon, immigration was recognised to be of structural significance;
from having been discussed largely in terms of manpower needs
and economic necessity, immigration was conceived also as a 'social
problem' and a problem of assimilation and ethnic balance; from
having been largely marginalised in France, immigrants became
increasingly politicised and involved in conflict and struggle.

According to the statistics of the Ministry of the Interior, the
number of foreigners in France in 1970 stood at 3,061,000, or 6
per cent of the total population. This was the highest recorded
figure since the war. The number had risen to 3,600,000 by 1972
and 3,700,000 by 1 January 1973. Annual entries reached a peak
by the end of the 1960s: 195,130 in 1969 and 212,785 in 1970. By
1 January 1974 the two largest foreign populations were the
Algerians (846,000 according to Ministry of Interior statistics) and
the Portuguese (812,000). These had now displaced the Italians
(573,000) and the Spanish (571,000). Immigration from the other
North African countries had taken the Moroccan population to
270,000 and the Tunisian population to 150,000 by the same date.
Immigration from the West African states of Mali, Mauritania and
Senegal totalled 77,000 whilst Yugoslavs stood at 79,000 and
Turks at 46,000.

It was a period in which a high level of immigration was still
welcomed by the authorities. The *Revue Politique et Parlementaire* of
December 1969 confirmed the importance of immigration in the
following terms:

> We can therefore claim that by underplaying its demographic
> potential and constituting itself instead as an immediate econ-
> omic resource, foreign labour has clearly been an important
> factor in economic stability. We might even go so far as to regret
> the fact that, in terms of French economic growth, this resource
> has not been even more substantial.
>
> (quoted in Centre d'Information sur
> le Développement 1972: 2)

Not surprisingly, many employers saw things in the same way.
The magazine *L'Usine Nouvelle* reflected this view:

> The presence of this immigration gives our economy more
> flexibility, since it is a question of people who are extremely
> mobile, are willing to change firms and regions and, if needs be,

go on the dole. Immigration is therefore beneficial in that it allows the country to save on education costs (which are incurred by the country of origin) and to help balance the nation's budget. As they are young, the immigrants often pay more in taxes than they receive in allowances.

(26 March 1970, quoted in Gaspard
and Servan-Schreiber 1985: 29–30)

In 1971 the Minister of Labour and Population, Joseph Fontanet, also underlined the economic and demographic advantages of immigration: 'It remains a fact that the refusal by the French to do certain jobs coupled with demographic stagnation means that the need for foreign workers is crucial' (Bulletin GIP 1971: 14). This attitude towards immigration was also echoed in the Sixth Plan (1971–5): 'The Sixth Plan suggested the necessary increase in their numbers to respond to our economic needs: these needs, which corresponded to 60,000 extra entries each year until now, will mean 80,000 annual entries from 1971' (Centre d'Information sur le Développement 1972: 2)

Yet the end of the 1960s also marks a radical change in approach to immigration policy. This change in thinking will be discussed in more detail in Chapter 3. Let us just note here the broad outlines of this redirection in approach and the resulting changes in immigration policy. In certain official circles, fears were expressed about the social problems caused by the more recent immigration from Africa, and especially from North Africa. It was suggested that a new immigration policy should be based on a quota system which would favour those more likely to adapt to the norms of French society (although how new this was will also be discussed further). A system of selective controls would therefore be effected, partly through differential quotas based on the criterion of assimilability and partly through suppressing the practice of regularisation and firmly establishing control of immigration through the ONI. It was not economic slow-down and manpower surplus which provided the initial justification for immigration controls in the modern period (indeed the above statements all express a continuing need for immigrant labour); it was more a question of ethnic 'balance' and fears of the social tensions which would ensue if this balance was not maintained.

On 1 July 1968 France unilaterally limited Algerian immigration to 1000 per month (subsequently fixed at 35,000 per year by the Franco–Algerian agreement of 27 December 1968 as a response to Algerian displeasure).[4] The other measure intended to regain control over migration flows was the circular of 29 July 1968 which suppressed the process of regularisation for unqualified workers and made receipt of a residence permit conditional on already having a job. This attempt to revitalise the ONI produced results which were 'not negligible' (Tapinos 1975: 91), the number of ONI introductions passing from 24 per cent in 1968 to 56 per cent in 1972.

However, it was the so-called Marcellin–Fontanet circulars of January and February of 1972 which had a far greater impact. Taking their name from the ministers responsible for their introduction (Marcellin was the Minister of the Interior, Fontanet was the Minister of Labour), the circulars again concerned restrictions on the issue of work and residence permits. Regularisation would be granted only to those who could provide evidence of a work contract for one year and proof of decent housing. Expulsion from the country was the penalty for failing to satisfy this condition. The circulars therefore merely extended the logic already contained in the circular of July 1968 – a fact which is often forgotten, since it was the Fontanet circular of 23 February 1972 which had such a large effect on public opinion whilst the 1968 circular received relatively little attention (Tapinos 1975: 99).

In the spirit of the comments made in the Calvez report of 1969, the intention of the circulars was to guarantee state control of immigration through the ONI, eradicate illegal entry and favour French workers and those foreigners already in France whose situation was legally correct. In practice, the consequences were more far-reaching. Not only 'clandestins' were liable to be expelled. An article in *Le Monde* (4 February 1973) entitled 'The punishment of the victims' pointed out how the policy of linking residence to possession of a work permit could affect *all* foreign workers, including those who were in possession of a residence permit but had subsequently been made unemployed. This might include foreigners who had been living and working in France for several years. Furthermore, the circulars allowed for expulsion to be carried out without the traditional right of appeal for 'offenders' (Verbunt 1973: 714).

The circulars sparked off immediate protests: hunger strikes in Valence, Toulouse, Paris, La Ciotat, Lyons, Bordeaux, Strasbourg, Mulhouse, Lille, Nice, Montpellier, Aix-en-Provence and St

Etienne; a strike of 367 foreign workers in April 1973 at the Boulogne-Billancourt factory of Renault; sit-ins in offices by foreign workers; and numerous demonstrations and meetings in Paris (Verbunt 1973: 707; *Lettre* 1973). These were the first signs of a widespread mobilisation by foreign workers against discriminatory legislation and racism. The hunger strike was to become the favoured tactic of resistance in the 1970s in the struggle against repressive controls and the threat of expulsion. Wihtol de Wenden suggests (1988a: 165–9) that the politicisation of the immigrant movement and the emergence of immigration onto the political scene can be located in the months of struggle which followed the application of the Marcellin–Fontanet circulars.[5]

However, there were also other significant developments in the discussion around immigration. Social conditions, and especially pitiful housing conditions for many foreigners, received more media attention in the early 1970s. A range of terms were used to describe these: 'bidonvilles', 'caves', 'hôtels de fortune', 'baraques de chantier'. The deaths by asphyxiation of five African workers on the outskirts of Paris in January 1970 had drawn attention to the appalling level of housing and chronic overcrowding for many foreigners. After a visit to the scene of the tragedy in Aubervilliers, the Prime Minister Jacques Chaban-Delmas promised to eradicate all 'bidonvilles' by 1973. But this was to prove a wildly optimistic forecast. October 1970 saw the creation of the GIP (interministerial group for the reduction of slum housing). Other measures that year aimed at eradicating the nefarious practices of many unscrupulous landlords and employers. But the extent of the clandestine traffickers in foreign labour ('trafics de main-d'oeuvre') and of the dealings of unscrupulous landlords (nicknamed 'marchands de sommeil') in the 1960s, to which governments had turned a blind eye or had even encouraged, was such that state intervention in this area was a difficult process. The law of 6 July 1973 which prohibited illegal trafficking in foreign labour and penalised employers who were involved in such dealings was criticised by the Left for not going far enough to tackle the problem effectively.

The state was not accustomed to dealing with the housing of foreign workers. It is true that the SONACOTRA had been established to create hostels for foreign workers. But this agency dealt with only a small proportion of the foreign population. Housing had traditionally been the responsibility of the employer not the state. This link was even reaffirmed in the Marcellin–Fontanet circulars, at the very time when officials were beginning to talk more of an interventionist policy in the area of social conditions of foreign workers and their families. The link established between employers and immigrants' housing was clearly in keeping with the idea that the social aspects of the immigrant's life are subsumed within his economic function. A sort of feudal or plantation logic underpinned the relationship between employer and foreign worker in France. The fact that the Marcellin–Fontanet circulars emanated from the ministries of the Interior and Labour are indicative of the narrow way in which questions of immigration were still circumscribed at this time (Verbunt 1973: 713 and 715). The question of education for 'second-generation' immigrants was another area where virtually no initiative had been instigated by the state (Centre d'Information sur le Développement 1972: 5).

The period 1968–74 was therefore one in which a traditional non-interventionist approach by government to the social aspects of immigration still persisted whilst, at the same time, fresh moves were made by the authorities to regulate in areas previously outside the legislator's domain. A law of 27 June 1972 gave the same rights to foreigners as to French nationals for election as delegates to company committees. Another law of 1 July 1972 was the first of its kind to outlaw incitement to racial hatred and racial discrimination. Other measures which aimed at facilitating the process of integration of foreign workers into French society were also introduced (circular of 30 May 1973, circulars of 27 March and 12 June 1973, decree of 22 October 1973). However, these measures which aimed at integration through extending the rights of foreigners in the country seemed to be undermined by the new measures of control which often made the position of foreigners far less secure. This tension, or contradiction, between the two poles of the new policy on immigration has been a major feature of the policy practised by all governments over the last twenty years.

Certainly, the protests at the end of 1972 and in 1973 were in reaction to the more repressive arm of government legislation (especially the Marcellin–Fontanet circulars) and the new racism in France. In June 1973 the extreme right-wing organisation 'Ordre Nouveau' launched a campaign against 'uncontrolled' and illegal immigration. That summer saw an outbreak of racial violence – largely directed at Algerians – including a number of deaths. The unions and the Communist Party were more vociferous in their support for demands for equal rights of foreign and French workers (although they were far more circumspect over the tactic of hunger strikes as the best weapon for achieving this goal; see *Le Monde*, 4–5 February 1973). Such was the level of racism and the unwillingness of the authorities to prosecute the perpetrators of racist attacks that the Algerian government, fearing for the safety of Algerians in France, announced on 19 September that it was suspending all further emigration to France (*Le Monde*, 21 September 1973).[6] Over the space of a few years, questions of immigration and racism had risen rapidly up the political agenda; in the years to come, they were to take on greater political significance.

## 1974–81: INTEGRATION OR REPATRIATION

By the mid-1970s, the foreign population stabilised at between 3.5 and four million. (The 1975 census put the number of foreigners in France at 3,442,415, whilst the Ministry of the Interior recorded a figure of 4,128,312 on 31 December 1974.) There had been a big increase in immigration from Portugal, especially after the Franco-Portuguese agreement of 1963. At the time of the 1954 census the Portuguese population stood at 20,000; the census of 1975 showed that it had risen to 758,000 and now constituted the biggest immigrant community in France alongside the Algerians (710,000).

The 'new' approach to immigration fashioned between 1968–72 provided the framework for immigration policy during the years of the presidency of Valéry Giscard d'Estaing (1974–81). Officially, immigration was viewed primarily as a 'problem of society' (Secrétariat d'Etat aux Travailleurs Immigrés 1977: 20) and inextricably related to the economic recession and rising unemployment of the 1970s. The right of free movement of nationals of member states of the EC and the liberal regime for Portuguese nationals meant that the 'problem of immigration' was, in effect, a euphemism for the problem of 'those of non-European origin'.

Two major developments at the beginning of Giscard's term of office were fundamental in signposting the approach to immigration: firstly, the creation of the new post of Secretary of State for Foreign Workers and, secondly, the temporary suspension of immigration announced through the circular of 5 July 1974. The creation of the post of Secretary of State was evidence of the advances made by immigration towards centre stage of the political arena. Like the official political recognition accorded the movement for women's rights (the post of Secretary of State for Women was created in 1974), immigration was now firmly on the agenda of major political issues. During the seven years of Giscard's presidency there were three holders of the post. The first Secretary of State, André Postel-Vinay, resigned after only six weeks in office when he was refused the budget he had requested to improve the level of housing of immigrants. His successor, Paul Dijoud, occupied the post until 1977 and was then replaced by Lionel Stoléru who was responsible for immigrants until 1981.

Postel-Vinay was in post long enough to preside over the suspension of immigration, and to issue, shortly after, another circular (19 July) suspending family reunification ('la réunification familiale' or 'le regroupement familial'), that is, the right of families to rejoin their spouse/parent already resident in France. The ban on primary immigration was never lifted and is still in force today. The right to family reunification was restored by the circular of 21 May 1975 (after the Conseil d'Etat had ruled that its suspension was unconstitutional) and then redefined according to certain stringent conditions by the decree of 29 April 1976.

France was not alone in stopping immigration in the early 1970s. All the major countries of immigration in Western Europe adopted the same approach to the strict control of migration flows at about this time. The principal argument used by the authorities justifying this measure was the economic recession and the rise in inflation and unemployment. Just as it was 'evident' in the 1960s that there was a link between a mobile new labour force and immigration, so it was soon 'common sense' in the 1970s that there was also a link between a shortage of jobs and the presence of immigrants in the country.

However, strict controls were also justified on other grounds. Official rhetoric during this period constantly emphasised the importance of controlling the migration flows to France in order to allow for the integration of those 3.5 to four million foreigners already in the country. The link between integration and control (see Chapter 3) had already been established in the 'new' approach to immigration in the late 1960s and early 1970s. The new administration in 1974 adopted the discursive logic of integration and control and presented it, through the new Secretary of State, as a new and coherent package.

In October 1974 a programme of twenty-five measures was announced along these lines: the commitment to maintain the suspension of immigration in order to stabilise the immigrant population, the progressive improvement of rights of foreigners so as to bring them into line with those of French nationals, the provision of better housing for immigrants, new programmes of training, improvements in the reception and orientation of immigrants newly arrived in France, promotion of cultural differences of immigrant communities and closer cooperation with EC partners on a more integrated approach to immigration policy. There was also to be the encouragement of a return to their country of origin for those foreigners who desired it, and the attempt to replace, where possible, foreign workers with French nationals.

It was envisaged that the policy of integration would be effected largely through agreements and cooperation between the state and municipalities with a considerable immigrant population. On a visit to Marseilles in February 1975, Giscard initiated, in discussions with the socialist mayor Gaston Defferre, a pilot programme of this sort. Emphasising his hopes for a genuine integration of immigrants into French society, he declared: 'These immigrant workers who are a part of our national economic community must have a place that is worthy, humane and fair in the French society that I am trying to organise' (*Le Monde*, 1 March 1975).

However, when one looks at the steps taken in the area of immigration to achieve this 'fair' and 'open' society, it is difficult not to remark cynically on the gap between rhetoric and reality. Perhaps the fact that, from the very beginning of Giscard's presidency, insufficient money was allocated to improve the housing conditions of immigrants was a sign of the lack of will to back up the rhetoric with effective action. Postel-Vinay suggested precisely this in his letter of resignation as Secretary of State for Foreign Workers to the Prime Minister, Jacques Chirac (letter of 22 July 1974, quoted in Mangin 1982: 61). As Postel-Vinay predicted in his letter, the government's programme to improve housing conditions of foreign workers continued to be severely underfunded. Consequently, there was little improvement in housing and many immigrants continued to live in sub-standard accommodation. Certain municipalities refused to house more than a certain number of immigrants in the name of the theory of the 'threshold of tolerance' ('seuil de tolérance') which suggested that the social fabric was threatened if the number of foreigners surpassed a certain threshold – somewhere between 10 and 30 per cent of the total population in any given environment (see Chapters 3 and 4).

Housing continued to be a major focus of concern throughout the 1970s, and also a major focus of struggle. In 1975 15,000 residents of immigrant hostels established by the SONACOTRA went on strike. They were protesting at the level of rents and the severity of the rules which operated in the hostels. The strike went on until 1980 and became the longest ever to have taken place outside the work-place. It was of major significance in terms of the struggle by foreign workers for a recognition of social rights as residents in France rather than merely instruments of the economy.

The Giscard administration did not only renege on its promise to improve housing conditions for foreign workers and their families. The government's training programme and budget for social assistance were also underfunded, whilst the money allocated for the reception and orientation of foreigners entering France was progressively suppressed (Mangin 1982: 27). The law of 11 July 1975 allowed for foreigners to be trade union delegates. Yet this was merely the realisation of a bill proposed by the former Minister of Labour, Georges Gorse, in October 1973. The creation, in May 1975, of the 'Office of Cultural Promotion' – whose task was to promote art exhibitions, television and radio broadcasts and other cultural activities dedicated to representing cultural diversity – must also be seen against the background of continued social deprivation of immigrant communities, the persistence of inequalities between French nationals and foreigners, and the evident lack of real will on the part of the administration to tackle these problems.

The administration's diagnosis of immigration as a 'social problem' met with a remedy which was strong on rhetoric but totally inadequate on social action (Mangin 1982: 29). The barrage of legislation which was imposed without negotiation, excluding foreigners from the whole process, was indicative of the contradiction between rhetoric and action (Lochak 1976; Wihtol de Wenden 1988a: 200–1) and between the theory of Giscard's 'open' democracy (of which immigrants were to be an important part) and its practice. The real problems of racism, discrimination in job applications, difficulties at school and so on were not tackled seriously. The struggle for a recognition of fundamental rights, which had taken off dramatically after the Marcellin–Fontanet circulars in 1972, continued in diverse forms throughout the 1970s. Rent strikes, strikes at the work-place, hunger strikes, strikes against racism, marches and demonstrations were all means by which effective 'political' action was accomplished outside the normal, institutional political channels which were blocked off to immigrants. This 'politicisation of the non-political' (Wihtol de Wenden 1987: 140–58) was a way of challenging the institutional and bureaucratic structures of French society which effectively excluded immigrants from participation in society.

A more fundamental contradiction to the declared programme of security, equality and right to difference for foreigners in France was provided by the other major strand of immigration policy, namely, the programme of controls. Although the closing of the frontiers and the effort to suppress clandestine immigration were announced as a necessary part of the stabilisation and integration of the foreign population in France, it was soon clear that measures of control had other effects which seriously jeopardised the security of immigrants. The policy of linking residence to work and suppressing the process of regularisation, laid down in the Marcellin–Fontanet circulars of 1972, was reaffirmed by the circular of 2 May 1975 and the decree of 21 November 1975. At a time of economic recession and increasing unemployment, this meant that any foreigner who lost his or her job was, after six months, likely to be expelled from the country. Attempts to suspend or restrict family reunification (July 1974, November 1977) were overturned by rulings of the Conseil d'Etat, yet the harsh conditions governing its re-introduction, imposed by the decree of 29 April 1976, were not in keeping with the spirit of humanism, equality, generosity and respect advocated by Giscard and Dijoud.[7]

However, Dijoud's regime as Secretary of State for foreign workers seems relatively liberal compared to that of his successor Lionel Stoléru. From 1977, the rhetoric of choice and pluralism was largely dropped from the official language of immigration. The major debates around immigration focused on the immigrant as antithetical to the interests of the nation-state, thus giving credence to the argument advocating substitution and repatriation. These debates included the costs/benefits of immigration to the nation, immigrants taking the jobs of French workers, the money sent by immigrants in France to dependants in their country of origin (so depriving France of that money), the ways in which immigration impeded the process of modernisation (so maintaining archaic practices and preventing France from competing with other major producers) and illegal immigration. Under Stoléru, the main priorities were therefore the tighter control of entry and residence rights, the substitution of French workers for foreign workers, the fight against illegal immigration and the removal of immigrants through voluntary, financially aided repatriation. This whole policy of control and repatriation was aimed especially at Algerians (Weil 1990: 10).

Two measures in particular highlight this effort to control and reduce the immigrant population. The first was the repatriation scheme introduced by Stoléru in 1977 ('aide au retour') which offered 10,000 francs as an encouragement to immigrants to return to their country of origin. Known familiarly as the 'million Stoléru' after the Secretary of State's declared aim to remove one million foreigners from French soil in five years, the measure proved to be a failure: only 57,953 took up the offer, most of whom were Spanish and Portuguese workers (not the expected non-Europeans) who had already decided to return to their countries of origin.[8] (The scheme was eventually suppressed by the socialist government on 31 December 1981.)

The second measure was the Bonnet Law (after the Minister of the Interior, Christian Bonnet) of 10 January 1980. This introduced a stricter regime defining entry and residence rights in France and was designed to combat illegal immigration. This law has to be seen in the context of the government's creation of new definitions of 'irregularity', which were linked to employment. In other words, this logical connection between unemployment of immigrants, their 'illegal' status and their consequent expulsion from the country was cemented in law. As immigrant workers were often in jobs under threat, the logic of the Bonnet/Stoléru initiatives threatened the security of all those in France subject to this regime.

## 1981–91: THE POLITICS OF IMMIGRATION UNDER MITTERRAND

During the 1980s the question of immigration became a major (if not the major) political issue in France. There was a barrage of legislation, a major debate about nationality and national identity, the rise in political fortunes of the racist FN under the leadership of Jean-Marie Le Pen and the parallel development of anti-racist activity and new forms of cultural expression. There was also an enormous literature and discussion devoted to the subject – in parliament, official reports and statements, books, articles in journals, magazines and newspapers, television and radio programmes. 'Second-generation' youth became the major focus of attention (instead of the 'immigrant worker') as the 'problem' became articulated more around ideas of the permanent rather than the temporary presence of immigrants, and around social questions rather than economic ones.

The 1982 census put the number of foreigners in France at 3,680,100, or 6.8 per cent of the total population.[9] (The Ministry of the Interior recorded a figure of 4,223,928 at the end of 1981.) The first report of the Council for Integration (February 1991) suggests that there is nothing to indicate that this figure will have varied significantly when the latest census figures of 1990 become known. This is also confirmed by André Lebon in his annual survey of statistics relating to immigrants and foreigners for the Ministry of Solidarity and Health (1989: 39).

Since the supension of primary immigration in 1974, the number of foreigners in France has therefore remained fairly stable. To offset the small increase through family immigration, births of foreigners in France and refugees, there have been departures and expulsions (though the numbers of these are not so well known; Voisard and Ducastelle 1988: 16–17). The 1982 census put the number of Algerians at 795,920, Portuguese at 764,860, Moroccans at 431,120, Italians at 333,740, Spanish at 321,440 and Tunisians at 189,400. Commentators on changes in the foreign population during the 1980s have often remarked on the increased 'feminisation' of immigration, the rise in the number of young people of 'immigrant origin' and the high degree of concentration of foreigners in France, with more than half (57 per cent) in the three major industrial conurbations, Ile-de-France, Rhônes-Alpes and Provence-Côte d'Azur (for example, Mestiri 1990: 19–21). However, we shall see in the following chapters how the focus on women, youth and the visibility/concentrations of immigrants is itself problematic in that it constructs a specific dichotomy between the nature of contemporary immigration and past immigrations.

There was an enormous increase in legislation on immigration during the first half of the 1980s. Between May 1981 and March 1986 there were 16 laws, 79 decrees, 62 'arrêtés' and more than 220 circulars (Costa-Lascoux 1989: 6). Socialist policy was heavily determined by preceding events and practices – a fact which has occasionally been overlooked in recent literature on the subject. The description by the socialists of their immigration policy between 1981–6 as 'a new immigration policy' (cf. Ministère des Affaires Sociales 1986) should therefore be taken fairly sceptically. Let us remember that the formulations at the end of the 1960s and the beginning of the 1970s were also characterised as 'a new immigration policy', whilst the booklet produced by the office of the Secretary of State for Immigrant Workers in 1977 was called 'The New Immigration Policy'. (The ideological uses of this formulation will be considered in the next chapter.) In fact, there has been a broad political consensus on immigration which has spanned the last twenty years. The journalist Robert Solé was fairly accurate when, at the time of a major debate on immigration in parliament on 6 June 1985, he claimed that 'on fundamental issues, the positions of the major political parties are far closer than one would think' (*Le Monde*, 8 June 1985).

The booklet produced by the Ministry of Social Affairs in 1986 defined the socialists' immigration policy as a wide-ranging and coherent programme on immigration, as opposed to what were characterised as the random series of pragmatic measures which had gone before. Indeed, this was the way the programme was presented early in 1981: that is, as a programme that would consider all aspects of the question, from the problems faced by 'second-generation' children at school to the wider considerations of migration and international cooperation. However, by 1983, when racist attacks were on the increase and the FN had broken through the 10 per cent barrier in municipal elections, the government responded in the most pragmatic way possible by tightening its controls and stepping up its campaign against the 'clandestins'. Furthermore, the consensus on integration and control, which the socialists inherited from the Giscard era, was also to form the basis of their own policy. Any sense of a 'coherent' policy was soon submerged beneath the sea of contradictions which this inevitably threw up.

However, the difference between the two administrations did appear considerable in the first year of socialist rule. Under Giscard, it was said, the emphasis had been on expulsion of immigrants; their existence in France had been one of constant insecurity and fear. In the first euphoric days of socialist victory in 1981 – with a political programme designed to challenge more than twenty years of right-wing rule – the emphasis was very much on the need to put an end to the insecurity of immigrants and to improve the situation inherited from the past. Some early measures introduced in 1981 were designed to achieve this: the supension of all expulsion of foreigners born in France or having entered France before the age of ten (circulars of 6 July and 7 August); the retrospective regularisation of all foreign workers who had entered France illegally before 1 January 1981, thus legalising about 130,000 'clandestins' (circular of 11 August); the right of association granted to foreigners, thus bringing into line in this domain the rights of foreigners and French nationals (law of 9 October); the suppression of Stoléru's repatriation programme (25 November).

These measures were nevertheless accompanied by the familiar rhetoric on controls ('la maîtrise des flux migratoires'). This took the form of stricter definitions of entry and residence rights (law of 29 October 1981; see Wihtol de Wenden 1988a: 282, 285) and a firm commitment to eradicate illegal immigration ('la lutte contre le travail clandestin'; Council of Ministers, 23 July 1981, 2 September 1981, 28 April 1982). In May 1982, decrees concerning entry and residence rights led to such a large number of foreigners being refused entry that President Chadli of Algeria lodged a formal protest (Bruschi 1985: 51). Mitterrand was subsequently obliged to put an end to these excessively severe measures. The contradictory messages given out by this process of outlawing 'immigration' whilst 'integrating' immigrants and removing their fears of insecurity will be considered further in the following chapters. Let us note here that severe statements on controls and the backtracking on the pledge to grant immigrants the vote in municipal elections (contained in Mitterrand's 110-point manifesto programme for the presidential elections of 1981) made some proponents of rights for immigrants quickly disillusioned. In the words of Albano Cordeiro, they soon saw, in the new government's approach, 'more elements of continuity than of rupture with regard to previous measures introduced' (Cordeiro 1984: 105). Indeed, the law of 29 October 1981 actually made the conditions for entry even more restrictive than the severe Bonnet Law of 1980 (Lochak 1987: 10), whilst the number of expulsions rose from 2861 to 8482 between 1982–4 (and was 12,364 in 1986; Hannoun 1987).

Viewed in this way, the more repressive stance taken by the government in 1983 was an extension of a long-standing rigour rather than a complete about-turn. However, there were other reasons at this time for adopting a stricter approach to immigration. The early socialist experiment with nationalisation and public spending projects had already been replaced by austerity measures; unemployment was continuing to rise; racism was on the increase and the FN polled over 10 per cent of the vote at the municipal elections of March of that year on an anti-immigrant ticket.[10] Fearing being dubbed by the extreme Right and elements of the conventional Right the party of 'laxity' which was sacrificing France to the (North African) immigrants, a number of socialists favoured a tougher line on immigration. In response to strikes by immigrant workers in the car industry, the Prime Minister Pierre Mauroy blamed the workers' action on 'religious and political groups whose action is based on criteria which have little to do with the social realities of France' (27 January 1983, quoted in *Le Monde*, 11 February 1983). This statement was echoed by the Minister of Labour Jean Auroux (*Le Monde*, 11 February 1983).[11] The brochure *Vivre Ensemble: les Immigrés Parmi Nous* (Secrétariat d'Etat Chargé des Immigrés 1983) was not released by the government after its publication in February. During the campaign for the March elections, Gaston Defferre, the Minister of the Interior and mayor of Marseilles, prided himself on being ideally placed to expel immigrants and fight against delinquency (thus suggesting and reinforcing the association between the two: *Le Monde*, 12 March 1983); the day before the elections, Pierre Mauroy more or less blamed the immigrant question for the loss of votes to the extreme Right, rather than condemning the wave of racism aimed at immigrant communities.

In response to these and other events in 1983 (especially an alliance of the conventional Right and the FN to capture Dreux in the by-election of September; see Gaspard and Servan-Schreiber 1985), the meetings of the Council of Ministers of 31 August 1983 and 4 April 1984 spelled out the government's tougher line on immigration: increased controls, a clamp-down on 'clandestins' and a new scheme of financial aid for voluntary repatriation. The

introduction of this latter scheme (decree of 27 April 1984) highlighted the gap between the rhetoric of a coherent immigration
policy and a pragmatic approach responding to racist, anti-immigrant feeling of the time. The scheme was dressed up as a financial
package aimed at helping the return and reintegration of immigrants into their country of origin. It was consequently termed
'aide à la réinsertion' – to distinguish it from the Stoléru scheme
of 'aide au retour' – and would be effected through negotiation
and agreement with the countries of origin (thus taking their own
economic problems into account as well). In practice, the scheme
was thwarted from the outset by the refusal of the countries of
origin to negotiate agreements of 'reinsertion'. (This refusal was
officially described in a delightful euphemism as 'a certain re-
ticence on the part of the countries of emigration', Ministère des
Affaires Sociales et de la Solidarité Nationale 1986: 42.) They
showed little enthusiasm for a project which encouraged a mass
return of their own nationals at a time of economic hardship. This
led to the scheme being introduced unilaterally by the French
government. Following its introduction, there were relatively few
takers for any aspects of the scheme, for it was seen by many to be
little more than a device for reducing the numbers of immigrants
in France at a time of high unemployment and growing racism –
the very criticisms made by the socialists of Stoléru's repatriation
scheme.

Two other measures introduced in 1984 highlight the contradictions in a policy of integration and control. The law of 17 July
introduced a single residence and work permit ('la carte unique').
This had for long been a demand of immigrant associations, for
the different durations of the separate permits had been a bureaucratic nightmare for immigrants. The new law rationalised the
previous system by stipulating that all foreigners over the age of
sixteen residing in France must be the holders of either a residence
permit (valid for ten years and automatically renewable) or a
temporary residence permit (valid for one year but renewable
thereafter). This measure at least removed a major barrier to the
security of immigrants in France.

However, the decree of 4 December pulled in the opposite
direction. It imposed such strict requirements for family reunification that the legal right of members of a family to join their
relative became virtually meaningless. The measure required the
member of the family already residing in France to show proof of

adequate housing and finances at a time when immigrants occupied the worst housing stock and were more likely to be unemployed or in low-wage jobs than the French. This form of discrimination against non-EC nationals clearly contradicted the socialists' declared aim to situate its immigration policy within 'a judicial framework defining the status of the migrant, founded on the principles of human rights and equality of treatment between foreigners and "nationals"' (Costa-Lascoux 1985: 20). It also contradicted the terms layed down in the 'Convention relating to the juridical status of the migrant worker' to which France had become a signatory in the same year.

Hence, between 1983–6 the contradictions between integration and control grew and immigration became a political and electoral football. The electoral successes of the FN and the increase in racist attacks (*Différences* 1983) were met by a huge mobilisation of anti-racist support expressed in marches in 1983 (the march for equality) and 1984 (Convergence 84) and the formation of a new anti-racist organisation, SOS Racisme (autumn 1984). Opting for a high-media profile, slogans ('Hands off my pal'), rock concerts (300,000 people attended the concert in the Place de la Concorde in June 1985) and a fairly close relationship with the Socialist Party, SOS Racisme was from the outset viewed sceptically by a number of other associations and anti-racist movements. The older-established MRAP (Movement against Racism and for Friendship Between Peoples) with its links with the Communist Party,[12] the League of the Rights of Man, LICRA (the International League against Racism and Anti-semitism) and smaller associations were critical of its concern with image, the glamour status quickly achieved by its leader Harlem Désir, its financial support from within the government and its lack of concern with the real problems of racism and exclusion.

In 1985 a new organisation was formed called France Plus, which appealed directly to the new generation of French nationals 'from immigrant parents', known popularly as 'les beurs'.[13] Not politically aligned, its major aim was to bring in more 'beurs' as candidates on the election lists of all parties, and to encourage others to participate in the electoral system and to make full use of their rights of citizenship.[14] France Plus is integrationist and opposed to any reference to the cultural difference of the 'beurs' which might lead to 'differences in rights and duties and to apartheid' (*Le Quotidien*, 17 September 1990). In opposition to the earlier anti-racist slogan 'the right to difference' ('le droit à la différence'), the major slogans of France Plus have been 'the right to resemblance' ('le droit à la ressemblance') and 'the right to indifference' ('le droit à l'indifférence'). France Plus has also been criticised by other grassroots organisations for its appeal to a narrow élite of 'upwardly mobile' 'beurs' (thus ignoring the vast majority of 'second-generation' youth and the more concrete problems of discrimination and exclusion).

During 1984–5 the debate on immigration also shifted onto a more general discussion of national identity, through conferences organised both by the New Right Club de l'Horloge and by socialist clubs, and the appearance of a number of books on identity (Griotteray 1984; Le Gallou 1985; Le Club de l'Horloge 1985; Espace 89 1985). The attempt by the socialist government to appease both 'sides' in the more polarised debate around immigration (messages of support for SOS Racisme whilst announcing more severe measures of control) led to deep contradictions in policy.

The right-wing government of Jacques Chirac (1986–8) had a slightly different problem, in which the appeasement of anti-racism played little part. The question was rather how the Right could take up the nationalist and anti-immigrant mantle paraded so successfully by Le Pen without actually forming an open alliance with his party (Chirac apparently had no objection to the numerous alliances between the FN and Chirac's own party, the RPR, on local councils). The increased police powers of on-the-spot identity checks, used predominantly against North Africans (or those who 'looked like' North Africans), were an early indication of how the socialists' policy of controls and the fight against illegal immigration had taken on a far more sinister air. The Pasqua Law of 9 September 1986 (named after the Minister of the Interior, Charles Pasqua) extended the severe conditions defining entry and residence rights already fixed by the Bonnet Law of 1980 and the law of October 1981. It also stipulated that decisions regarding expulsion from the country be taken not by the judiciary but by local prefects, thus making them part of administrative rather than legal practice and speeding up the whole process considerably. The result was a doubling in numbers, over the next three months, of those deported from France (Voisard and Ducastelle 1988: 69). The reintroduction of visas for all non-EC nationals (14 September

1986) was a further move to control the frontiers (Silverman 1989: 94).

Pasqua's scant regard for human rights led to the illegal deportation of 101 Malians in October 1986 and an alarming rate of deportations after that. In May 1987 he showed himself capable of sinking to the same rhetorical depths as Le Pen when he promised to deport illegal immigrants in train-loads. The full significance of this remark can only be appreciated when one notes that it was delivered at the start of the trial of Klaus Barbie for crimes against humanity, amongst which was the despatch of sealed train-loads of Jews from Lyons to the extermination camps.

The most significant political and public debate connected with the question of immigration in this period – and the clearest sign that the right-wing coalition government was intent on stealing the clothes of the FN – was the bill presented in October 1986 to reform the Code of Nationality. The main thrust of the proposal was to remove the long-established principle of the 'jus soli' governing the attribution of nationality, by which all children born in France of foreign parents (and having resided in the country for more than five years prior to the age of majority) are automatically French nationals at the age of eighteen. The government proposed to change this automatic right into a voluntary request for French nationality (which could be refused according to certain conditions; for example, to those who had served a prison sentence of more than six months).

The intent of the bill was to 'safeguard' national identity. Throughout the 1980s the ideologues of the New Right and the Front National had been putting forward just such a project to 'purify' France (Griotteray 1984; Le Gallou 1985). This bill had the potential for creating stateless subjects. It caused an outcry, was rejected by the Conseil d'Etat on 30 October and was then put in limbo whilst a special commission was set up (the so-called 'comité de sages') to look into the whole area of nationality. The proposal was finally postponed indefinitely in September 1987 when Chirac announced that the issue was too sensitive and controversial to be dealt with during the run-up to a presidential election. However, the televised sessions, in which the commission listened to a wide cross-section of opinion, proved a fascinating national debate and debate about the nation (see the transcripts of these sessions in Commission de la Nationalité 1988: Tome 1). On 7 January 1988 the commission published its sixty propositions, amongst which was the reaffirmation of the 'jus soli' (Commission de la Nationalité 1988: Tome 2).

Since the return of a socialist government in 1988, under the premiership of Michel Rocard (1988–91) and then Edith Cresson, 'immigration' has remained at the centre of political attention. The Rocard government perpetuated the same contradictions around integration and control that characterised the immigration policy of previous socialist administrations in the 1980s. The coupling of the terms 'rigour' and 'humanism' (Mestiri 1990: 45) in the law of August 1989 on entry and residence rights for foreigners (the Joxe Law after the Minister of the Interior, Pierre Joxe) was indicative of the need to legitimise all decisions with this contradictory discourse. This law attempted both to 'humanise' the drastic procedures for expulsion introduced by the Pasqua Law of 1986 and at the same time to maintain the 'rigour' of control which successive governments of Right and Left have introduced over the last twenty years.

If the debate on nationality was the centre-piece of the Chirac years, the debate on the headscarf played a similar role at the end of the decade. We have already mentioned that the exclusion from classes of the three female students at Creil, a town near Paris, in October 1989 quickly became a national affair. Following a ruling by the Conseil d'Etat (27 October 1989), the government's response to the exclusion was equivocal: the Minister of Education, Lionel Jospin, argued both that the secular state system was inviolable and that the state had a duty to include all children, irrespective of their background and origin. The debates around nationality and the headscarf were clearly symptomatic of much wider crises which political interventions were not only incapable of tackling but exacerbated considerably (see Chapters 4 and 5).

'Integration', 'the problems of the suburbs' and 'racism/anti-racism' became the major topics of discussion in the new decade. Rhetoric and gestures by the government seemed to take the place of any serious change in policy. To defuse the tensions generated by the headscarf affair, in December 1989 Hubert Prévot was named Permanent Secretary to a newly created cabinet committee responsible for integration (he was frequently referred to as Secrétaire Général à l'Intégration). The Council for Integration was created in the same month, and officially installed in March 1990. Set up to consider and recommend ways of 'integrating' immigrants more effectively in society, based on a thorough understanding of historical and statistical evidence on immigration, the Council's first meeting (19 December 1989) discussed instead the necessity for stricter controls on immigration and the fight against illegal immigration and abuse of the right of political asylum. It is true that subsequent meetings concentrated on housing (11 January 1990), schools (31 January 1990) and training and the cities (10 May 1990).[15] Yet there have, as yet, been few concrete measures arising from these deliberations, and too little money provided by the government to aid local councils in their attempts to improve social conditions, accusations that were frequently made by SOS Racisme (as for example at the third national congress of the anti-racist organisation, 28–30 April 1990). The continued confusion in the brief of the Council between social measures and measures of control was evident in the first report of the Council (February 1991).

The views expressed in this report were largely the consensus cross-party views which prevail today. Despite the Right's attempt to point the finger at the government over its handling of 'immigration' – as in the opposition conference on immigration (31 March–1 April 1990) – the closeness of the Right and Left over the question of immigration was evident in the cross-party round tables on racism (3 April 1990) and immigration (29 May 1990). After the meeting on immigration, Michel Rocard praised 'the unanimously shared will to control immigration and to work for the integration of legal foreigners'.[16]

The political rhetoric on integration belied the deepening crisis in social cohesion. This crisis – which manifested itself especially in the suburbs around Paris, Lyons and Marseilles and in the schools – extended far beyond 'inter-ethnic' tension, yet was consistently represented as an 'immigrant problem'. The 'ghetto-suburbs' became a euphemism for immigration.[17] Riots in Vaulx-en-Vélin in the suburbs of Lyons (6–7 October 1990) (reminiscent of the 'hot summer' of riots in the suburbs of Lyons in 1981) and Sartrouville (26–7 March 1991) in the Seine valley near Paris highlighted the frustration and social exclusion of 'second-generation' youth, whilst demonstrations in the schools (24 October 1990) were also the expression of frustration over inequalities and bad conditions. After a special conference on the suburbs in December 1990 ('les assises de Banlieues 89' at Bron), Michel Delebarre was named Minister of State with responsibility for the cities (19 December 1990). In early April 1991 Delebarre and

Michel Rocard visited some of the main suburbs in crisis. Yet their professed concern about the problems of the suburbs (like that of the Tory Government in Britain over the problems of the inner cities) was regarded sceptically by many residents themselves and by anti-racist organisations (see *Le Quotidien*, 8 April 1991). The riots and demonstrations were signs of a much deeper crisis in social cohesion, born from the social and economic marginalisation and exclusion of a growing number of young people (see *Le Nouvel Observateur*, 25–31 October 1990) and the breakdown in channels of social and political mobilisation (the massive decline in support for the Communist Party, the disenchantment with political parties in general and with institutionalised anti-racism) (Wieviorka 1991; Dubet in *Libération*, 30–1 March 1991). The sociologist Alain Touraine described French society as a huge machine capable, at one and the same time, of 'sucking in and repelling, integrating and excluding' (*Le Figaro*, 28 December 1990).

In this climate of social crisis, racism continued to flourish. Acts of physical racial violence did not increase in 1990 compared to previous years, but there was a significant increase in acts of symbolic racial violence (report by the Commission nationale consultative des droits de l'Homme 1991). The desecration of Jewish graves in Carpentras (9–10 May 1990) was the most publicised example of symbolic racial attacks, but the increase in graffiti, racist tracts and revisionist history denying the Holocaust, anonymous telephone calls and so on were other examples of what the report by the national commission on human rights mentioned above called the 'banalisation of racism'. The huge march against racism and anti-semitism after the Carpentras desecrations (14 May 1990) – which was joined by Mitterrand and Rocard in a glare of publicity – and the adoption by parliament of the Communist-inspired proposals to tighten up the provisions of the 1972 law against racial discrimination were themselves largely symbolic responses to racism rather than a serious attempt to tackle its underlying causes. Racism and anti-racism became both 'banalised' and politicised (see, for example, articles in *Politis*, *Le Nouvel Observateur*, *L'Evénement du Jeudi*, *L'Express* and *Le Quotidien* between 10 and 20 May 1990). The moral and symbolic outrage at racism had little effect on the popularity of Le Pen or on the extent of racism in society.

Anti-racism was under attack from outside and deeply divided from within. The Gulf War accentuated the division between France Plus (pro-war) and SOS Racisme (anti-war) and led to a split within SOS Racisme itself when a number of its luminaries (including the philosopher Bernard Henri-Lévy and the director of the Paris opera, Pierre Bergé) resigned over the movement's position against the war.[18] At the same time, relations between Jews and Arabs in the organisation were put under even greater strain.

The divisions between anti-racist organisations mentioned previously were indicative of a crisis in the anti-racist movement and a need for a more serious reflection on how to combat racism. SOS Racisme was seen by many disadvantaged 'beurs' and foreigners as merely part of the institutional political and media machinery. Conscious of this criticism, SOS Racisme began to distance itself from the Socialist Party in 1989 (especially over the Joxe Law of 1989) and concern itself more with social problems, through the slogan of 'integration'.[19] The heady years between 1984–9, in which anti-racism became synonymous for many with SOS Racisme, were now seen by some critics to have been counter-productive (Taguieff 1991). During those years anti-racism had become fixated on Le Pen and had failed to situate racism in its wider social, economic and ideological context.[20] Some researchers suggested the need for a more serious reappraisal of the nature of contemporary racism and a reformulation of strategies for anti-racism (Taguieff 1991; Wieviorka 1991).[21]

After ten years under a socialist president, France was profoundly marked by a sense of national and social crisis. The term 'immigration' had become a euphemism for this crisis. Although the FN benefited most from this association, the causes of the politicisation of immigration in the 1980s lie far beyond the extreme Right itself. Caught in the glare of the national racism of Le Pen – 'like rabbits trapped in the headlights of an oncoming car' (Grillo 1991: 43) – anti-racism (and the organised Left in general) not only lacked the necessary vision and strategy to cope with the wider social crisis but frequently perpetuated a discourse which contributed to a confusion of racism and anti-racism. The next chapter considers the development of this discourse in contemporary France and the construction of today's consensus meanings on immigration.

# Chapter 3

# The 'problem' of immigration

The end of the 1960s was a transitional period in the evolution of the discourse of immigration in France. It was then that a different way of perceiving immigration began to evolve and the first measures of immigration control in the modern period were introduced. Not that this signifies a complete break with the past and the construction of a new and discrete episteme. There are continuities and discontinuities in the development of the discourse of immigration which do not correspond to changes in government and make any fixing of temporal 'periods' fairly arbitrary. The following discussion will therefore look back – and forward – to situate the developments of the 1970s in a wider context. It will nevertheless suggest that a new consensus on immigration was constructed at the end of the 1960s and the beginning of the 1970s which laid the foundations for the contemporary debate on immigration. At the heart of this consensus was a new racialisation of the question of immigration, leading subsequently to the racialisation of wider socio-economic and political questions. This process of racialisation of social relations was effected largely through a reconstructed discourse of cultural and national difference.

## PROBLEMS AND SOLUTIONS

Most recent histories of immigration in France have located this time as the point at which official policy on immigration changed. As we have seen, what has been described as the 'laissez-faire' approach of the early and mid-1960s switched to a more interventionist approach by the state. This intervention took the form of both controls on immigration and measures to facilitate the integration of the three million immigrants already in the country. The reasons for this change in policy are, in large part, attributed to the changing nature of immigration itself: from an 'immigration de main-d'oeuvre' to an 'immigration de peuplement', that is, from an economic immigration of manpower to a social immigration of dependants, and, similarly, from immigration as a temporary phenomenon to a permanent immigration ('immigration sédentarisée'). Immigration was therefore no longer deemed to be merely of economic but also of social significance. Immigration was now responsible for social problems which needed addressing; hence the justification for a new intervention by the state.

This rationale for a change in immigration policy was not only established in official circles but generally accepted by writers on immigration policy. However, there are a number of problems with this historiography of immigration (see Noiriel 1989). In terms of the evolution of the process of emigration, immigration and settlement, it is over-reductive to suggest that there is ever a neat divide between a temporary immigration for economic reasons and permanent settlement in the country of immigration. Many immigrants had already settled in France before the suspension of primary immigration in July 1974. For example, at the time of the end of the Algerian war in 1962 there were some 350,000 Algerians in France, including more than 50,000 families (Sayad 1985: 34). North African immigration during the 1950s and early 1960s was both an economic and family immigration (Nair 1988: 262). In any case, is it ever possible to say precisely whether an immigrant is temporary or not, whatever might have been his or her thoughts on an eventual return to the country of origin? More importantly perhaps, the historiography outlined above suggests that at a certain moment immigration shifts from being an economic to becoming a social phenomenon: as if the social and the economic can be compartmentalised in this way and the immigrant is ever merely a unit of labour.

Of particular interest are the terms used at this time to describe the process of migration and settlement. Previous migrations were not described in the same way even though, as Abdelmalek Sayad has remarked, 'economic immigration has always finished by becoming an immigration of settlement, and one can say that there has never been an immigration of so-called settlement which was not primarily an economic immigration' (Sayad 1983: 40). Considered in this light, the use of the dichotomies between temporary and permanent and economic and social forms of immigration to describe the post-war period might then appear to be not so much a reflection of a reality but a construction of one. It is in this sense that I will be considering the discourse of immigration in contemporary France. The end of the 1960s and the beginning of the 1970s are significant not so much because of a 'real' shift from temporary to permanent and economic to social forms of immigration, but because the evolution of immigration began to be constructed in this way. Viewed like this, the so-called 'problem of immigration', conceived as a social and cultural problem, is a construction, though, like all ideological constructions, one which has very real effects on social relations.

It is not only necessary to problematise the notion of the 'problem'; the notion of the 'solution' should also be viewed critically. They come hand in hand. Immigration was constructed as a 'problem' which warranted a 'new approach', soon to become known as 'the new immigration policy'. To put it another way, the new approach was legitimised by the idea of a new problem, namely that immigration was no longer simply an economic but also a social phenomenon and therefore required state intervention.[1] The dichotomy between a 'laissez-faire' approach in the 1950s and 1960s and the need for a firmer interventionist approach by the state at the end of the 1960s (Secrétariat d'Etat aux Travailleurs Immigrés 1977; Ministère du Travail/Secrétariat d'Etat aux Travailleurs Immigrés 1977: 33; Ministère des Affaires Sociales et de la Solidarité Nationale 1983: 9) is also part of the same redefinition of immigration.

The main point here is that this elaborate historiography of post-war immigration, constituted by numerous dichotomies produced and reproduced by officials and researchers alike, is in fact a euphemistic language effacing the 'real' problem – that of the assimilation of 'these' immigrants compared to previous ones.[2] As Sayad says (1985: 29), the distinction between an 'economic immigration' and a 'family immigration' 'is, at bottom, merely a disguised way of describing – through an apparently "neutral" and "objective" vocabulary – the opposition between an "assimilable" and an "unassimilable" immigration'.

At the heart of the story of the contemporary discourse of immigration is the reformulation of the concept of assimilation: the 'unassimilables' were no longer the Italians (end of the nineteenth century) or the Poles (between the wars), but the non-Europeans, and especially those from North Africa. The focus on their 'installation' and eventual naturalisation is profoundly linked to a new questioning around the legitimacy of immigration (or rather 'these' immigrants) and the development of a discourse on families, fertility, illegality ('les clandestins') and social and national crisis. The reformulation of immigration at the end of the 1960s transformed the term 'immigration' into a euphemism for non-Europeans (particularly North Africans) and delegitimised it. It is important to consider the nature of this reformulation of immigration, since the major issues underlying this process are often effaced in the euphemistic language of 'the problem of immigration' and 'the new immigration policy'.

These terms were introduced in official circles at the end of the 1960s (or rather reintroduced but with different meanings, as we shall see). In May 1968 the Economic and Social Council asked Corentin Calvez to produce a report on 'the problem of foreign workers'. The report of the same name was presented to the Council and adopted in February 1969. Other important voices were also prominent at this time in a reappraisal of the question of immigration; notably Michel Massenet, head of the Population and Migrations section at the Ministry of Labour (and formerly, from its inception in 1958, director of the FAS), and Maurice Schumann, the Minister of Social Affairs. The ideas proposed by Calvez, Massenet and Schumann were significant in defining 'the problem' and producing the 'new' approach to immigration.[3]

Their argument hinges on the fact that France, though traditionally open to mass immigration, could no longer maintain an open-door policy. This idea was of course not unique to France. All countries in western Europe which had received large numbers of immigrants after the war were coming to similar conclusions at about this time (or before in the case of Britain). France is presented as a unified nation within which successive flows of migrants have easily, even spontaneously, become absorbed through the process of assimilation (Calvez 1969: 1; Schumann 1969: 934; Massenet 1970: 20).[4] This traditional process is at risk today due to the change in migration flows to France over the previous ten or fifteeen years; that is, from a predominantly European migration to a largely African one (Massenet 1970: 22). The 'cultural proximity' of the previous immigrants, which facilitated the process of assimilation, is contrasted to the 'cultural distance' of the new immigrants, which hampers assimilation and threatens social cohesion. Massenet puts it like this:

> Not only has immigration ceased to be a marginal phenomenon, owing to increasing numbers of immigrants, but it has also ceased to be a natural phenomenon, that is to say a process which gives rise to a spontaneous adaptation. The problems that immigration poses to our society put at risk society's future cohesion.
>
> (Massenet 1970: 22)

Here the qualitative change in immigration (from predominantly European to largely non-European sources) is accompanied by a quantitative change: the argument around 'different cultures' defining the 'problem' is never far away from the argument around increased numbers. A demographic discourse is also invoked. Massenet (1968: 2, 6; 1970: 21) and Schumann (1969: 934) compare the fertility rates of immigrants with those of the 'native' French ('Français de souche'). They both point out that foreigners are breeding ten times as fast as the French. Calvez makes the link between the projected growth in numbers of Algerians and the problems of assimilation into French society:

> Demographic projections put forward to appreciate, for example, the probable numbers of Algerians in France in the year 2000 have suggested a figure of 2.5 million people. This would lead to the presence, in France, of an unassimilable island, at a time when it is not certain that the Algerians themselves wish to belong definitively to the French community. It is therefore in the common interest to avoid the appearance of these ethnic problems.
>
> (Calvez 1969: 2; cf. Conseil Economique et Social 1969: 6)

It is not merely a question of numbers here but, more importantly, a question of concentration and the creation of ghettos. The fear of ghettos ('îlots inassimilables') is at the heart of the theory of the 'seuil de tolérance', or 'threshold of tolerance'. This quota theory based on racialised criteria is invoked by Calvez to guarantee assimilation and the maintenance of social cohesion:

> In a general way, the immigrant presence in France leads us to recommend the precise studies carried out on the thresholds of tolerance which should not be exceeded in the areas of housing,

schools and the work-place; that is, thresholds necessary to maintain a suitable social balance, founded on the proportion- ate levels of foreigners, and variable according to the ethnic group. It is also necessary to be aware of the high fertility rates of Algerian families.

(1969: 2)

Massenet's views (and even his vocabulary) are very similar to those of Calvez. It is worth quoting these at length, for the racialisation of immigration and social relations in the 1970s owes much to formulations of this kind:

As we hope that our society should contain no forms of segre- gation (even implicit), we should not underestimate the risk of seeing the appearance in our country of islands of people impermeable to the traditional processes of assimilation, which have, over the centuries, woven the unity of France from very diverse elements. Due to the concentration of immigrants in five regions, in a number of zones of rapid urbanisation, the presence of the foreign population in certain communes has reached what one mayor in the Paris region has called a 'critical threshold'.... The thresholds beyond which the host population closes itself to the foreign population and risks expressing more than simple indifference have been classified according to em- pirical measurements. In a primary school class, the presence of more than 20 per cent of foreign children slows down the progress of all the pupils. In a hospital, problems of coexistence arise when foreigners represent more than 30 per cent of the number of patients. In a block of flats, it is not wise to go beyond the proportion of 10 to 15 per cent of families of foreign origin when these families are not accustomed to life in a modern environment.

(1970: 23–4; cf. Freeman 1979: 158–9)

It is not clear from this exposition of the theory of the 'seuil de tolérance' which immigrants present the greatest problems. At times in this text (and others) Massenet makes it perfectly clear that it is North African immigration which poses the major prob- lem, and, more specifically, Algerian immigration (1970: 22, 24). At other times, he uses the general terms 'immigrant' or 'étranger'. Calvez and Schumann also slip between the same specific and general terminology. As suggested above, this is indicative of the elision being made between immigration and non-Europeans (especially North Africans), which has become the standard association in the political and popular discourse of contemporary France.

It is also not clear what empirical evidence there is to confirm the different percentages listed above. Why hospitals should be able to function with a higher percentage of foreigners than schools or housing estates before social cohesion is put at risk is not explained. However, pursuing the logic of the racist theory which he is propounding, Massenet concludes 'our immigration policy must be orientated according to a new notion: that of the immigrant's capacity to adapt in our country' (1970: 24).[5]

How new the notion of 'adaptability' actually is will be discussed shortly. For the moment, let us consider the ways in which the 'problem of immigration' is formulated in the views expressed above. Previous immigrants (predominantly European) assimilated naturally and spontaneously; but recent (non-European) immigrants are either not able or refuse to assimilate. It is *their* inassimilability which would create problems (not French racism). These problems are *social* problems of cultural and 'ethnic' relations. Their increasing numbers (due to a prolific birth-rate) will cause increased ethnic tension and will therefore be a growing threat to social cohesion.

This is not to say that fears are not also expressed about the damaging *economic* consequences of continued and uncontrolled immigration. These anxieties centre around the 'slow-down' effect of the immigrant work-force on the modernisation of French industry (Calvez 1969: 2; Conseil Economique et Social 1969: 5), and the threat this work-force poses to French jobs (Massenet 1970: 21–2). However, these economic arguments are closely linked to the social, cultural and ethnic arguments (although sometimes in contradiction to them as well). Immigration *per se* was not to be stopped; it was, in Massenet's words, to be reorientated according to the criteria of assimilation, ethnic balance and social cohesion.

It was noted in the previous chapter that the economic arguments in favour of immigration were heard throughout the 1960s and well into the 1970s. Industrialists, employers and economic planners argued that the French economy still needed a substantial immigration to provide a cheap and mobile work-force. Maurice Schumann said in 1969 'nobody should underestimate the economic and human value of immigration and the contribution of immigrants to the development of our country' (Schumann 1969: 940). The sixth economic plan (1971–5) talked of the necessity for more than 60,000 new immigrants each year for the duration of the period covered by the plan. Some employers continued to argue for the need for immigration even after the suspension of primary immigration in July 1974 (Cordeiro 1984: 88–93; Wihtol de Wenden 1988a: 205).

Clearly there are contradictions between the demographic, economic and social/cultural/ethnic arguments. The attempt to construct a coherent approach from this disparity was suggested in Massenet's remarks on a reorientation in approach mentioned above. It was given more flesh in the proposals outlined in the Calvez report. They suggest that the new policy should be based on an easily assimilable European immigration, a use of North African immigrants for temporary manpower needs, stricter mechanisms for reinforcing this orientation in controls, and renewed efforts to improve the trade union rights, housing conditions and education of immigrants already in the country. Immigration controls (of non-Europeans) were therefore justified, indeed essential, to maintain social cohesion. These are the origins of the policy of control and integration, which has become the bedrock of the immigration policy of all French governments over the last twenty years.[6]

The year 1968 saw the introduction of measures (albeit fairly limited in scope) which were already in line with this reorientation: the restrictions on the procedure of regularisation (July), the introduction of free circulation for workers from EC countries (October) and the Franco–Algerian accord limiting the number of Algerian workers entitled to enter France each year to 35,000 (December) (see Tapinos 1975: 87–8). The desire to tap European rather than non-European labour reserves is equally clear when the Franco–Algerian accord of 1968 is compared to the Franco–Portuguese accord of 29 July 1971, which allowed for an annual contingent of 65,000 workers. Portugal was now deemed to be the principal source of foreign labour (Tapinos 1975: 94).

Immigration controls in contemporary France were not at first the result of the economic crisis of the 1970s; instead, they were influenced largely by concerns about assimilation, ethnic balance and social cohesion. The terminology used in official and research circles to describe this reorientation in the approach to immigration has frequently effaced these considerations. But how 'new' were the 'problem of immigration' and the 'new policy' when concerns about immigration and assimilation had been voiced on a number of occasions in the past?

## STATE DETERMINATIONS AND DETERMINATIONS OF THE STATE

I have been arguing that the 'problem of immigration' was not a natural result of the changing pattern of migration flows and their effect on French society; it was the result of the way this evolution was perceived and interpreted at the end of the 1960s by a number of influential officials. However, I am not suggesting an intentionalist conspiracy theory. It is important not to confuse individual, psychological determinations with the wider conditions of possibility of a certain way of thinking. It is the latter which concerns us here; specifically, the role of the state in this process.

The expressions 'the problem of immigration' and 'a new policy' (problem and solution) have the effect of masking the active role of the state in constructing so-called 'problems'. The 'problem', it appears, is located with the presence of others rather than with the wider structures of society which produce this categorisation of others as a problem at a particular historical moment. And the 'solution' is legitimised as a justifiable reaction to the new problem. My critique of this formulation has been to suggest, instead, that the 'new approach' was not simply a response to a perceived and verifiable 'problem' but was active in actually producing the parameters of the debate and creating a new consensus.

The reappraisal of the historiography of contemporary immigration policy quickly leads to a rejection of the limited idea of problems (caused by certain immigrants) and solutions (provided by the state). Yet neither is it a question of reversing this formula to suggest that the state is itself the origin and source of new ways of conceptualising social relations. This view is a highly mechanistic vision of the social formation and leaves no space for the idea that there are always contradictions in dominant formations and a process of struggle over dominant meanings. The state cannot be discussed satisfactorily in functionalist terms for it does not simply impose ideologies from above onto civil society below. It is not a simple case of one-way traffic; nor is it a simple case of a clear dichotomy between the two. The state is not a homogeneous and monolithic structure, just as civil society is not an autonomous domain separate from the state. Both are constantly traversed by diverse and often contradictory processes; both are therefore *always already constituted*. Determinations of economic and social organisation (and the construction of relations of power) are part of a complex process which the reductionist language of origins merely simplifies and mythologises.

This complexity can best be shown (at least in part) if we consider the state's 'new immigration policy' in a wider historical context. The discourses of demographic, economic, social, cultural, ethnic and national necessity which are in play here – and which are frequently pulling in different directions – are the very discourses which have shaped the question of immigration over the whole of the modern period. We have already mentioned, in Chapter 1, the contradiction at the end of the nineteenth century between the criteria of economic necessity, on the one hand, and assimilation and naturalisation of foreigners on the other. This is at the heart of the tension between viewing immigration either as a potential work-force ('immigration de travail') or as a potential demographic and national support ('immigration de peuplement') (see especially Sayad 1985: 29; and 1988: 178).

The end of the 1960s was clearly not the first time that this contradiction had surfaced. Neither was it the first time that it had gone under the name of 'the problem of immigration'. In his analysis of immigration between the wars, Georges Mauco (1932) described the 'problem' in terms very similar to those used more recently: competition between immigrants and nationals in the labour market (1932: 57–8), the economic and geographical concentration of immigrants (1932: 58) and assimilation (1932: 60, 518–20). Treating the same period, Schor also points up the arguments at the time for the use of ethnic criteria in the selection of immigrants as a guarantee for a successful assimilation (1985: 501–4, 511–29). From 1931 the frontiers were closed to new foreign workers; the law of 10 August 1932 protected the national labour force and gave priority in employment to French workers by instituting quotas for foreign workers according to profession. It led the way towards large-scale repatriation of thousands of foreigners (especially Poles) (Tapinos 1975: 8; Perotti 1988: 63); in 1934 a law was passed forbidding naturalised French men and women to practise at the bar for ten years after naturalisation; in 1935 the financial encouragement to voluntary repatriation instituted the previous year took a more rigourous turn when some forced returns were organised, especially affecting Poles (Ponty 1985).

It will also be remembered that questions of manpower, population growth and assimilation were at the heart of the discussion around immigration after the war. The brief originally assigned to the ONI at its inception in November 1945 was to regulate immigration according to insufficiencies in specific areas of employment which could not be filled by domestic manpower reserves. The ordonnance which created the ONI explicitly maintained the principle established by the 1932 law (mentioned above). It would also institute a selection process in which Europeans would be encouraged to settle permanently whilst non-European immigration would be on a temporary contract basis. The ideas expressed by Georges Mauco before the war on the use of ethnic criteria for an assimilationist immigration policy (which were not implemented at the time) were more prominent in 1945 with the creation of the ONI (Weil 1990: 13). Mauco was named by de Gaulle as Secretary General of the newly created Committee of Population ('Haut Comité de la Population') and introduced his ideas on the selectivity of immigrants according to 'ethnic desirability' (Weil 1990: 18). In 1945 de Gaulle himself talked of the introduction over the following years of 'good elements of immigration into the French community' (speech by General de Gaulle at the Consultative Assembly, 2 March 1945, quoted in Tapinos 1975: 18). The arguments which then took place between demographers (amongst whom the voice of Alfred Sauvy was the most prominent) and economic planners highlighted the old tensions between economic and ethnic criteria for the development of a 'new' immigration policy (for an overview of the main arguments at this time, see Tapinos 1975: 15–19).[7]

The concept of a 'problem of immigration' at the end of the 1960s and the reformulation of immigration policy according to a system of contract labour organised on ethnic lines and maintaining the principle of 'national preference' in employment were therefore not new ideas. The major discourses within which questions of immigration were constituted had for long been those of manpower, ethnic/cultural proximity and demography. Coined in official circles at the end of the 1960s, the term 'new policy' creates the impression of a fresh response by the state to the transformed social landscape. As I have already suggested, this implies that the

state is merely the independent arbiter of problems created elsewhere. In fact, there were a number of continuities between the
'new' approach and past traditions.

The concept of a 'new' policy at this time to tackle a 'new'
phenomenon is best viewed as part of the standard historiography
of post-war immigration in France discussed previously. It runs in
tandem with the notions of a change from temporary to permanent and economic to social forms of immigration. Its fundamental
message is to establish a dichotomy between the easy assimilation
of previous (European) immigrants and the inassimilability of the
new (African) immigrants. This dichotomy is at the heart of the
contemporary racialisation of immigration. The 'newness' of the
'new policy' therefore lies not so much in the measures themselves
but in the reformulation of the past history of immigration which
it implies. It is the retrospective reconstruction of the idea of
assimilation which is most significant here.

Much work on immigration has shown that the notion of the
easy assimilation of past (European) immigrants is a myth. It has
revealed how fears of the inassimilability of immigrants are not
new and that immigration has often been seen as a threat to social
and national cohesion. Yet this work has not always been critical
enough of the vocabulary and formulations used in the construction of this myth. Indeed, as I suggested earlier, it has frequently
(re)produced the standard historiography of immigration – now
the consensus view – and has therefore produced (implicitly) the
very myth of the change in the process of assimilation which
(explicitly) it has tried to combat (cf. Noiriel 1989).

The suggestion that the idea of assimilation is retrospectively
reconstructed in the contemporary period assumes that assimilation is not a continuous and unchanging process but is re-formed
and re-articulated at different periods. So, although the concept
of assimilation is an integral part of the formation of the nation-
state, it is not simply the same phenomenon from one period to
another. This is valid too for many of the major terms being
discussed here: immigration, nation, 'race', 'problems' and so on.
Their meanings are always different depending on which historical configurations they appear in. The fact that the 'problem'
between the wars signified Poles, Slavs, Jews and so on whilst the
'problem' today signifies, predominantly, North Africans is not at
all insignificant in this respect. For the question of immigration in
contemporary France is profoundly formed in the image of ex-

and post-colonial structures and cannot be understood outside that history. This contextualisation of immigration takes analysis out of the realm of a generalised terminology and places it firmly in the realm of history.

The discussion of the reconstruction of the process of assimilation in the post-colonial world will be developed in the next chapter. For the moment let us consider briefly the 'problem of immigration' in the context of other important contemporary developments. 1968 in France is, of course, better known as the time of anti-state demonstrations than the time of a reformulation of immigration policy. Yet the latter is bound up with the former (in a way that goes far beyond the fact that many immigrants participated in the May demonstrations and strikes). Both were responses to the quickly changing economic and social landscape: the modernisation and internationalisation of industry, the de-population of the countryside and the over-population in towns, the major housing crisis and the growing contradiction between an over-centralised state and the diversity of spaces created through new economic and cultural practices. Both were symptoms of a breakdown in the consensus around social cohesion.

The 'new approach' to immigration should therefore be seen in the context of the crisis of the state at this time and the struggle over the contours of the national state in the post-colonial era. This crisis and struggle are relevant to the way in which North African immigration became a major focus for anxieties in the 1970s. This issue became one of the major sites for the contemporary struggle over conflicting concepts of the nation-state.

We cannot here explore the full complexity of the time. What we can say, in a general way, is that the 'new' analysis of immigration at this time was an attempt to construct a new discursive coherence (the solution) at a time of perceived social instability. The state's construction of a problem/solution of immigration is therefore both symptomatic of a much wider social and national crisis, and instrumental in producing the new framework within which social relations are perceived henceforward.

## INTEGRATION AND CONTROL

As we have seen, the official solution to the 'problem of immigration' was not simply the control of non-European immigration; as in Britain during the 1960s, it was a dual approach which linked *control* of those wanting to come in with the *integration* of those already in the country. Henceforward, the link established between integration and control is to become the most distinctive feature of official and political discourse on immigration in the contemporary period.

It is not simply a question of aligning two distinct elements to form a coherent policy. All descriptions of the policy clearly establish that the success of the programme of integration of immigrants depends on the ability to maintain strict controls on new immigration and, especially, to stem the tide of illegal immigration and illegal employment of foreigners. Repeatedly, this equation has been presented as a self-evident truth. The following are, in chronological order, just a few examples of the dominant official approach to immigration which was established at this time and which continues to be the 'common-sense' view today:

> It is clear that, in the present climate of expansion, immigration is necessary for growth in France.... But it must be controlled and organised if we want to offer to those foreign workers we receive on our soil decent work and living conditions comparable to those of the French, and at the same time fulfil the needs of our own development. We must combat illegal and uncontrolled immigration.
>
> (Georges Gorse, Minister of Labour, 14 June 1973)

> Control is a duty to ensure the future of immigrants in France.
>
> (Secrétariat d'Etat aux Travailleurs Immigrés 1977: 29)

> Measures of prevention... must ensure a better control of entries, for without this action all attempts to improve migrants' working and living conditions are likely to fail.
>
> (Ministère du Travail/Secrétariat d'Etat aux Travailleurs Immigrés 1977: 33–4)

> The suppression of illegal immigration, the struggle against employers of foreigners without papers, and the control of migration flows form the primary objective. Failure to do this threatens the integration of foreign communities legally installed in France.
>
> (Mission de liaison interministérielle pour la lutte contre les trafics de main-d'oeuvre 1983: 19)

If immigrants are allowed to enter the country without controls,

France risks losing its equilibrium. The increased effort to suppress illegal immigration will facilitate the necessity to improve immigrants' living conditions more rapidly

(Max Gallo, spokesperson for the Elysée, September 1983)

Today the effort to control migration flows fully is a permanent objective of the government's policy. It is the complément of its policy of integration.

(Ministère des Affaires Sociales et de la Solidarité Nationale 1986: 45)

The best possible integration must be the primary objective. ...To achieve this it is necessary to maintain the suppression of illegal immigration. ...This is an indispensable element in a sound immigration policy.

(Michel Hannoun 1987: 146)

A policy of integration is only effective if migration flows are more or less controlled.

(Robert Solé outlining the 'new' policy on integration to be implemented by Hubert Prévot, Secrétaire Général à l'Intégration, Le Monde, 9 February 1990)

These statements show that the same formula has been produced and reproduced under right- and left-wing governments. A consensus has been established which clearly transcends political factionalism. Like the theory of the 'seuil de tolérance' discussed earlier, the formula of 'integration and control' suggests that harmonious social relations, economic well-being and national cohesion are dependent on limiting the numbers of 'ethnically different' people in French society. Social, economic and national problems are therefore caused not by failures of government, the crisis of international capitalism, the inadequate social programme in the large cities and so on, but by the numbers and concentration of non-European immigrants in those cities. To guarantee social cohesion it is necessary to police not only the external frontiers between France and non-European countries but also the internal frontiers between these groups. The fundamental contradiction of 'integration and control' springs from the message contained in the formula: successful social relations can be achieved only through the implementation of ethnic/racist controls. (North African) immigrants are represented as both a threat and a problem to society and as potential citizens within society.

This contradiction cannot be satisfactorily explained as merely hypocrisy on the part of the state. The policy of integration is not simply a deliberate sop to liberal sentiment whilst the state gets on with the real job of implementing racist immigration controls. As I have already suggested, this implies a degree of wilfulness by the state which exaggerates its ability to direct and control ideological meanings and presents the state as a fairly monolithic institution. It therefore fails to grasp the real crisis of legitimacy faced by the state at this time and the search for a new consensus to explain social cohesion. The policy of integration and control produces a new racialised paradigm for the understanding of social relations, yet one whose coherence and legitimacy is constantly threatened by the contradictions which the new paradigm both introduces and attempts to mask. Of all the (euphemistic) terminology discussed previously concerning the new historiography of immigration, 'integration and control' is the quintessential sign of the contemporary reconstruction of assimilation. Its very 'newness' implies that these immigrants are not like previous ones, therefore justifying the need for a different approach.

The contradictions of the 'new' racialised immigration policy were not long in coming to the fore. As we have seen, the Marcellin–Fontanet circulars of 1972 were accompanied by a number of 'social' measures of integration in 1972 and 1973 (including the passing of the law of 1 July 1972 against racial discrimination). At the same time – and in direct response to the harshness of the Marcellin–Fontanet circulars – came the wave of demonstrations, protests and hunger strikes by immigrants throughout France (in a show of immigrant resistance the like of which had not been seen before in the post-war period) and the racist campaign by 'Ordre Nouveau' in June 1973.

These developments did not occur in a simple cause and effect manner. They were a product of the new racialisation of the question of immigration which was taking place which aimed to exclude those of African (especially North African) origin. Immigration was now no longer merely confined to the technocratic discourse of economic planners. Nor was it merely a question of agreements with the countries of emigration concerning numbers, arrived at behind closed doors between officials, far removed from the area of political debate and public discussion (Freeman 1979). Clearly immigration never had been simply this. Yet, as we have noted, the social, political and other implications of immigration had not (up until this point) penetrated the public domain. Now immigration had entered the political and public arena in the form of the social problem of ethnic/cultural relations.

At the same time, official discourse (in exemplary fashion) had to attempt to defuse and depoliticise the very racialised categories which it had been deeply implicated in producing in the first place. So, for example, Georges Pompidou's response at a press conference in September 1973 to the events of the summer of racial violence was to say: 'France is profoundly anti-racist.[8] The French government is fundamentally anti-racist and we detest everything that resembles racism.' The response of Pierre Messmer, then Prime Minister, was similar:

> In France equality is independent of nationality. All those who work here have a right to equal treatment.... If I don't speak here of racism – which I have fought against all my life and which disgusts me – it is because the discourse and the articles of faith of anti-racists serve no purpose other than to give anti-racists themselves a clear conscience.
>
> (quoted in *Le Monde*, 6 October 1973)

Georges Gorse, Minister of Labour, reacted to the Algerian decision to suspend emigration by suggesting an over-reaction on the part of the Algerians and denying any real problem:

> I understand and share the emotion raised by certain regrettable incidents. I caution against all artificial dramatisation of the situation. The task of solving the problems which might arise is best left to the negotiations and the social action which we are developing. The government has clearly shown its determination to control immigration and to give foreign workers and their families decent living conditions, and to guarantee their security and their dignity. The government will pursue its action according to the lines already laid down.
>
> (quoted in *Le Monde*, 21 September 1973)

Yvon Chotard, Vice-President of the CNPF (the French equivalent of the British CBI), also denied the existence of racial discrimination: 'In French firms there is no discrimination of any sort' (quoted in *Le Monde*, 21 September 1973). Like any denial or disavowal, these statements were symptomatic of a far more deepseated crisis which threatened to expose the illusory coherence of the new approach.

The formulation of integration and control therefore instituted a new racialisation of the discourse of immigration. It articulated ideas of ethnic balance, social cohesion and national homogeneity in a new consensus; yet clearly the racist assumptions of this approach could not be officially recognised. From the outset, it was riven by contradictory assumptions about assimilation and difference, inclusion and exclusion. This tension was at the heart of the new consensus. It manifested itself in the ever-widening cracks in the social contract during the 1970s, and especially in the ambivalent notion of cultural difference. The report produced by the office of the Secretary of State for Immigrant Workers in 1977 entitled *La Nouvelle Politique de l'Immigration* is a classic example of this tension, for it is constructed on the shifting sands of the new contradictions.

On the one hand, the report discusses the 'problems of immigration' using assumptions close to, if not the same as, the 'seuil de tolérance'. It declares eternal truths about the nature of social interaction and development:

> History teaches that all human groups whose living standards and place in society are evolving positively tend towards a spontaneous control of their numbers, since this is the most crucial element in any improvement in their situation. This rule is valid for the immigrants: without stabilisation there can be neither integration nor advancement.
>
> (Secrétariat d'Etat aux Travailleurs Immigrés 1977: 50)

It is true that the authors of the report object to the way the theory of the 'seuil de tolérance' pays too much attention to numbers and not enough to other factors regulating the interaction of ethnic groups – 'environmental characteristics, height and comfort of block of flats, levels of sound; make-up and behaviour of the surrounding communities; character and quality of relationships between individuals'. However, this statement is contradicted by others elsewhere in the text; for example, 'the main source of tensions comes from the excessive concentration of the immigrant population in certain quarters and in certain cities' (1977: 28).

The report makes the distinction between immigration from Africa over the previous ten years and the predominantly European immigration up to the 1960s. It describes how the cultural difference, or cultural distance, of the new immigrants has led to greater difficulties in integration:

> This cultural and human diversity has given rise to a diversity
> in the difficulties of integration and advancement. These diffi-
> culties increase, in general, in proportion to how recent
> installation has been. If, today, the first immigrants from the
> Mediterranean European countries have very largely assimi-
> lated into our society, North Africans have instead met
> numerous obstacles, whilst those from Black Africa remain on
> the margins of French life and take refuge in a debased form of
> communal existence.
>
> (1977: 21)

This description of the recent history of immigration in France
follows the classic argument defining the 'problem of immigration'
which we discussed previously: European immigrants are por-
trayed, retrospectively, as assimilable, and therefore constitute a
successful immigration, whilst the more recent immigration from
Africa is non-assimilable, and therefore constitutes a problematic
immigration.

According to the argument outlined above the source of the
problem facing France is the cultural difference of the new immigrants. However, in the same text, cultural difference, cultural
diversity and pluralism are also heralded as major signs of the new
'open' democracy being forged by the President, Giscard d'Estaing. The programme of twenty-five measures for immigration
announced by Giscard's first government in October 1974, which
outlined the policy of integration and control, mentioned the need
to promote the cultural differences of immigrant communities.
The Office of Cultural Promotion was subsequently set up in May
1975. In his introduction to the report of 1977 quoted above, Paul
Dijoud, the Secretary of State for Immigrant Workers between
1974 and 1977, situated the new policy on immigration within
Giscard's vision of a democratic and pluralist society:

> The President of the Republic offers France the vision of a
> pluralist society. Pluralism begins with the recognition of dif-
> ferences, and especially considers them as a source of
> enrichment. To live with the immigrants, to help them at each
> moment to integrate professionnally as well as personally –
> would that not be the clearest sign of the success of pluralism?
>
> (1977: 7)

Dijoud suggests that the way France treats its immigrants will be a yardstick by which to measure the advances made towards the acceptance of differences and the creation of this pluralist society (1977: 7). Judged by these criteria and considering the deplorable record on immigration during Giscard's term of office, France does not come out of this in a very favourable light. However, it is not a question here of cynically pointing up the hypocrisy of the authorities. This would once again be to suggest that the discourse of cultural pluralism was merely a consciously designed ploy by the state to mask the real business of racist controls. It is more relevant to consider the ambivalence over cultural difference in the 1970s.[9] The theory of the 'seuil de tolérance' and ideas of cultural diversity are both products of this ambivalence; both are grounded in a theory of social relations as 'ethnic/cultural' relations.

The quotations from *La Nouvelle Politique de l'Immigration* above demonstrate the ease with which the language of 'difference' can slip between a racist and pluralist perspective. Rather than being polar opposites, these perspectives share much common ground. This has been a major problem for anti-racism. The slogan 'the right to difference' became a rallying cry in the 1970s in the same way that Black Power and 'black is beautiful' did in the USA and Britain in the 1960s. Yet more recently (in the 1980s) the New Right has exploited, for racist ends, the very terminology of 'difference' and 'culture' used to counter racism before. These questions will be considered further in the following chapters. However, it is important to situate the contemporary racialisation of politics in the context of the development of the ambivalent ethnic/cultural discourse of the 1970s.

## RACIALISATION AND THE NATION

In the 1970s the language of 'difference' and 'culture' became increasingly mobilised in the discussion of social, economic and national questions, as well as questions of identity. In the latter half of the decade the debates around 'the economic crisis', employment, housing or crime were frequently articulated within a differentialist/racialised framework. For example, the rate at which French industry had become sufficiently modernised to meet the demands of a new, competitive, internationalised market-place was invariably discussed in terms of the benefits or disadvantages to the nation of immigration. As we have already seen in Chapter 1, even those who rejected the proposition that immigration was responsible for the maintenance of antiquated economic practices or those who disproved the argument that immigration was a financial burden on the state (like the inter-ministerial report directed by the communist deputy Anicet Le Pors in 1976)[10] were invariably drawn into accepting the national/racialised parameters defining the debate in the first place (see Sayad 1985: 35–9; 1986).

In the area of employment, few statements were made which did not equate immigration with unemployment in some way, either explicitly or, as with the costs/benefits debate, by merely accepting the agenda which had been set. In January 1976 in a televised broadcast, the Prime Minister Jacques Chirac made the link between immigration, unemployment, the economic crisis and substitution of foreign for French workers perfectly clear:

> A country which has 900,000 unemployed but more than two million immigrant workers is not a country in which the problem of jobs is insoluble. It requires a systematic revalorisation of the condition of manual workers in sectors which are being abandoned by French workers.
>
> (quoted in Wihtol de Wenden 1988a: 206)

Shortly after, the Minister of Labour, Michel Durafour, wrote in *France Soir* on 10 February 1976:

> Why should we hide the fact that the employment situation in France has an absurd side to it: there are a million unemployed people but at the same time there are two million immigrant workers, of whom a considerable number have greater resources than certain workers in the much sought-after tertiary sector. Who can fail to see a contradiction in that?
>
> (quoted in Wihtol de Wenden 1988a: 206)

By the time of the report entitled *Immigration et 7e Plan* in 1977, these links had become common-sense assumptions: 'At a time of crisis, the simultaneous presence of a high level of unemployed French workers and large numbers of foreign workers in the factories is bound to raise questions' (Ministère du Travail/Secrétariat d'Etat aux Travailleurs Immigrés 1977: 156). Giscard's second Prime Minister, Raymond Barre, shared the belief held by his predecessor that 'there is a case for replacing the immigrant work-force with French workers', whilst Lionel Stoléru, minister

responsible for immigrants between 1977 and 1981, made numerous pronouncements in the same vein: for example, 'the task of
the French government is to reduce the number of immigrant
workers in France'; and 'it is not worth poking fun at foreigners
when we are not capable of collecting the rubbish in our own
country' (quoted in Sayad 1979: 19). As a candidate in the
presidential elections of 1981, Giscard encouraged the departure
of immigrants as part of the struggle against unemployment
(Mangin 1982: 30). The link made between immigration and
unemployment in the notorious slogan of the FN in the early 1980s
– 'two million unemployed, two million immigrants' – was not
invented by Le Pen, merely exploited by him.

The appeal of this 'logic' owes much to the way in which
(non-European) immigration became politicised, popularised and
racialised from the end of the 1960s, that is, represented as an
economic, social and national problem. Hence the following official rationalisation of a policy of repatriation acquires its
'coherence' through a repetition of links made consistently elsewhere (in official circles and in the media) between immigration,
the economic crisis, unemployment and the ideas of substitution
and national preference:

> [The question of 'return'] acquires particular importance today
> because of the serious employment problems facing the French
> economy.... New aspects of the problem of jobs necessitate the
> progressive replacement, in certain jobs, of foreign workers by
> French workers. This is an essential and irreversible develop-
> ment, which will be effected through the upgrading of manual
> jobs and a better use of available French workers.
> (Secrétariat d'Etat aux Travailleurs Immigrés 1977: 123)

In the second half of Giscard's presidency, this re-nationalisa-
tion of social and economic relations according to the new
racialised criteria was intensified. In official discussion of immigration, talk of integration was progressively dropped in favour of a
more determined approach to police the frontiers between what
Abdelmalek Sayad (1984b) has termed 'the order of immigration'
and 'the order of the nation'. This was the period when Lionel
Stoléru introduced the voluntary scheme of financial aid for repatriation (1977), and then presided over a barrage of legislation
aimed at regulating the phenomenon of immigration and facilitating the process of expulsion from the country (which was often

carried out in the form of circulars, thus averting open discussion in parliament, but was particularly facilitated by the Bonnet Law of 1980). This was also the period when official attention became particularly focused on the frontier people 'par excellence' – the 'clandestins' (see Chapter 5).

Yet the attempt to fix and control the frontiers more effectively between 'the order of immigration' and 'the order of the nation' was also a symptom of the growing struggle around notions of inclusion and exclusion and the growing contradictions in republican structures. In its diverse forms, the resistance by immigrants to repressive controls (mentioned in the previous chapter) was a challenge to and redefinition of the political, economic, social and cultural 'spaces' of the republic. Those who were being categorised more systematically as 'outside the nation' were in fact refusing to accept this classification; and this resistance to racist controls highlighted inequalities between French nationals and non-European foreigners, that is, highlighted the institutionalisation of racialised categories in the ordering of the nation.

Indeed, the increased racialisation and 'nationalising' of the discourse of immigration could not but help reveal fundamental contradictions in the organisation of the republican nation-state. We have seen, in responses by some ministers to the violence of the summer of 1973, how difficult (indeed impossible) this was for the authorities to confront head on. Rationalisations, denials and so on were called for. One of the major principles at stake here was that of equality, so dear to the liberal republican tradition. The republican rhetoric informing Pierre Messmer's quote of September 1973 – 'in France equality is independent of nationality' – looked increasingly hollow as racist controls met with growing resistance. What became more and more apparent during the 1970s was precisely the contradiction at the very heart of this republican discourse, that is, between the universalism of the Rights of Man and the particularism enshrined in the link between citizenship and nationality. The very fact that the resistance to racist and exclusionary measures had to be 'non-political' in the traditional sense (strikes at the work-place, hunger strikes, rent strikes and so on) was a sign of the absence of political rights for foreigners; measures like the Marcellin–Fontanet circulars and the Bonnet Law highlighted the precarious nature of life for non-European foreigners in France; measures aimed either at suspending the right of family reunification (measures which were judged

unconstitutional by the Conseil d'Etat) or its grudging re-introduction under extremely severe conditions highlighted the
different conceptions of family life for nationals and non-nationals.

It was becoming clearer that immigrants did not have the same
rights as French nationals and that equality was not independent
of nationality. Messmer's quote is only one of many such rationalisations and denials of this major contradiction in republican
discourse. All rhetoric of equality will eventually come up against
the juridical distinction between nationals/citizens and non-na-
tionals/non-citizens. To be an immigrant was automatically to be
a second-class citizen. 'Citizenship and nationality' became a major
debate in the 1980s (see Chapter 5) but the discriminatory assumptions underlying the link between the two were being unlocked in
the developments of the 1970s.

The developments described here concerning the new racialisation of the question of immigration were a fundamental part of
wider contemporary social processes; they were not merely confined to specific aspects of the economy or society. We have already
seen how the question of immigration was always this, yet had been
marginalised (even effaced) in the standard historiography of
France. In the 1970s, the politicisation of immigration therefore
highlighted major aspects of (and contradictions in) French society
and ideology which had received little attention up to that point,
aspects which transcended the Right/Left divide and went far
beyond political or class divisions. More precisely, they cut across
these divisions. This was particularly revealing in the case of the
Left.

It will be remembered that, under the Third Republic, it was
the Left which had often provided the greatest impetus to colonial
expansion (Galissot 1986). At the beginning of the 1920s the
communist-led trade union, the CGT, was against all foreign
competition for jobs (Noiriel 1988a: 118). In the 1930s, the non-
communist and communist Left was as 'contaminated' by racism
as the Right (see especially Schor 1985: 257-75, 562-4). In the
immediate post-war period, the leading voice in the Ministry of
Labour, the communist Ambroise Croizat, held the view that the
domestic work-force should be protected from the competition of
foreign labour. In the 1950s and 1960s (as we have seen) the
communists and the CGT proclaimed both slogans of solidarity
with immigrant workers from North Africa and demands for a
protection of national interests. In the 1970s the Left and the trade

unions found themselves consistently caught between the contradictory solidarities of class and nation (cf. Grillo 1991).

In unlocking many of the contradictions of Jacobin republicanism, the racialisation of social relations in the 1970s therefore posed serious problems for the Left. As we have seen, the affirmation of cultural difference was itself double-edged; and anyway it was always at odds with the conflicting solidarity of class and conflicting ideas of assimilation (see Galissot 1984a: 59). The Left as a whole has consistently failed to provide a fundamental challenge to the contemporary nationalisation/racialisation of social relations. This is largely because the republican Left has itself been thoroughly impregnated with the nationalised and racialised ideology of republicanism. The following chapter will consider this more fully, and especially the way the Left has been torn between theories of assimilation and difference (as the headscarf affair of 1989 clearly demonstrated).

The construction of the 'problem' of immigration, the 'new' formula of integration and control and the ambiguities of the discourse of cultural difference (all of which traverse the Right and the Left) are fundamental factors in the development of the politicisation of immigration in the 1980s. This is why the tendency to focus on the rise of racism in the 1980s and, frequently, to link this phenomenon with the FN is misleading. By locating it within the extreme Right, this approach marginalises racism. The terminology of the FN in the 1980s only emerged from the wider discussion of immigration in the 1970s; but so too does the terminology of anti-racism. The following discussion will therefore concentrate on broad aspects of the new paradigm.

# Chapter 4

# Assimilation and difference

In the previous chapter I argued that the definition of the 'problem' of immigration at the end of the 1960s and beginning of the 1970s involved a retrospective reconstruction of assimilation. The dichotomies between temporary and permanent, single male and family and economic and social forms of immigration formed the new vocabulary through which this reconstruction took place. As we have seen, its effect was to suggest a major distinction in terms of assimilability between European and non-European immigrants based on cultural differences. This redefinition of past and present immigration was a major factor in the contemporary racialisation of immigration and wider social, economic and political questions. This chapter will develop this argument to consider other discursive aspects of this process, the wider historical determinations of this new paradigm and the problems it has posed for anti-racist movements.

## THE 'SEUIL DE TOLERANCE' AND THE GHETTO

In an interview on 10 December 1989 for the television channel Antenne 2, François Mitterrand declared that the threshold for numbers of immigrants in France had been reached in the 1970s. This comment was seized upon by the media and became a major debating point during the following weeks (despite Mitterrand's subsequent attempts to distance himself from the remark; see *Le Monde*, 12 January 1990). The former Prime Minister under Giscard, Raymond Barre, suggested in an interview shortly afterwards that a coherent immigration policy (which would include financial aid for repatriation) would reduce social tensions and avoid 'large concentrations of immigrants in certain quarters or certain towns' (quoted in *Libération*, 12 January 1990). The newspaper *Libération* published a series of six reports based around the notion of the 'seuil de tolérance' (22–9 January 1990; see also *Le Figaro*, 10–11 May 1990; *La Croix*, 11 May 1990; *L'Evénement du Jeudi*, 10–16 May 1990; *L'Express*, 28 March 1991). More recently, the leader of the right-wing RPR and former Prime Minister Jacques Chirac reminded everyone that

> we risk exceeding the threshold of tolerance, whose existence has been recognised by the President. It is not sensible to deny it in the name of some anti-racist ideology or other.... We must have an immediate moratorium on family immigration.
>
> (*Le Monde*, 22 February 1991)

Mitterrand's statement was provocative for at least two reasons: firstly, it was a not very diplomatic intervention by the President in the headscarf affair which, at that time, was splitting France into opposing camps; secondly, it was highly embarrassing for the Socialist Party since it revived the use of a term which the socialists had cast as part of the Right's discourse on immigration, and belonged in the dustbin of useless (and racist) concepts for describing 'ethnic relations'.[1] However, in practice the grand lines of policy and discourse on immigration proposed during the 1980s (integration and control) came from the Left and Right alike; and, as we have seen, this consensus was founded on ideas close to (even the same as) those informing the 'seuil'. After all, at the same time that Mitterrand was talking of the 'seuil', his Prime Minister, Michel Rocard (7 January 1990), and Minister of the Interior, Pierre Joxe, were constantly assuring everybody that France 'could not accept all the world's poor'. This statement did not cause the same embarrassment for socialists. Clearly it does not have the same disputed history as the 'seuil'. Yet it is doubtful whether it does not offer the same view as that enshrined in the 'seuil', namely that certain problems of French society are attributable to the growing numbers of 'Third World' nationals in the cities.

At the same time another term was also much in evidence in the media: the 'ghetto'. Once again the use of this term does not shock French liberals in the same way as the 'seuil'. Nevertheless it has very similar connotations. As with the 'seuil de tolérance' the ghetto equates concentrations of (certain) immigrants with social problems. The 'ghetto' has become the new shorthand way of referring to the problems of the suburbs, especially through the

composite term 'cité-ghetto' ('cité' here referring to the large
estates of 1960s council housing or HLM in the suburbs). Newspapers and magazines frequently introduce reports on the suburbs
through headlines like: 'Eliminate the cité-ghettos' (*La Croix*, 2
May 1990); 'Cités: the end of the ghettos?' (*L'Evénement du Jeudi*,
21-7 March 1991); 'Cités-ghettos: a history of disaster' (*Le Figaro*,
1 April 1991); 'Ministers at the front-line of the cités-ghettos'
*Libération*, 4 April 1991). The problems of the suburbs are thus
designated as 'immigrant problems' or part of 'the problem of
immigration'. Yet, despite this connotation, the word is used as
much by the Left as the Right, and by 'anti-racists' as much as
'racists'. The need to break with the logic of the ghetto was the
major theme of the third congress of SOS Racisme (27-30 April
1990). Harlem Désir (and virtually the whole of the political
establishment) has consistently used the term to denote the division of France into separate communities and counterposed it to
the French tradition of integration on an individual basis (see, for
example, interviews in *Le Nouvel Observateur*, 7-13 June 1990, and
*L'Humanité*, 20 March 1991). Thus the logic of this dichotomy
between today's 'ghettos' and yesterday's individual assimilation
is, once again, that today's 'immigrants' are different from previous ones.

Two features invariably accompany the use of the term 'ghetto'
in France to imply that it is a phenomenon which is alien (until
recently, that is) to the French tradition: it is described both as a
recent phenomenon in French cities and as part of the 'Anglo-
Saxon' tradition. For example, an extensive enquiry into ghettos
in the journal *Politis* (8–14 January 1990), under the titles 'Long
live the ghetto' and 'The integration machine has broken down',
described aspects of the French situation as 'an American-type
development'. Harlem Désir saw this ghettoisation of minorities
as totally alien to the juridical and social traditions of France, yet
one which had now reached such a pitch in France that minorities
'are more impoverished than in Anglo-Saxon society'. To avoid
this 'americanisation' of France, SOS Racisme suggested the creation of a Ministry of Integration.

A report in the weekly *L'Express* (12 January 1990) on the
housing of immigrants, entitled 'Immigrants: danger of the ghetto', compared the situation to that of the Bronx and commented
'if appropriate measures are not taken one cannot rule out the
possibility of the appearance in France of concentrations of ethnic

minorities, badly housed and badly integrated, comparable to those that prevail in the big American cities'. The next day *La Croix* treated the same story with the headline 'No to all the immigrant ghettos'. The article described immigrant housing conditions as 'new forms of ghettos' (*La Croix*, 13 January 1990). An article in *Murs, Murs* (no. 15, January 1990) on London ('London: saint town or ghetto city?') described how the British multicultural approach can lead to 'veritable ghettos'. Robert Solé in *Le Monde* (9 February 1990) outlined how the government's 'new' approach to 'integration' would take particular care to 'avoid "the ghettos", that is to say, to combat excessive concentrations'. The newly appointed Secretary General of the Inter-ministerial Committee on Integration, Hubert Prévot, was asked in an interview in *L'Express* (9 February 1990) whether he feared 'the explosion of certain ghettos, along the lines of the English or American experience'. In his reply he said that France did not have the same 'gigantic concentrations'.

This discourse spans not only the domains of politics and the media but also informs 'serious' research. Dominique Schnapper has compared France's assimilationist tradition with the 'minorities' tradition of the Anglo-Saxon world in the following way:

> It is essential to know how to resist what is contrary to one's own values and England does not always manage to do this.... Since the arrival of populations from the former Commonwealth, that country has witnessed the creation of ghettos.... A ghetto is a quarter defined by the national origin of its inhabitants. In France the local councils have always been careful not to allow the constitution of quarters inhabited by people of a single ethnic group. There are quarters where one finds many immigrants but they cohabit with others from different nationalities, and there are always French as well. We do not have the phenomenon of ghettos in the English or American sense.
>
> (*Le Nouvel Observateur*, 23–9 November 1989)

The demographer Hervé Le Bras (1989) outlined two possible scenarios for the future: either a rapid integration or 'the appearance and reinforcement of ghettos' (along American lines). Once again, the ghetto is represented as a new and alien phenomenon for France. These analyses not only show a profound ignorance of what is referred to as the 'Anglo-Saxon' model; they also show little understanding of the realities of the 'French' model. They are firmly entrenched in the 'two model' theory of the nation outlined in Chapter 1, which serves to produce misleading ideas of both France and 'Anglo-Saxon society'.

The appearance of the discourse of the ghetto at the end of the 1980s was not the first time this term had been widely used in the contemporary period to express a fear of ethnic concentrations. In the early 1980s the affair of Vitry-Saint-Maur (1980) – when a communist council, arguing that it had more than its fair share of immigrants, bulldozed a hostel for Malians (Lloyd 1981) – was accompanied by a media focus on the 'ghettos' constituted by certain housing estates (see de Rudder 1982). The theory of the 'seuil de tolérance', on the other hand, can be situated at the end of the 1960s and the beginning of the 1970s (de Rudder 1980: 6–7). The later appearance of the 'ghetto' is perhaps due in part to the need for a more 'neutral' and acceptable term once the 'seuil de tolérance' had been rejected as a valid social scientific category (see *Sociologie du Sud-Est* 1975). It is clear that the opprobrium attached to the term did not necessarily extend as far as the idea, the practice or the 'logic of too many is too many' (Barou 1984: 116–17).[2]

Whatever the explanation, we can say that both terms accompany the contemporary construction of the 'problem of immigration'. With regard to the use of the term 'ghetto', Véronique de Rudder has remarked that France 'has continued to make immigration into a problem itself. The ghetto became a convenient term to designate it' (1982: 53). And, as with those other terms already discussed which constitute the idea of a new problem, the 'seuil' and the ghetto also reformulate the past to imply the cultural homogeneity of France, the assimilation of previous (European) immigrants and the inassimilability of African immigrants in contemporary French society. This proposition has become a subtle common-sense assumption behind much 'liberal' discourse today, as in the question 'Is France, for so long a land of welcome, becoming the victim of a sudden increase in intolerance?' (*Le Nouvel Observateur*, 23–9 November 1989); as if intolerance has not figured in France before the contemporary period.

The idea that the ghetto in France is both a recent and an alien phenomenon needs to be considered in this light. The notion that concentrations of ethnic (or other) groups is unhealthy for the 'social body' was not invented twenty years ago; rather it was reconstructed in the context of the new 'problem' of assimilation of African immigrants. As we noted in Chapter 1, a reappraisal of the national development of France suggests that the republican nation-state has never been an unproblematic machine for assimilation but rather one founded on the tension between assimilation and difference. The idea, then, that assimilation has been a constant practice until the new immigration, whilst ghettos are a recent and alien phenomenon born of this immigration needs to be reformulated to take account of far more complex practices of spatial (and other) inclusions and exclusions. The discourse on ethnic concentrations discussed above marginalises spatial/racialised exclusion instead of viewing it as a constant practice of the modern nation-state. Rather than polar opposites, 'assimilation' and the 'ghetto' are part of the *same* history. Noiriel confirms this in the following way:

> All the statistics at our disposal from the beginning of the nineteenth century refute the commonly held notion that the constitution of immigrant 'ghettos' is a recent, post-Second World War phenomenon. Already under the Second Empire, foreigners were concentrated in the large, dynamic industrial centres like Roubaix, the highly populated suburbs of Lille (Wazemmes, Saint-Sauveur...) or Marseilles. Afterwards, each new influx of immigrants resulted in the appearance of new 'ghettos': in the mines in the north and in Lorraine, in the Paris region, and in the valleys of the Alps and the Pyrenees.
> (1988a: 171; also Dubet 1989a: 30)

'Ethnic' concentration of this kind is a complex phenomenon. Strictly speaking, the term 'ghetto' is a misnomer in that it is very rare that whole quarters or communes were or are really ethnically homogeneous (cf. Lapeyronnie 1987: 296). This is why Schnapper's comment above about ghettos in England today is absurd; there is no area in the country that is ethnically homogeneous in the way she suggests. Indeed, no space can ever be so sealed off from the surrounding social and economic environment that it is not marked profoundly by the traces of that context. Furthermore, these areas served the different interests of a diverse range of people – from employers to the immigrants themselves (in terms of strategies of resistance).

Leaving these considerations aside, the point that I wish to make here is that an unproblematised notion of assimilation is totally inadequate to describe the complex process of political, social and (especially) economic organisation. Economic interests contradicted any political warnings on the dangers of foreign concentrations and the need to spread the new immigrants as widely as possible (Noiriel 1988a: 172–3). The historian Benjamin Stora confirms this view: 'concentrations' were formed not according to 'a policy of ethnic segregation but an economic logic'. Immigrants looked for the cheapest lodgings, and therefore inevitably went to the popular and industrial areas (*Le Monde*, 7 March 1991). Furthermore, we have already mentioned that the construction of the national state under the Third Republic and the institutionalised differences between nationals and immigrants contributed to a marginalisation of immigrants on the political, social and ideological levels as well. As Noiriel again points out:

> republican legislation excludes foreigners from the benefits of the welfare state accorded quite 'naturally' to nationals, and constructs increasingly widening 'reserved zones' for the French (in the civil service and in the liberal professions of the 'public sector'). This first, and essential, means of channelling foreign labour into sectors of penury is complemented by a second means, equally important, which concerns the administrative forms of control of immigrants. We can see here a good example of the way in which juridical, sociological and economic processes are articulated in reality.
>
> (1988a: 306)

In fact, these same processes (accompanied by the same fears of concentrations of 'undesirable' elements) had first been used not to segregate immigrants from nationals, but the 'dangerous classes' from the bourgeoisie. This was the case in Britain and France. The nineteenth-century fear of working-class ghettos – zones, it was believed, of criminality, disease and rebellion – was redirected towards immigrant ghettos in the twentieth century (MacMaster 1991: 14–15). René Galissot points out that 'the social history of the nineteenth century is brimming over with a 'racism' directed at the dangerous classes, in which their morals and customs are represented as hereditary diseases' (Galissot 1984a: 63). Etienne Balibar argues that the first racism was an anti-working class racism established through the 'ethnicisation' of the work-force (Balibar and Wallerstein 1988: 273–87).[3] The anti-racist argument that Jacobin assimilation was responsible for the destruction of minorities does not take this 'ghettoisation' into account. The 'Jacobin' nationalisation of the state and society also *constructed* minorities through new rules of differentialism, segregation and exclusion.

However, as far as immigrants were concerned, assimilation was never really intended for them anyway: 'assimilation – including, indeed especially, that of the Left – was promised to the peasants, those from the provinces, and the overseas "évolués" rather than to immigrants' (Galissot 1984a: 62). Galissot exposes the myth that many immigrants were assimilated in the inter-war years through the process of 'naturalisation' (that is, the approved request for French nationality by those not born in France). He points out that the number of naturalisations was, in fact, low; the main form of obtaining French nationality was through 'acquisition' (that is, automatic acquisition of nationality at the age of majority by children born in France of foreign parents) (Galissot 1986: 13; also 1985b: 61–2). Despite the fears of ethnic concentration and the problems this posed to assimilation (Mauco 1932: 518–20; Schor 1985: 517), this did not actually prevent the constitution of such 'concentrations' (in the mining regions, for example; see Schor 1985: 517).[4] Nor has the rhetoric of assimilation/integration more recently prevented the economic determinations of urban 'concentrations' on the edges of large French cities (Barou 1980).

The clearest example of the limitations of assimilation is to be found in the colonial context. The number of Muslims in Algeria who were naturalised was very low (30,000 in 1939) (Krulik 1988: 70). So too was the number who went to French schools – supposedly the institution *par excellence* for the dissemination of French culture and values and the assimilation and equalisation of all the children of the republic. And, as we have seen, those who were 'assimilated' always carried the traces of their origins – and therefore their 'difference' from French citizens – for they were categorised as 'évolués' or 'French muslims'. For Jews in France, the rigours of 'assimilation' were perhaps the hardest, for they were subject to its fundamental ambivalence: the constant tension between inclusion and exclusion.

The concept of assimilation (or integration) is therefore a smoke-screen for the complex ordering of social relations, in which a process of racialisation and racism has played a fundamental role. A number of works in recent years have challenged the historical amnesia and exposed the myth of assimilation by pointing up particularly the racism directed at Italians and Belgians at the end of the nineteenth century, and Poles and Jews between the wars, and the concentrations of immigrant groups in cities like Paris or Marseilles, where they sometimes constituted 20 per cent of the total population of the city (see Noiriel 1988a; Schor 1985; *Vingtième Siècle* 1985; also Lorreyte 1988). Schnapper's view (quoted above) that France has avoided English-type ghettos because of the care taken by local councils 'not to allow the constitution of quarters inhabited by people of a single ethnic group' completely ignores the fundamental paradox of this approach: the only way that ethnic groups can become invisible depends on their prior designation as an ethnic group to be monitored and dissolved. The 'care taken by local councils' referred to by Schnapper is often the racist threshold theory and unofficial quota system. As Barou has rightly pointed out:

> There is therefore a paradox in the policies of the French state with regard to minority groups, who are both invited to merge into the national fabric by renouncing their attachment to origins, yet who are also the object of particularist designations with which they are subsequently reproached.
>
> (1984: 118)

In other words, policy preaches invisibility whilst constructing visibility. Barou's article (1984) is an interesting analysis of the way in which (in particular) housing policy for immigrants has been perpetually caught in the paradox of 'invisibility'. This is precisely the paradox of assimilation.[5]

However, the point that concerns us here is not simply that assimilation (in relation to immigrants) contains a fundamental paradox or that it is a myth, but that it is a myth constructed at a particular time and has a very specific effect on an understanding of the present. Myths of the past are always functional in the present. I have suggested that the recent discourse on the ghetto equates ethnic concentrations with the Anglo-Saxon tradition of minorities and segregation, and implies (through comparison) the assimilationist tradition of France. It is therefore part of the wider reformulation of assimilation in contemporary France, whose primary effect is to reconstruct cultural differences between Europeans and non-Europeans (especially Africans).

The 'new' racism of cultural difference (which, as we have said, is not so new at all) shows that the notion of 'race' continues even if the word 'race' is, in France, virtually non-existent (Guillaumin 1984a, 1986). Yet this evolution must also be historicised. Balibar points up the problems with an analysis which concentrates on the discursive shift without considering the wider historical shift which made it possible:

> Certain theorists of discourse analysis examine this kind of shift in terms of a discursive strategy which allows the circumvention of certain taboos and, in the end, reproduces the same old practices in contemporary societies. However, this is not enough. There must also be some cultural transformations. Racism in the form of cultural differentiation comes from the post-colonial period, from a period of international circulation of labour and, to a certain extent, from the crisis of the nation-state. It relates to our national and cultural identity crises in the same way that the biological hierarchy of races related to that long period in history in which European nation-states were carving up the rest of the world and instituting first slavery and then colonisation. This is not the only determinant but it is a concrete and absolutely essential one.
>
> (1991: 79–80)

The myth of assimilation (for immigrants) should also be seen in this light; that is, in the context of the globalisation of capital and the end of the high era of colonial expansion. Without wishing to put a precise date on this change, we can say in general terms that this was a post-war phenomenon. Assimilation functions, then, as a 'retrospective illusion' and as a post-war myth (Galissot 1985a: 73–9; 1986: 12–13; see also Balibar 1984: 1741). Galissot suggests that it is then, with the new ideas of national reconstruction, repopulation and a policy of nationalisation (advocated fervently by the Left and the extreme Left as much as, if not more than, the Right), that assimilation became the consensus view on national origins:

> It is at that moment that the idea of assimilation – whose origins are certainly to be found in Left republicanism but without any reference to immigration – is enlarged to become the doctrine of an immigration policy, and even a false idea serving to reformulate the preceding history of migration.
>
> (1986: 12)

This point is crucial. In the immediate aftermath of the war, 'immigration' not only became a subject worthy of economic and demographic interest, but the considerations of origins, ethnic balance and assimilation – which were to be the defining criteria for the new 'scientific' approach to immigration – were used retrospectively to analyse previous migrations. In other words, immigration was brought into focus as an issue worthy of serious analysis (though not yet of central political and public concern) in the context of, and to serve the interests of, an 'ethnic/cultural' assimilationist concept of the nation, whose immediate predecessors were the racist nationalists Drumont and Barrès and the architects of Vichy (cf. Noiriel 1988a: 34–43, section entitled 'The "shameful" origins of the history of immigration in France').[6] The desirable 'ethnic' orientation of an immigration policy for the new France was proposed by de Gaulle during his brief period as President in 1945:

> On the ethnic level, it would be appropriate to limit those from the Mediterranean basin and the East, who have profoundly modified the composition of the French population over the last half-century. Without going as far as the United States and using a rigid quota system, it is desirable that priority should be accorded to naturalisations of those from the North (Belgium, Luxemburg, Switzerland, Holland, Denmark, England, Germany, etc.). One could envisage a proportion of 50 per cent of these elements.
>
> (quoted in Noiriel 1988a: 39)

The use of 'etc.' is most telling here. It already presupposes the existence of an ethnic division between north, on the one hand, and south and east Europe on the other. This common-sense 'ethnic division' will, of course, be modified in the post-war period to bring in Italians, Spaniards and Portuguese, in the context of a wider process of Europeanisation, and to exclude Africans. It is also worth noting de Gaulle's use of something approaching a 'seuil de tolérance' in his conception of assimilation and 'ethnic balance' (see also André Siegfried discussed in Noiriel 1988a: 342–4).

The construction of the question of immigration after the war, the use of a transformed (retrospective) concept of assimilation applied now to immigrants, and the economic and ideological reconstruction of France at this time should be considered together as part of the same historical process. This historical perspective on the meaning of the term 'assimilation' suggests the need to reappraise the common conflation between assimilation, Jacobinism, universalism and republicanism. These are all problematic terms, not simply because they are too general to account for complex processes, but because none of them has a continuous history; instead, they are, at different times, reconstructed and take on different meanings. The retrospective use of assimilation is part of a reformulation of the nation and nationalism after the war, especially around Gaullism: that is, grafting a retrospective unity, uniformity and continuity on to the image of the nation after the chasm of occupation and collaboration. It is, perhaps, already a part of the marginalisation of the occupation and Vichy from the grand narrative of the history of France.

The use of the concepts of the 'seuil de tolérance' and the ghetto in more recent times should be considered historically in the same way; they are also part of the post-war assimilationist discourse underpinning conceptions of immigration and retrospective constructions of national homogeneity. Their usage functions both retrospectively and comparatively, placing national identity within a racialised Europe and distinguishing it from the new immigrants from the South. This perspective allows us to make certain comments about the new racialisation of immigration, which will consider both the discursive shift in the discussion of immigration and the wider historical context within which this has occurred.

## PROXIMITY/DISTANCE: COLONIALISM/POST-COLONIALISM

Two significant features of the new post-war order were a) a retreat from empire and b) the construction of a new European-ness. This historical process is well known. So too is the fact that patterns of post-war migration flows into Europe to a certain extent mirrored this process in reverse: that is, there was an increase in migration from the former colonies compared to pre-war migration flows. In other words, if the pattern of migration was largely (though by no means exclusively) European during the colonial era, then in a number of European countries the pattern has been an increase in (ex-)colonial migrants during the 'European' era. The following discussion considers aspects of this post-war reversal.

The concept of assimilation suggests the cultural proximity of

Europeans compared to the cultural distance of those from North and sub-Saharan Africa. We have already remarked that this view of other Europeans was not one that was much in evidence at the time of the racist violence directed at Italians and Belgians at the end of the previous century, or at Poles, Czechs and Jews of diverse European nationalities in the inter-war period. The world had clearly moved on and one feature of this evolution was the reconstruction of 'cultural proximity' in the post-war period. The line between proximity and distance is not a fixed one and can be drawn and redrawn in an infinite number of ways. Yet history is in the habit of mapping dominant or hegemonic lines (cf. Noiriel 1989: 216–17). Why should the boundary be Europe rather than say, in the French case, the Mediterranean basin? After all, culturally speaking, France has much more in common with the Maghreb than with Scandinavia or Britain (cf. Nair 1988: 265). Clearly the answer to this question involves a highly complex series of historical, economic and ideological determinations. The following discussion concentrates specifically on the colonial/post-colonial context and considers some aspects of the spatial configurations of proximity and distance in the post-war period.

It is significant that the line defining proximity in the post-war period has, in the dominant discourse, become progressively 'European-ised', at the very time that an increased number of non-European and, for the most part, ex-colonial immigrants have settled in France and have therefore occupied the same geographical space. In other words, their increased proximity – on economic, social, cultural and other levels – has been accompanied by an increased effort to distance them from the idea of France and present them as a problem. The line separating 'two worlds' – the 'metropole' and the colonies, the dominant and the dominated – has become increasingly blurred in this period (not that it was unproblematic in the past). This is a source of profound anxiety. As Véronique de Rudder has remarked, the foreigner 'is no longer from elsewhere, but from here: a colleague at work, a neighbour in the same flats. The far-off has never been so close.... So the question has become how to keep the foreigner at a distance' (1982: 53).

Keeping the foreigner at a distance can be accomplished through a variety of exclusions, not the least important of which is the barrage of terms which define his or her difference as distance. At the time of the construction of the 'problem of immigration' twenty years ago, the conditions of the shanty-towns ('bidonvilles') on the outskirts of the big French cities became a major focus of political and media attention. The condemnation of the appalling living conditions often used a language which suggested that there was a correspondence between 'under-developed' housing and 'under-developed' people; 'imported living conditions by an imported population' (de Rudder 1982: 60). The phenomenon of the 'bidonville' is detached from the surrounding political, economic and social context and located as a feature from the 'Third World' which has no part in French society. As with the discourse on the 'seuil de tolérance' and the ghetto (ethnic concentrations alien to the French tradition), these housing conditions were frequently represented as an external phenomenon and not indigenous to France.

Yet, in this discourse, it is not simply a question of marginalising the 'bidonvilles' in the past or the ghetto today. At the same time, these representations carry with them an ambivalence about lines of demarcation: these 'distant' forms of social organisation ('exogenous') are present in 'our' current forms of social organisation in the here and now ('indigenous'). The contemporary 'problem' of immigration (expressed, above all, as a social, cultural and ethnic problem) is constructed precisely at that moment. This is the implication of de Rudder's statement quoted above: the necessity to keep (certain) foreigners at a distance arises at the moment when they are said to have transgressed the boundary between 'here' and 'there'. The dividing line has been breached; it must be fortified. But that very process of fortification cannot hide the anxiety which gave rise to it in the first place, and which it is at pains to efface.

The same ambivalence also characterises the use of those other dichotomies discussed in Chapter 3: those who should be a temporary outside presence (untroubling to the natural and national order) are perceived as a fixed and durable presence in 'our' cities. In his excellent analyses, Abdelmalek Sayad has shown how the immigrant is defined according to 'his' *temporary* and *economic* status; he is 'a labour force which is provisional, temporary, in transit', encapsulated in the composite term 'immigrant worker' ('travailleur immigré') (1979: 7; also 1984b, 1985).[7] The notion of the 'installation' ('sédentarisation') of these immigrants at a specific time then appears to be a contradiction in terms and is deeply unsettling to this image: it implies a link with the earth, a kinship structure and a social existence which are denied (or repressed) in the stereotype of the nomadic, male labourer.

It is significant, then, that the discourse of the 'bidonville', the 'seuil de tolérance' and the 'ghetto' has been used primarily in connection with the primary social space, that of residence. Even though the 'seuil de tolérance' has been applied to hospitals, schools (see Montfermeil) and even holiday camps, its main use has been in connection with housing (MacMaster 1991). It is rare (if not unheard of) that concepts of undesirable 'ethnic' concentrations and quotas are applied to the work-place. The selective use of such concepts is a further demonstration of the way in which the immigrant has been defined principally according to 'his' place in the productive machine (de Rudder 1980: 13). The definition of immigration as a social problem (first and foremost) is therefore symptomatic of a transgression of geographical and social space.

Those who clearly do not fit the old category of 'immigrant worker' are the young. The terms used to describe them are part of the same drama: immigrants, second generation, youth of immigrant origin and so on. These categories express an ambivalent status between the nomad and the resident, the ('ethnicised') foreigner and the ('non-ethnicised') national. According to Sayad, this is the fundamental paradox of the immigrant; 'not to be totally present at that place where one is present' (Sayad 1985: 33). Those born and socialised in France, who are the same in virtually every respect as 'the French', are therefore caught between the structures of sameness and difference, proximity and distance (cf. Lapeyronnie 1989: 326–7). The gap between their cultural and social similarity and their economic and ideological marginalisation can be a profound source of contemporary racism (Dubet 1989a: 105–6). Clearly, concepts of identity are not simply imposed on unwilling victims; many have mobilised around one or the other of the terms in these dichotomies, or around a mixture of the two in their struggle for identity and rights.[8] Yet, as I shall argue, this has led to a constant sliding between the language of sameness and difference which has presented problems for anti-racism (not the least of which is frequently finding itself sharing a discourse with the New Right).

I argued in Chapter 1 that this ambivalence of assimilation and difference (the double-bind behind the concept of assimilation) is a product of the modern nation-state. Its essential mechanisms have therefore been in place for much longer than the contemporary period and have been a frequent explanation of anti-semitism; racist constructions of the essential difference of the other become more marked in situations of greater similarity between minority groups and the 'host' society.[9] In considering the reasons, then, why in France today this underlying ambivalence about proximity and distance and sameness and difference should be focused specifically on North Africans (especially 'youth of North African origin') we must recognise the fundamental importance of colonialism. Contemporary racialisation is thoroughly dependent on the colonial experience (though this is not the sole determinant). Balibar argues that this experience is crucial to an understanding of the retrospective comparison of the old (European/assimilable) and the new (non-European/non-assimilable) forms of immigration: the pre-war immigrants are 'close' because they were never colonised, whilst the non-European, post-war immigrants are 'distant' because they were colonised (1984: 1741; also Bourdieu 1987; Dubet 1989a: 70–1).

Thus, spatial configurations of distance and proximity are over-determined by the historical realities of colonialism. The position of Algerians in France is a classic example of the ambivalence of proximity and distance. Algeria was both incorporated into France in the form of three departments and yet not like those departments in metropolitan France itself. The problems of terminology for defining Algerian immigrants indicates the level of this ambivalence: from the expression 'colonial workers' ('travailleurs coloniaux') of the early decades of the twentieth century to the expression 'French Muslims working in the metropole' ('Français-musulmans d'Algérie travaillant en métropole') and the current use of the terms 'Muslims' or 'Arabs', there has been a continual racialisation of those who are similar yet different (Galissot 1985a: 33).[10] The colonial relationship between France and Algeria has created a hybrid identity (Galissot 1984b: 118), '"subjects" who are neither totally French nor totally foreigners' (Sayad 1985: 37).

The 'post-colonial' era is not a clean break with the colonial past; it is thoroughly determined by it. Those from the former colonies and their families are *in* the former metropole; post-colonial proximity is superimposed on colonial 'distance'. The idea of the 'colonial legacy' is important if it is interpreted not simply as a reproduction of colonial structures but as the confrontation between those structures (institutions/ideologies) and the post-colonial migration of people and products, and (most significantly) the internationalisation of culture and communications. The new racism is different from colonial racism in that it is born from this confrontation, that is, from the breakdown in the distinction between 'there' and 'here'. It is much more to do with place and space, belonging, frontiers, mixing and inclusion and exclusion (yet, as I shall argue, it is also to do with rights and equality).

## HEADSCARVES AND THE ENLIGHTENMENT

A number of the issues mentioned above were crystallised in the headscarf affair of 1989. Elements which, it was said, were from another culture and another tradition were now posing problems in this one. Yet, as we have already seen in relation to 'ethnic concentrations', those elements deemed to be alien to the French tradition only appeared in that light due to a mythologised reconstruction of the development of the French nation. The constructed dichotomy between the assimilationist/universalist tradition of France and the differentialist/particularist tradition of other countries (notably the USA and Britain) created fundamental contradictions for the Left and anti-racism, as it had throughout the 1980s.

Viewed from the outside (that is, outside France), one of the ironies of the whole affair appears to derive not from the divisions which it caused amongst the Left, anti-racism and feminism, but rather from the fundamental similarities between them and a large part of the Right. For example, whatever differences there were between those who agreed with the exclusion from school of the three girls for wearing their headscarves and those who favoured the approach of the Education Minister Lionel Jospin which allowed them to wear their headscarves in school, a much deeper consensus over the French model of universalist secularism united the warring factions. Secularism is the sign *par excellence* of the rational, progressive, equal, universalist tradition of the French republic, counterposed to the particularist tradition of the 'Anglo-Saxon' model. The idea of the individual-led French model is constantly placed in opposition to the community-led Anglo-Saxon model, the concept of integration (assimilation) as the polar opposite of ghettoisation. The headscarf affair therefore gave a remarkable insight into the way in which the Enlightenment is signified today in France. The following comments focus primarily on the ways in which this dichotomy is constituted and the consequent problems posed for anti-racism.

The classic way in which the affair was constructed was in terms of the binary opposition between secularism and difference, as, for example, in the headlines 'Islam in the schools of the Republic' (*Le Monde*, 7 October 1989) and 'Islam and secularism' (*Le Monde*, 19 October 1989 and 20 January 1990). Like most binary oppositions, the two terms in question are signified both differently and hierarchically (cf. Said 1981). Islam denotes religion whereas the secular republic is beyond religion; Islam is a particularism whereas the secular Republic is neutral; Islam is obscurantist and anti-rational whereas the secular Republic is founded on the rationalist principles of the Enlightenment. It is therefore through 'the school of the Republic' ('l'école de la République') that children can be saved from the obscurantist particularism of religion.

This view was clearly expressed by the socialist group of militant assimilationist republicans ('Socialism and Republic') led by the then defence minister Jean-Pierre Chevènement. It was also expressed by five intellectuals (Elisabeth Badinter, Régis Debray, Alain Finkielkraut, Elisabeth de Fontenay, Catherine Kintzler) in an open letter to the Education Minister published in *Le Nouvel Observateur* (2–8 November 1989) entitled 'Teachers, don't give in!', which supported the exclusion of the three girls from classes. In this text the secular state system of education is described in terms of a rhetoric of emancipation, neutrality, universality and liberty in opposition to the constitution of a mosaic of ghettos.

Yet those who supported Jospin's stand (against exclusion) and were in favour of a 'new secularism' were no less likely to develop the same dichotomy as that expressed above. These included the anti-racist organisations SOS Racisme and MRAP and the feminist 'second generation' group Nanas Beurs. Harlem Désir proposed the opposition between the rational, progressive and neutral education system and the obscurantism of the sect: 'Schools must welcome all children for it is only in that way that they can escape from obscurantism' (*Le Figaro*, 20 October 1989). Nanas Beurs were against the private sphere of religious schooling because it inevitably leads to the oppression of women: 'Only the secular system will allow emancipation and integration' (quoted in *Le Monde*, 28 October 1989). Like many other commentators on the affair, Souad Benani, president of Nanas Beurs, situated the contemporary struggle in terms of the old struggle between

Church and state at the end of the nineteenth century prior to the institutionalisation of the separation in 1905. She reinterprets Jules Ferry's opposition between 'science' (secularism) and the Church a century ago in terms of the choice today between integration and fundamentalism.[11] In response to the letter by Badinter *et al.*, Harlem Désir, Alain Touraine and three others opposed the old-fashioned secularism of the Debray type with a more open brand of secularism which would place the secular school 'above particularisms' but 'in respect for these'. Their opposition to the exclusion of the three girls was based on the fear that this merely 'feathers the nest' of both the fundamentalists and the FN (*Le Monde*, 10 November 1989). This idea was echoed in a different way by the writer Bernard Henri-Lévy (*L'Evénement du Jeudi*, 9–15 November 1989). He suggested that the best way to 'emancipate' young Muslim girls from the oppressive embrace of Islam is not to exclude them from school but, quite the opposite, to subject them to a good dose of Rabelais and Voltaire in the well-worn universalist tradition of the secular school: 'We have young "beurs" who arrive at school impregnated with beliefs, taboos and a form of servitude inherited from their families. The secular school must speak to them and liberate them.' He concluded that if this was not done they would end up 'immured in their ghetto'.

Finally, in this defence (or construction?) of the French tradition of secularism, let us mention the voice of the historian Michel Winock, for his is a profoundly informed description of the crisis. Having situated the headscarf affair within the historical struggle to establish the modern form of secularism in France, he concludes as follows:

> Two scenarios can be imagined. Either we are disposed to allow the formation – contrary to our tradition – of religious communities living according to their own rules, constituting different ghettos in society, a state within a state, with its own specific laws, customs, tribunals; and then we enter into the logic of segregation in the name of 'difference'. Or, faithful to our history, we believe that Muslims can, if they want, become French citizens, in which case their religion – a minority religion in a pluralist society – will accept the concessions which Catholicism was obliged to make in the past.
>
> (*L'Evénement du Jeudi*, 9–15 November 1989)

The points that I wish to make about the above comments are not primarily partisan ones. My comments focus instead (as they have throughout this chapter) on the ways in which the history of the republican nation-state is frequently signified (by the Right and the Left) in terms of universalism and assimilation. It is a history (or historiography) in which the particularist ideas of difference are presented as constituting an alternative and non-French tradition and having therefore played no part in the development of the French nation. It is this polarisation and construction of a (Manichean) binary opposition which is the cause of such confusion, for, as we have seen, that universalist and assimilationist past has not always been devoid of racialised (and often racist) concepts of the nation.

Winock's 'two scenarios' and 'two traditions' – the Enlightenment *as opposed to* the differentialist model, the individualist *as opposed to* the community-led model – need to be considered more problematically. It is true that there are differences between French and 'Anglo-Saxon' models of nation-building. But it is far too simplistic to characterise each in fixed and absolute terms and, as part of the same process, to lump together Britain and the USA (under the tag of 'Anglo-Saxon'). The idea of a dichotomy between secularism and difference constructs the myth of the secular Republic as a neutral space, free of cultural, ethnic and religious input, a space untouched by ideology and socially constructed differences (class, gender and so on). Elisabeth Badinter, one of the signatories to the open letter to Lionel Jospin, presented the secular tradition as follows: 'People must be reminded that the secular state school means neutrality imposed on everybody.... It is the only way to cement our national community' (quoted in *Le Monde*, 25 October 1989). Gisèle Halimi, the founder and co-president of the movement Choisir and the then deputy leader of SOS Racisme, echoed these sentiments in another open letter to Jospin. She argued for the exclusion of any religious signs worn ostentatiously 'whose intention is to compromise the neutrality and therefore the serenity of the state school' (*Le Monde*, 27 October 1989). (She resigned from SOS Racisme over its pro-Jospin and what she saw as its anti-feminist stand.) The same process is at work here as in the discourse on the 'bidonvilles' and the ghettos: religious, ethnic and other particularist definitions are not part of the French tradition of organisation of public space (which is 'neutral') and can only trouble the 'serenity' of that space.[12]

Yet the separation between religion and the state, the private and the public is not as simple as that. It is true that over the last century there has existed a compromise between the state and the Catholic Church but this has left notable religious (that is, Catholic) traces in the public sphere which have made Catholicism an 'invisible' religion in France and 'more equal than the others' (Balibar in *Libération*, 3 November 1989): the major holidays in France are Christmas, Easter, Assumption and All Saints; the traditional half-day at school was arranged to accommodate catechism classes; the contractual relationship between the private schools (predominantly Catholic) and the state includes a certain amount of state subsidy for private (religious) education; the tax-payer similarly contributes to the maintenance of the (Catholic) church and so on (cf. André Chambraud, one of the founders of SOS Racisme, in *L'Evénement du Jeudi*, 9–15 November 1989).

Furthermore, the strict universalism, secularism and neutrality of schools had been breached on numerous other occasions (*Le Monde*, 7 October 1989). In the mid–1970s Paul Dijoud, the Secretary of State for Immigrant Workers, had already introduced criteria that one might call 'ethnic' by identifying the nationality of parents of pupils with a view to considering their 'foreign culture' and, it was assumed, their use of a 'foreign language' (see Henry-Lorcerie 1989a). Dijoud's discussion of the importance for the identity of immigrants of conserving their 'culture of origin' was part of the contemporary racialisation of society during the 1970s discussed in the previous chapter (for the 'ethnicisation' of the terms 'Français' and 'immigré' in a circular of 25 July 1978 on the schooling of children of immigrants, see Henry-Lorcerie 1989b). This 'differentialist' ideology in schools was abandoned with the arrival of a socialist government in 1981 (and specifically rejected by the profoundly secular republican socialist Jean-Pierre Chevènement when he became Minister of Education in 1984).

Clearly, history is all-important in explaining the power of the myth of neutrality today, especially the classic representations of the Revolution and the creation of state secularism a century later: the former as the struggle between rationalist universalism and the particularist privileges of the monarchy and the aristocracy, the latter as the struggle between scientific universalism and the particularist privileges of the Church. In both cases, particularism is associated with anti-rationalism and obscurantism and is therefore represented as alien to the basic premises of the rationalism of the Enlightenment. Republican principles, enforced particularly through state education, offer, at one and the same time, a vision of the 'equalisation' of citizens and 'the cult of national unity threatened, in more or less imaginary terms, by "difference"' (Balibar in *Libération*, 3 November 1989).

In the headscarf affair this 'vision', in its most extreme form, was often polarised in terms of the Republic *or* fundamentalism (secularism or fanaticism), the Republic *or* separate development (integration or apartheid). The problem for large parts of the Left was that they were often sharing the same discourse as Le Pen who used the affair to warn against 'the islamicisation of France'. Elisabeth de Fontenay (another signatory to the open letter to Lionel Jospin) accused Jospin of surrendering 'education to the interests of the communities and religion' (debate by the Socialist Party, 4 December 1989). And in a splendid example of the either/or choice facing France, in which there is a convergence of many of the discursive elements mentioned above, the Prime Minister Michel Rocard announced, on 2 December 1989, that France cannot be 'a juxtaposition of communities', must be founded on common values and must not follow the Anglo-Saxon model which allows ethnic groups to barricade themselves inside geographical and cultural ghettos leading to 'soft forms of apartheid' (quoted in *Le Monde*, 7 December 1989). Harlem Désir echoed these sentiments (and many of the same words) a few days later when he described the situation in the housing estates as one not of integration but of despair:

> Thus a model which has come from elsewhere is establishing itself little by little in our towns: that of the Anglo-Saxon world. It is a most serious challenge to the French melting-pot. How many ghettos do we have to have to introduce a specific policy?
> (*Le Monde*, 10 December 1989)[13]

This sort of polarisation is symptomatic of a fundamental problem: a conceptual/linguistic crisis in the naming of social relations, for the language does not match the reality. France, like Britain, is clearly riven by concepts of alterity. The problem is that these frequently inform policy and opinion (quotas and thresholds for housing, racist attacks and so on) yet are continually denied in legal and official channels. Of course, the 'Anglo-Saxon' model of the

institutionalisation of 'race relations' is itself beset by a whole range
of different problems, not the least of which is the objectifying of
the socially constructed concept of 'race' (which is one of the
powerful reasons for its rejection by most French commentators).
However, one of the effects of denying its existence is to leave the
door open for Le Pen and others to exploit that territory which
resembles reality for many people. The intellectual New Right has
done precisely this; it has made a racialised and Europeanised
discourse of cultural difference its own.

The intervention in the headscarf affair by one of the founders
and leading figures in the New Right, Alain de Benoist, is most
significant in this respect. He exposes the false neutrality of secularism, argues in favour of the right of the three girls to express
their cultural difference and challenges the imperialism of western
assimilation and universalism from a 'Third World' perspective
(see his article in *Le Monde*, 27 October 1989). For those not already
familiar with his pedigree, his approach could easily be taken for
a 1960s-inspired, anti-imperialist, Left critique of the West. His
discourse is a prime example of New Right cultural differentialism
which now occupies that ground ceded by the Left in its disorien-
tation over the categories of assimilation and difference (for an
analysis of de Benoist and the New Right in general, see Taguieff
1985,1988b). De Benoist's article highlights the measure of the
problems for the Left: the language of racialised cultural difference has been appropriated by the New Right and cannot easily
be used for anti-racist purposes. The Left is therefore either
thrown back on an assimilationism (under the term 'integration'),
with the consequent problems discussed above, or forced to com-
bine an assimilationist and differentialist approach, with the
consequent contradictions in strategy.

The final section in this chapter considers these questions in a
more general way. Yet it is worth emphasising the problems posed
for 'democracy' by relegating concepts of alterity to a dangerous
and 'non-French' world. Michel Winock cites the article by de
Benoist as an example of where the differentialist road leads. For
Winock it is a question of either the French tradition of the rights
of the individual or a Balkanised version of organic societies
(*L'Evénement du Jeudi*, 9–15 November 1989). However, one might
argue that more people are likely to take the road advocated by
de Benoist if alterity is *not* recognised (in some form) as a part of
the *de facto* reality of contemporary France. In which case, what is

more dangerous is the perpetuation of the myth that it does not, and never has, formed part of the French tradition. So that, when the first report of the Council for Integration (which was established as a direct result of the headscarf affair) describes the major criterion on which the concept of integration is founded as that of 'the equality of individuals before the law, irrespective of their origins, race, and religion... to the exclusion of the institutional recognition of minorities' (Haut Conseil à l'Intégration 1991: 10), one can point to all those times when origins, 'race' and religion *have* been used in the past (and are certainly used today) to categorise people. At the height of the headscarf affair, it was therefore a salutary reminder of 'hidden' elements of France's 'tradition' to read Patrick Weil's description of the ideas which, as we have already seen, informed the new immigration policy of 1945:

> They favoured an ethnic immigration policy based on quotas, rather like the American model. ...The ordonnance was prepared by the provisional government of Général de Gaulle. Its authors, like Georges Mauco the pioneer of research on immigration, suggested at first an immigration composed of 50 per cent from Northern Europe, 30 per cent from the Latin countries of Europe, and 20 per cent of Slavs.
>
> (*Libération*, 8 November 1989)

## RACISM/ANTI-RACISM

The dicussion so far has attempted to reconsider the distinctions between assimilation and difference, and universalism and particularism as alternative models for the formation of nation-states. These terms have been constructed as polar opposites (often in Manichean fashion) yet are in fact part of a far more complex and contradictory interweaving of elements in the national/social formation. I have also attempted to show how sections of the Left and anti-racism today are as much victims and perpetrators of these dichotomies as anyone else. They continue to be trapped within the concept of a distinctive paradigm of national formation, as the affair of the headscarves so clearly illustrated. They are therefore unwittingly reinforcing the use of a retrospective concept of individualist assimilation to define the French nation, and a retrospective concept of neutrality to define republican secularism. At the same time these views, *in extremis*, implicitly contribute to the idea that today's 'immigrants' are a threat to this tradition.

All this makes opposition to racism highly contradictory. Since what is at stake here is the national question, whose institutional/ideological structures traverse the Right and the Left, anti-racism frequently shares the very language of its adversaries. The dichotomy between racism and anti-racism is another of those alternatives which simplifies, and confuses, reality. The final section of this chapter therefore considers the problematic nature of the opposition between racism and anti-racism and outlines some of the difficulties for anti-racist strategy.

The structural nature of racism within the nation-state (so blandly effaced in simplistic notions of the universalist, individualist and assimilationist tradition) creates problems for the Left's opposition to racism, as the nationalist tradition is also a fundamental part of its own ideology. Given the fact that the high era of colonialism during the Third Republic was inspired more by the Left than the Right, one might even say that, at times, the Left has been even more culpable than the Right. We cannot here explore in any detail the long history of the Left, national identity and racism (see Sternhell 1983). However, the following points serve as reminders that the major problem for an anti-racist strategy of the Left has frequently been its attachment to republican nationalism. As Galissot has noted, anti-racism is 'caught in the trap of national identity' (1985a, cf. also Gilroy 1987). Yet analysis of racism has too often perceived it as *external* to the national/social complex rather than *internal* to it. Hence racism has been marginalised and ghettoised in numerous ways.

Racism is frequently depicted as the dark side or underside of modern, western, liberal democracies. This analysis is founded on a Christo-Manichean model of the nature of society: racism is the *evil* which is a constant threat to the enlightened tolerance of democratic society. Or racism is depicted as *irrational* behaviour, which suggests that the solution to racism would lie in an extra dose of rationalism. In both these ways racism is divorced from liberal democracy and the Enlightenment rather than located as the product of modernity. As Taguieff has pointed out, this tendency is founded on 'a postulate in the form of an alternative: democracy or barbary. The difficulty with this type of vision is that what is designated as barbaric is also a product of modern democratic society' (1988a: 154).

The efforts to counter racism by proving the non-scientific status of the term 'race' (see the articles by François Jacob, Albert Jacquard and Jean Hiernaux in *Le Genre Humain* 1986) are also founded on a Manichean opposition between science (presumed neutral) and ideology (presumed value-laden). The problem here is twofold: firstly, the scientific delegitimisation of the term 'race' does not abolish racist practice. Guillaumin has demonstrated this in a number of illuminating articles (see especially 1984a and 1986). The efforts to disprove the scientific status of 'race' (prompted especially by the work done through the UNESCO to conjure away racism through science after the war) come up against the same problems of language and social practice that we noted previously: namely, that the banishment of the term is no guarantee of the banishment of the practice.[14] This is implied in Guillaumin's idea that the *concept* of 'race' might have virtually disappeared in France, but the *notion* is alive and well (in the form of cultural differentialism).

Secondly, science can equally well be used to legitimise different racist theories (Gobineau, social Darwinism, sociobiology and so on). Science is perhaps the most ubiquitous modernist discourse; racism and anti-racism have constantly resorted to it to legitimise their arguments. Scientific anti-racism is therefore merely a double of scientific racism and is consequently trapped within a racist logic. As Guillaumin has pointed out, 'to remain on the terrain of race – of its existence or its non-existence – is to situate oneself inside the racist logic... and not even to challenge the whole range of its presuppositions' (1984a: 218)

Psychological or psychoanalytic and economistic Marxist analyses have also invariably succeeded in pathologising or marginalising racism. The former's concern with the process of othering (fear or hate of the Other, as in Albert Memmi's (1982) concept of 'heterophobia'), fear of the self, refusal of difference and so on locates racism within the dualistic model of self and other or master and slave. Racism is here situated within interpersonal relations of the couple. It is pathologised (therefore removing it from a social context) and universalised (therefore removing it from a historical context). Economistic Marxist analysis, on the other hand, certainly locates racism historically but restricts it to a functionalist role within capitalist development (cf. Wallerstein in Balibar and Wallerstein 1988). It is an extra element in capitalist exploitation (rather than an integral part of the formation of modern national states). This is a variation of the idea of racism as the perverse face of reason or as the perpetual Other of liberal democracy. In Galissot's words 'racism would always be simply the manifestation of the ultimate truth of a Hell: the Hell of the self, the Hell of the couple, the Hell of inter-personal exclusion or the Hell of capitalism' (1985a: 28).

These remarks are inevitably general. We cannot here explore or do justice to the full range of analyses of racism. Nor is it implied that, for example, psychoanalysis and historical materialist analysis are inadequate tools for the understanding of racism. On the contrary, I believe that they are both fundamental, provided they are used in less exclusive and more flexible ways. The point that I wish to emphasise here is that anti-racist approaches to racism have often marginalised racism by failing to challenge its real sites, or worse still, have merely mimicked racism in its discursive strategies. To think of racisms rather than racism would avoid removing it from specific historical contexts and universalising it; to think of the relative mobility and flexibility of the signifier 'race' (and others like 'culture') – which can articulate with numerous other discourses in different historical conjunctures – would avoid reifying and fetishising racism; and to think of racism as a total social phenomenon would avoid marginalising it from the social complex.

Let us consider, for example, the way in which anti-racism mimics racism in its use of a biological discourse and its representation of the national/social complex as a body. The 'seuil de tolérance' is dependent on the use of biological metaphors to describe social cohesion: the national body must either absorb or digest these foreign bodies (assimilation, integration and 'insertion' all have connotations of absorption) or expel them (expulsion, repatriation and so on).[15] Yet anti-racism too describes racism as a sickness infecting the body politic which must be cured (cf. Galissot 1985a: 24–5). Both racism and anti-racism conceptualise society as a pure body which has been invaded by a foreign virus.[16] It is as if the disease comes from outside and must be repelled; it is *in* the social body but not *of* it. Racism and anti-racism are at one in locating the essential problem as outside the body, rather than seeing the body itself as the source of the problem (or even the very representation of society as a body).

As we have seen throughout this chapter (and specifically in relation to the headscarf affair), the major problem of mimicry for anti-racism today can be seen in the ubiquitous use – traversing racism and anti-racism – of the discourses of assimilation and difference. In his magisterial work on the nature of racism and its 'doubles', Pierre André Taguieff (1988a) locates two major forms of racialisation which he terms 'hetero-racialisation' and 'auto-racialisation'. According to Taguieff, 'hetero-racialisation' (racialisation of the Other) leads to domination, oppression, exploitation and inequality; it finds its major forms of expression in slavery and colonialism; it is the universalising form of racism from which the idea of assimilation springs. 'Auto-racialisation' (racialisation of the self) is founded on the idea that 'we' constitute a particular 'race'; it leads to exclusion, segregation and, possibly, genocide; it finds its major form of expression in Nazism but also underpins the culturalist differentialism of contemporary 'new' racism; it is the particularist form of racism from which the idea of difference springs. The former racism aims to eradicate the Other; the latter aims to expel the Other. The former is an eradication of difference; the latter makes difference absolute.

Taguieff suggests that if there are therefore two racisms – which he names 'universalist-inegalitarian' and 'communitarian-differentialist' – there are, symmetrically, two anti-racisms which are completely contradictory. The first is a variation on the model of assimilation which would guarantee equal rights for all ('individuo-universalist anti-racism'). It suggests abolishing frontiers between groups (national, ethnic and so on) in the name of equality, for the idea that values and identity are located within fixed and specifiable groups or communities is seen as racist. It opposes differentialism by its slogan of mixing ('mixophilia'). The second form of anti-racism sees assimilationist universalism as a racism since the intention of assimilation is to eradicate differences through ethnocide or even genocide. It believes in the preservation of traditional values and that identity is located within the group ('traditio-communitarian anti-racism'). It promotes differentialism through its slogan 'the right to difference' (or 'mixophobia').

Taguieff's analysis of the discursive structures of contemporary racialisation highlights a number of the problems for anti-racism. Anti-racism is caught between assimilation and difference. It has both proclaimed the right to difference and the need to efface difference (mimicking the two major forms of racism). In the 1970s it swung from equality to difference, when assimilation was challenged through the concept of 'the right to difference'. In the mid and late 1980s there was a swing back again to equality, not (it was said) in the form of the old centralising ethos of assimilation but under the revamped concept of 'integration'; that is, an equality in rights but not necessarily a conformity of 'culture'. However, the difference between integration and assimilation, as we have already noted, is not necessarily as clear as that, for it is often difficult to see a clear break with the idea of assimilation.[17] Today, then, the two poles of anti-racism (assimilationist and differentialist) are frequently interwoven. Calls for plurality and diversity (difference) sit alongside calls for equality (integration/assimilation). The ultimate expression of this synthesis is to be found in the slogan 'equality in difference' proclaimed by numerous organisations (especially MRAP).[18]

Anti-racism is trapped within the same ambiguous language as its adversary. The slogan 'equality in difference' is virtually indistinguishable from the neo-racist slogan of the New Right 'equal but different'. And just as the New Right's slogan belies a naturalisation of differences and a hierarchisation of 'us' and 'them', so the anti-racist version of the same slogan is frequently caught up in the same ideological classifications. Yet, if the alternative to differentialism (or 'tribalism') is 'integration' (cf. Adil Jazouli in Le Monde, 15 February 1991), then anti-racism is perpetually locked into the classic topography of assimilation or difference. Most anti-racist organisations in France conceive of the option in terms of a dichotomy and choose 'individual integration' rather than 'tribalism'.[19] Yet, despite his own tendency to fit in precisely with this mode of conceptualisation, Harlem Désir has also recognised the underlying problem: 'there is a great confusion in people's minds. Nobody knows how to speak about immigration any more' (quoted in Le Monde, 28 April 1990). The new democratic forum launched by SOS Racisme in January 1990 posed a fundamental question: 'How to be anti-racist, therefore "differentialist", without effacing the aspiration to the universal present in all people?' (reported in La Croix, 31 January 1990). I would stress here that this question is relevant not simply to France but to other western nation-states undergoing a similar crisis in the formulation of democracy and rights today.

The two models of racialisation proposed by Taguieff are invaluable in an understanding of racialised discourse today. However, the models should not be taken as distinct and fixed. As

I have argued, assimilation and difference are not opposites; they are part of the same process. The ambivalence of assimilation is the result of its ever-present by-product which is differentialism. Taguieff's structural approach does not always capture this ambivalence (although it certainly captures the *ambiguities* for anti-racism). If it is true that colonial racism was a product of the assimilationist/individualist/universalist form, whilst Nazism was founded on the differentialist/particularist/ collectivist model, this should not suggest that the two forms are mutually exclusive.

This applies equally to contemporary racism. The discussion above of the ambivalent nature of concepts of distance and proximity in the post-colonial era suggests that the new racism in the former colonial metropoles is a blend of these two forms. Although the signs of cultural differentialism, segregation and exclusion are perhaps most apparent (at least these are the elements on which most analysts of new racism have focused), it is nevertheless the question of equality/inequality and rights which eventually emerges as the major source of conflict. As I have mentioned, it is at the moment when those people previously defined as an ethnic group want to be 'individuals', the moment when subjects want to be citizens, the moment when inequality is challenged in the name of equality that the contradictions of the republican nation-state come to the surface.

The problem then becomes what language and strategies are appropriate today to challenge these inequalities (Taguieff 1991). How can anti-racism go beyond the traps of assimilation and difference? In France in the 1980s (as in Britain) one response to these questions was that of a new 'identity' politics. This is founded more on the ambivalent 'différance' of Jacques Derrida than the essentialist 'difference' discussed above. It underpins the idea of 'mixing' and hybridity as opposed to diversity and pluralism. It is not a relativist differentialism but a contradictory and ambivalent differentialism. At its most sophisticated, it deconstructs the fixed identities of both the individual and the group. It also breaks the fixed opposition between them by highlighting contradictory affiliations, shifting alliances and hybrid collectivities. On one level, then, it destabilises the old individual/group, equality/difference model of social organisation. However, it tends to achieve this destabilisation from the perspective of identity (albeit fragmented and contradictory) rather than from the wider perspective of national/social organisation. At its worst it can appear like old-fashioned libertarianism. Yet even at its best it tends to understate the institutional/ideological dimension in the construction of the social complex, in order to accentuate the space of struggle and resistance. In this sense, its attempt to deconstruct binary oppositions from within a) pays insufficient attention to the wider historical determinations of 'identities', b) occasionally loses sight of power relations altogether in the effort to break the monolithic dualism of the master/slave model, and c) slips towards a liberal notion of a 'free' space of contestation outside the national/social complex. For these reasons it is questionable how effective new identity theories can be as a politics of contestation of racialised discourse. This applies equally to what in France is termed 'intercultural relations' (see, for example, Lorreyte 1985: 541; 1988: 24–7). Just like pluralism and cultural difference, hybridity too does not necessarily guarantee equality.

Another language which emerged during the 1980s in response to the crisis in the social contract and which is concerned with equality and rights is that of 'new citizenship'. It is therefore to questions of citizenship that we now turn.

# Chapter 5

# Nationality and citizenship

The marches of 1983 and 1984 put the anti-racist emphasis back on equality once again. It was not that rights had not been a major issue – indeed, *the* major issue – in immigrant struggles previously. But in the mid-1980s the demands for equality were reformulated by different actors in a different context. If the classic struggles of the past had been primarily in the work-place (or in the hostels), then the decline of old-style workers' struggles, on the one hand, and the presence of a younger population largely socialised in France led to a changed perspective in the 1980s. The struggles of 'immigrant' car workers in 1982 and 1983 became the exception rather than the rule for action.[1] The new social and political movements centred now around demands for participation in the political arena (the right to vote for immigrants in local elections, adopted by SOS Racisme and other associations;[2] the campaign to register young 'beurs' for voting in all elections, promoted especially by France Plus) and new cultural forms (the emergence of 'beur' movements, marches, independent radio stations, new magazines). Local collective action flourished in the mid-1980s, with an emphasis on uniting across ethnic and national lines (see *Migrations Société* 1989a). These new social and political movements form part of what is often referred to now as the new citizenship: movements that mobilised not simply through the institutional political channels but also within social and economic spheres in the attempt to redefine and repoliticise those spaces (see Wihtol de Wenden 1987: 168–9).

Like the slogan of equality, citizenship is a plastic term which can be used in a variety of ways to mean a variety of things. As a broad umbrella term which can incorporate the demands of diverse movements and associations, it inevitably contains conflicting and contradictory claims and discourses, including especially those discussed in the previous chapter. However, in a very general sense the reorientation of the debate in the 1980s onto rights was an important route towards reassessing the historical formulation of rights in France and, especially, questioning the link between rights and nationality.[3] For, at the heart of the citizenship debate is the association, established at the time of the Revolution, between nationality and citizenship. The fact that, today, about four million people resident in France are not entitled to citizen status because they are not French nationals has led analysts and activists alike to question the basis of entitlement to rights in the modern state, and to attempt a redefinition of the social contract for the contemporary era. A major demand, supported by many movements and associations, has therefore been to dissociate citizenship from nationality and to base it instead on residence (of at least five years in the country). This would certainly be a major step towards a greater equality of rights between nationals and non-nationals since it would give immigrants political rights (although at present only voting in municipal rather than all elections is being debated) and offer full protection against expulsion from the country.

However, a redefinition of the social contract clearly needs to go further than this. Nationality and citizenship have become systematically institutionalised in the formation of the nation-state, whilst juridical definitions of both have become tightly articulated with the concept of cultural conformity. From a wider perspective still, rights cannot be considered outside economic and social determinations. In their liberal sense, equality and citizenship are both blind to the wider structures of the national/social and international complex which limit the enjoyment of rights in numerous ways. Like the concepts of assimilation, universalism and individualism discussed in the previous chapter, citizenship too has acquired an idealised status in republican mythology which a new approach to rights must therefore problematise. Today, when racialised (and other) categories are used in discriminatory ways, it is a question of going beyond the abstract principles of universalism and equality before the law. The claim to dissociate nationality and citizenship allows for the possibility of viewing rights in other than a national and universalist framework; yet it, too, remains a mere slogan unless the complex process by which rights have become framed is fully reappraised.

The real merit of the claim lies in the fact that at least it opens up the possibility for a genuine reappraisal of rights today. For in pinpointing the way in which citizenship was 'hijacked' by the nation-state in the nineteenth century (and similarly 'hijacked' by the concept of cultural conformity), this approach provides the essential first step towards a far-reaching reappraisal of the French republic and the historical determinations of rights within the nation-state. Rights only became tightly articulated with the interests of the nation at a particular period of industrial growth and (as far as 'non-nationals' are concerned) the institutionalisation of differences between nationals and foreigners through an expanding state apparatus (see Chapter 1). The 'de-naturalising' of this process opens the way to a reconsideration of rights, the state and the nation. By showing that they are not inherently bound to be constructed in a common formation (but only came together at a particular moment in the growth of the nation), this approach has the potential for establishing a new perspective on rights (at a time of crisis of the classical form of the nation-state).

France is, I believe, further along this path than Britain. The debates around the crisis of the nation-state and a new citizenship have included a passionate reconsideration of republican traditions. And even if these debates are frequently characterised by mythologised reconstructions of those traditions (by Left and Right), at least the struggle over history is a fairly broad one – including researchers and activists alike – rather than confined to narrower groups as in Britain.

This chapter considers aspects of the recent debate around nationality and citizenship in France. First of all, it looks at the national framing of rights. Then it considers some of the contradictions surrounding rights today at a time of crisis of the nation-state through a) the focus on illegal immigration and the law, and b) the nationality debate of 1986 and 1987. Finally, citizenship will be situated at the intersection of diverse and often contradictory discourses; in a fluid situation, ideas for a new citizenship are always tenuous and at the mercy of unpredictable developments.

## RIGHTS AND THE NATION-STATE

We have already seen in Chapter 1 that it was during the second part of the nineteenth century that the social sphere became increasingly nationalised; the non-national was denied many of the rights of the national and was progressively removed from full participation in society. The institutionalisation of the distinction between citizens (nationals) and foreigners was enshrined in the construction of two different legal paradigms. For nationals/citizens equal rights were at the very heart of the universal natural heritage of all 'men' and were guaranteed through the rule of law ('le domaine de la loi'). For non-nationals/citizens of another nation, this natural entitlement to rights was deemed to rest with their country of origin, not with France. Rights enjoyed by foreigners in France were therefore not part of natural law but were restricted either to what was negotiated through bilateral agreements between France and other nation-states or to what was granted by the government. Foreigners were subject not to the rule of law but to the rule of administration ('le domaine réglementaire'). The area of the law defined the frontiers of the nation; the area of checks and controls governed the rest (see Sayad 1984b; Zolberg 1988: 213–14).

We have also seen that the juridical and administrative regimes introduced through colonialism established a similar division between citizens (enjoying full rights) and subjects (excluded from fundamental rights like the right to vote, as in Algeria) (Balibar 1984: 1744; Galissot 1986: 8). Subjects were 'French but not completely' (Bruschi 1989: 255). The last hundred years has therefore seen the construction of two distinct legal frameworks, founded on national criteria, which has institutionalised a two-tier system of 'subjectification': the first is empowering (the construction of the citizen), the second is disempowering (the construction of the subject). The hierarchical division of the domain of the law casts an oblique light on the much-vaunted 'juridical culture' of French republicanism founded on the rule of law and the Rights of Man. This is not to deny the complex pattern of exclusion/inclusion and variable power relations in the realm of citizenship itself (that is, for nationals) according to racialised categories, gender, class and so on. As I shall be arguing later in this chapter, questions of new citizenship extend far beyond the confines of the issue of immigration, even if that is defined in its widest sense as a French national/social question.

Yet for the moment let us stay with that institutional division between citizens and subjects and consider some of its concrete manifestations in contemporary France, especially at the level of local administration. For, despite recent progress in the acquisition of rights for immigrants (see Chapter 2) and the fact that different spaces have been opened up, challenging the structures of the national state and extending the concept of citizenship (Wihtol de Wenden 1987), one must also recognise the fragile and ambiguous nature of this progress, since the acquisition of rights is frequently undermined by other constraints in the social formation.

As non-nationals are removed from the natural rule of law, it is of little surprise that it was not until 1980 that the first law relating to immigration was passed (the Bonnet Law).[4] Prior to that date immigration was regulated by the state not through the passing of laws following open discussion in parliament but by means of the executive and administrative (and non-parliamentary) options open to law-makers in France, in the form of decrees, 'arrêtés' and circulars. Immigration was subject to an 'infra-droit' (Lochak 1976), that is, regulated administratively rather than through proper parliamentary and judicial scrutiny, and frequently totally outside the rule of law. It is significant that two of the most important measures of the modern period – the Marcellin–Fontanet proposals of 1972 (which, it will be remembered, reinforced controls and facilitated expulsions of 'irregulars') and the suspension of primary immigration in July 1974 – were implemented by means of circulars.[5] This was in keeping with the method of introduction of much legislation relating to immigration in these years. The circular is the most administrative of weapons in the French legal armoury. It is the text which has the least judicial force. As Myrto and Christian Bruschi point out, it is 'drafted not in general terms according to the criteria of respect for individual rights, but in the interests of the smooth functioning of the administration' (Bruschi and Bruschi 1984: 2023). In other words, the circular is the perfect instrument for constructing the immigrant as an object of control rather than an individual subject of law.

Nor could the rights of immigrants be guaranteed by bilateral agreements with the countries of emigration. As we have seen, in the twenty-five years following the Second World War the regulations defining the whole area of immigration were frequently limited to a discussion of numbers and manpower; the rights of immigrants in France were invariably not part of that agenda. Before the early 1970s, immigrants were frequently pawns in an economic game played by others (Galissot 1985a: 70–1), or even part of a modern form of inter-state slavery which inscribed racism within the structures of the state (Balibar 1984: 1743; Sayad 1988: 172-3). Furthermore, whatever measures concerning rights might be instituted at the level of the bilateral agreement, their implementation in practice could not be guaranteed. The contradiction between the place of law (international or national) and the practices of local administration and bureaucracy is central here. There can be a world of difference between a bilateral agreement between France and another state and actual administrative practice, especially when the state in question is a former French colony whose relations with what was the metropole are charged with complex historical association. International conventions on the rights of migrants are either unobserved, contradicted by state controls (Silverman 1989: 89–92) and the lowly position of immigrants in the labour market, or merely subverted by local administrative practice (Gollot 1990).

In the contemporary climate of the new racialisation of immigration, the practices of the local state can be the cutting edge of discrimination. As we have already mentioned, the measures of decentralisation introduced in the early years of socialist government at the beginning of the 1980s often worked against the interests of minorities for they gave greater powers to local politicians and administrators (Bruschi 1985: 58). The use of thresholds and quotas by municipal councils in housing and education is a good example of this. There is a considerable gap between the abstract government rhetoric of equality and non-discrimination and much local practice which has frequently responded to the material crisis in housing in the suburbs in racist ways. Even as early as the 1960s there are examples of the contradiction between national policy and racialised local policy. The Evian agreement (1962) marking the end of the Algerian war gave Algerians in France the same rights as the French, except for political rights (article 7). However, a circular of 1967 restrained the possibilities of family reunification and mentioned the necessity to limit this procedure when, locally, a quota or threshold of Algerians had been reached in a town or a suburb (Bruschi and Bruschi 1984: 2027).

Consequently, local and administrative practices can subvert the best of laws in theory. The law of the 17 July 1984 which introduced a single residence and work permit was generally welcomed by immigrant associations (see Chapter 2). In fact, even in the law itself – that is, even before it got anywhere near an administrator – there are ambiguities. Applicants for the new card had to prove that they had sufficient resources to maintain themselves and their families, and that they would observe the dubious notion of 'public order'. The first of these obligations reinforces the idea that, unlike French nationals, immigrants are defined primarily in economic terms. The second underlines the limits on freedom of expression and action for the immigrant compared to the national.

Yet further ambiguities have arisen in the application of the law, leading to uneven practices from one prefecture to another and resulting in a number of protests by anti-racist and pro-immigrant organisations. The newspaper *La Croix* (28 February 1986) noted that 'there are lengthy procedures, long waits, and mistakes leading to difficulties in obtaining housing and employment. As a result, a number of immigrants find themselves in a vicious circle which nullifies the initial progress made by the law.' Even a report on immigration for the Plan in 1987 underlined the arbitrary nature of the implementation of measures at the level of local services, offices and prefectures (quoted in Dubet 1989a: 92). This pattern is particularly noticeable concerning the right of family reunification (although here too there are also profound contradictions in the law itself). As for the laws governing entry and residence rights, there are numerous cases of local administrators making up their own rules.[6]

Even the simplest aspects of life for an immigrant depend on the good will of administrators. Whether it is to do with residence in the country, housing or living with his or her family, the immigrant must fill in forms. There is permanent contact with the administration (Wihtol de Wenden 1978) which is inevitably interiorised and contradicts the distinction between public and private life. As Christian Bruschi remarks, 'immigration has for too long been an area of "non-law" for there not to be the traces' (Bruschi 1989: 247).

The traces today are still significant: they include (for certain non-European and formerly colonised immigrants and their families) classification as citizens of another state and subjects of French state administration; designation as a group to be surveyed, administered, controlled, even expelled from the country according to national criteria; exclusion from certain fundamental rights; relegation to the worst jobs and housing according to national/racialised economic and social policy; the site of countless fears and anxieties ideologically. Any reformulation of rights is confronted with this deeply embedded historical construction of a two-tier national/social complex (cf. Costa-Lascoux 1987a; Bruschi 1989).

## THE LAW, TRANSGRESSION AND CRISIS: 'LES CLANDESTINS'

The forms of exclusion and classification mentioned above are effaced in the retrospective reconstruction of the homogeneity of France. An idealised republicanism does not confront the thorny question of discrimination in the meting out of the law. Yet, as we have already seen, a reformulated concept of assimilation to describe the past is mobilised only in response to a sense of crisis in the present. The contradictions of the model of universalism, 'the rights of Man' and equality before the law irrespective of origin became more acute as the question of immigration became increasingly politicised in the 1980s. In transgressing the (imagined) frontiers between universalism and particularism, assimilation and difference, individuals and communities, distance and proximity, the citizen and the subject, the private and the public, the administrative and the legal, the economic and the social, and so on, immigration became the site where those frontiers are thrown into sharp relief and where the whole nationalised structural apparatus of the state is destabilised.

Nowhere are these contradictions more visible today than in the discourse around illegal immigration ('la clandestinité'). All the fears discussed in the previous chapter of a foreign invasion of the republic's 'undifferentiated' public space are crystallised here. As with the discourse on assimilation and difference, the Left and anti-racism are as bound up in the contradictions of this discourse as the Right. This clearly poses problems for the demands for a new citizenship; for the language through which it is expressed is frequently trapped in the same ambivalent national model of social relations that we discussed previously.

One of the major problems for anti-racism lies in the link between integration and control (discussed in Chapter 3). The 'common-sense' policy of governments over the last twenty years is captured in the following statement: 'the government will reinforce the struggle against illegal immigration whilst consolidating the integration of foreign workers' (*Le Monde*, 1 September 1983).

In this statement, the couple 'integration/control' is dependent on the couple 'foreign workers/clandestins'. Indeed, François Mitterrand said at the Council of Ministers of 31 August 1983 that it was important not to confuse foreign workers who are part of the 'national reality' with 'les clandestins' who 'must be sent home' (*L'Humanité*, 1 September 1983).

Yet the hope of separating the foreign worker from the 'clandestin', the legal from the illegal at a time of the racialisation and illegalisation of immigration is as illusory as positing a binary opposition between assimilation and difference. In contemporary France they are profoundly entwined; the politicisation of immigration during this period has produced a relentless confusion between 'immigrants' and 'les clandestins', the legal and the illegal. This has been achieved through the construction of the 'problem' of immigration to refer to certain non-Europeans; through the conversion of what was called 'spontaneous immigration' in the 1960s, and openly encouraged by government, into 'illegal immigration' ('immigration clandestine') with the controls of the early 1970s and the suspension of primary immigration in July 1974 (cf. Marie 1990); through the attempts to curb the right of family reunification after 1974 (declared unlawful by the Conseil d'Etat); through the introduction of a voluntary scheme of financial aid for repatriation in 1977, and the introduction of the Bonnet Law in 1980 making expulsion of 'irregulars' an administrative rather than judicial matter (hence speeding up the process and removing it from the jurisdiction of the law) and so on. The qualities which were praised by Michel Massenet in the early 1960s – mobility, non-specialisation, and so on – which made immigrants well suited to the needs of the restructuring of French industry became the very qualities which in the 1970s and 1980s characterised the 'clandestins'. The measures mentioned above have transformed 'foreign workers' into 'clandestins' by defining certain 'immigrants', by statute and (ideologically) by example, as a problem, outside the law and outside the nation. At the end of the 1970s numerous official reports and papers appeared on the phenomenon of illegal immigration (see Wihtol de Wenden 1988a: 244–8).

The confusion is further compounded (rather than avoided) when the government itself is seen to adopt a tougher line on immigration in direct response to racist and anti-immigrant sentiment of the time (August–September 1983). Obviously, this 'confusion' is the very meat of the new racism which does not accept legality or French nationality as guaranteeing legitimacy. Jean-Yves Le Gallou, co-founder and Secretary General of the New Right Club de l'Horloge, puts the case cogently:

Is it as coherent as it seems to 'integrate' more fully the immigrants who are here in order to prevent the arrival of new immigrants? No. There is no evidence to show that legal immigration is less disturbing than illegal immigration. Denouncing the criminality of illegal immigrants is more to do with a precautionary language than an objective analysis: the few statistics that exist on crime and the prison population show that foreigners, especially from the Maghreb, are over-represented; but they do not distinguish between 'illegals' and legally established residents in the rise in insecurity. Moreover, the large majority of immigrants present in France entered illegally before being 'regularised'.

(1985: 26–7)

Le Gallou suggests that the distinction between 'legal' and 'illegal' immigration is a nonsense since the real problem is (North African) immigration in general. They are all the same, especially since yesterday's 'clandestins' are today's regularised immigrants. But of course he does not stop there. For yesterday's immigrants (legal or illegal) are also today's nationals, by virtue of naturalisation and automatic acquisition of nationality at the age of majority of children born in France. Yet this too does not distinguish them from legal or illegal immigrants for they are still attached to their non-French roots and culture:

A young North African born in France and having, in theory, lived here continuously between the ages of thirteen and eighteen, automatically acquires French nationality at the age of eighteen, but does not feel any more French, and is not thought of as any more French by his community.

(1985: 20)

The slippage from 'clandestins' to 'second-generation youth' is simple since 'their' ethnic origins will always place them outside the law and the nation.

Le Gallou's criticism of the distinction between legal and illegal immigrants has a powerful logic, with a racist pedigree which stretches back to the Action Française slogan of 'paper Frenchmen' (1926), used to refer to foreigners who were naturalised in

France, and before.[7] When the frontiers of national identity are racialised, neither legal immigrant status nor French nationality necessarily confer *legitimacy*. Economic illegality and national illegality are collapsed into a single reality (Marie 1988: 136; also 1990). The ambivalence of the process of assimilation of the Jews is the classic example; when the concept of nationality slips towards a cultural absolutist definition, then security cannot necessarily be guaranteed by the law. Le Gallou makes explicit what is implicit in official discourse on illegal immigration: it is an assault on and a delegitimisation of not only illegal immigrants or even (North African) immigrants in general, but all those who *might be thought to be* of North African origin. As Dubet rightly says: 'In effect the search for "clandestins" transforms every foreigner into a suspect whose offence would be that of having "the wrong face"' (1989a: 93). Or, as Sayad remarks, 'as if behind every immigrant lurked the danger of a potential spy' (1988: 174). When determinist criteria of this sort are being used, the law is flimsy protection. Sayad remarks elsewhere (though perhaps rather too deterministically): 'If it is true that the presence of the immigrant is a presence which is fundamentally *illegitimate*...there is absolutely nothing that could contribute to legitimise this presence' (1985: 35).

Mitterrand's plea not to confuse legal and illegal immigrants flies in the face of the contemporary social construction of 'immigration'. For example, let us consider the problems of definition discussed in a report on illegal labour ('le travail clandestin') (Conseil Economique et Social 1983). It is recognised in the report that the legal definition of 'illegal labour' makes no reference whatsoever to nationality (articles L. 324–9 and L. 324–10 of the Code of Labour). However, this has not prevented the term from acquiring the popular meaning of 'illegal *immigrant* labour', given the fact that 'le travail clandestin' has become a virtual synonym for 'l'immigration clandestine'.

The two are consistently confused even by those who dispense the law. In 1976 an inter-ministerial liaison group was established with responsibility for the struggle against the introduction, employment and housing of illegal immigrants (inter-ministerial 'arrêté', 10 August). In the annual report of the 'mission' for 1983 it is stated that:

> on numerous occasions it was the case that there was confusion, in the minds of those responsible for drawing up the records of

evidence, between 'le travail clandestin', as it is defined in article L. 324–10 of the Code of Labour, and the employment of a foreigner without work authorisation.

(Mission de liaison interministérielle pour la lutte contre les trafics de main-d'oeuvre 1983: 154)

It is also recorded in this report that treatment of the culprit(s) (foreign worker or employer or both) varied considerably from one area to another depending largely on how high a profile immigration had in the region.

The inevitable interconnections between state policy, the law and popular representations blur the contours between legal and popular terminology and connotations. The popular perception of the 'problem' of illegal immigration is itself largely constructed through the legal and discursive strategy of the state. The state, on the other hand, is equally likely to recycle popular representations. For example, popular images of foreign workers risking their lives to cross the frontiers and groups of organised racketeers who charge extortionate sums for illegal passports or for smuggling foreign workers into the country are not uncommon news items in reports on 'les clandestins' (see for example *Le Point*, 4 December 1989: 31). However, similar stories find their way into more official documents. The style of the following passage would seem to owe not a little to the more sensationalist sections of the press:

> Two fearsome 'passeurs' – one Spaniard nicknamed 'El Rubio', the other from Central Africa – organised their illegal network using methods not dissimilar to those of the Sicilian Mafia: abandonment of 'clients', bloody vendettas, the establishment of semi-official organisations operating in full view of the Spanish authorities who eventually began to take the matter seriously.
>
> (Mission de liaison interministérielle pour la lutte contre les trafics de main-d'oeuvre 1983: 73)

There is no reason to disbelieve this particular account but there is every reason to be sceptical as to its inclusion (in this particular style) in an official report on the 'realities' of illegal immigration. Clearly, the level of illegal immigration and non-declared foreign labour is impossible to measure accurately, as is the method of entry. The most substantial data were provided by the 'regularisation' of about 130,000 'irregulars' in 1981, the results of which formed the basis of a special report (Ministère des Affaires Sociales et de la Solidarité Nationale 1983). According to this survey, only 4.9 per cent of those questioned were irregular through illegal entry into the country (and only 5.6 per cent had forged papers). The vast majority (68.4 per cent) entered the country legally on a tourist visa and overstayed the three-month duration of their visa (1983: 26, table 1). These statistics, however unreliable, are the most comprehensive guide yet to the nature of illegal immigration in France. They clearly cast doubt on the status of the above description as a sober, official analysis of illegal immigration. The confusion of popular and official discourses makes the confusion of legal and illegal immigration all the more likely.

The question of illegal immigration is highly complex. The 'problem' has more to do with the North–South divide, the role of the informal economy as a structural part of modern capitalist economies, the use made by unscrupulous employers of cheap exploitative labour and so on (see Perotti and Thepaut 1983). It is both produced and repressed by the modern state, in the same way as contemporary racism. The state is gamekeeper and poacher at one and the same time.

This complexity poses a problem for anti-racism and movements for a new citizenship: how to challenge the construction of the illegality of immigration when this construction emanates from consensus views propounded by people right across the political spectrum. We have already seen how the consensus on integration and control (the success of the former dependent on the rigour of the latter) is at the heart of the illegalisation of immigration (immigration perpetuates the 'problems' of integration); and how the obsession with the 'clandestins' can affect all immigrants and many who are not immigrants at all (for a discussion of the level of racially motivated identity card checks – under the guise of a clamp-down on illegal immigrants – see Gaboriau 1984: 2009). Through a tendency to pathologise racism, anti-racism has frequently failed to situate racial discrimination within 'common-sense' practices and discourses like these.

The problem here, as always, is the way in which rights are framed within the highly ambivalent context of national belonging. So when the catchword for anti-racism *and* the government is 'integration', it is not always easy to separate its inclusionist aims (rights) from the exclusionist discourse which frequently accompanies it (controls). As a slogan for a new citizenship, 'integration' has too many links with the model 'inside the nation/outside the nation' for it not to be 'tainted' by that ambivalence. As Balibar remarks:

> I have always thought it extremely paradoxical to speak of the need to 'integrate' people who have been an integral part of the social structure of our country for one, two or even three generations. The question is how to confront or to minimize particular conflicts but not how to integrate those who are already inside social structures.
>
> (1991: 82)

The term 'integration' has all the problems of the term 'assimilation'; it too is a product of the ambivalence of the process of inclusion and exclusion constructed in the nation-state. If the primary task of a new citizenship is to dissociate citizenship from nationality (cf. Bouâmama 1989a) then the slogan of integration seems particularly ill-suited to achieve that end. The problem with any new discourse of rights in France is therefore how to move beyond the confines and contradictions of the national model. This is a major barrier to a reformulation of citizenship for, as we have seen, the language of racism and anti-racism is so thoroughly shot through with an ambivalent nationalist discourse.

The 1980s seemed to get stuck in the repetition of these contradictions. Mitterrand's statement of 31 August 1983 (mentioned above) was in response to the increased politicisation of immigration that year and the success of the FN in a by-election at Dreux. Yet six years later, following the increased politicisation of immigration through the headscarf affair, Mitterrand once again pronounced on integration and 'les clandestins', and advised the French people not to confuse legal with illegal immigrants (televised interview of 10 December 1989). Following this, another 'new' package of integration and control was announced by the government and the FN won an election at Dreux. The response of SOS Racisme was to demand a Ministry of Integration (although all they got was the Council for Integration).

In a wider sense, the focus on 'les clandestins' highlights the crisis of and struggle over the geographical and ideological frontiers of the nation in post-colonial, ex-metropolitan societies. The illegalisation of 'immigration' takes place at the same time as the 'penetration of the citadel'. These are not two separate processes but part of the same process: the confusion of the frontiers between difference and sameness, distance and proximity. Mitterrand's desire to maintain the distinction between legal and illegal immigrants is symptomatic of this crisis of naming and the struggle over the nation.

## THE NATIONALITY DEBATE

The major elements of this crisis were crystallised in the debate which followed the proposal by the Chirac government to change the Code of Nationality in 1986. In one sense, the whole nationality debate was a complete red herring. The attribution or acquisition of French nationality certainly guarantees those rights (especially political) reserved only for French nationals. Yet it is not a solution to the wider social and economic problems which lie behind the debate (cf. Solé in *Le Monde*, 17 March 1987, and *Le Monde*, 20 June 1987). Nor is it a protection against racism. The debate should not be about nationality but about the rights of all those resident in France and a redefinition of citizenship (cf. Costa-Lascoux 1987b: 114).[8]

The nationality debate was therefore indicative of the problem for anti-racism and the demands for a new citizenship: how to mobilise opinion around a reformulation of rights when the political and public obsession is with nationality? Once again anti-racism was obliged to accept the agenda of national identity established by the Right and the extreme Right and fight on the same terrain by adopting a 'pro' as opposed to an 'anti' immigrant perspective.

However, the debate is significant in a much more profound sense if we consider the broader determinations of this issue at this time. It has been suggested that it is paradoxical that 'the problems of nationality' have been linked to the 'problems of immigration', as there has in fact been a sharp decline in migration flows into France (Belorgey 1987: 71). This seems to miss the point, for it is not so much the migration flows themselves which are significant in this respect but the way they are represented. The construction of the 'problem of immigration' as the passage from temporary male workers to permanent families is founded on the idea that (non-European) immigration is a threat to social cohesion *and* national identity (see Chapter 3). In this paradigm, 'temporary' migrant labour is acceptable but 'established' communities sharing the same social space are perceived as a threat to national identity.

It is therefore precisely at the moment when immigration is represented as a social and cultural/ethnic problem (rather than simply an economic one) that questions of nationality become crucial. Far from it being a paradox that 'problems of nationality' have been linked to the 'problems of immigration', it is quite natural, given the way in which contemporary 'problems of immigration' have been constructed.

The contemporary debate around nationality exposes most clearly the way in which ideas of culture and assimilation are profoundly entwined with the juridical definition of nationality. Sayad comments on this articulation on the level of vocabulary:

> It is the whole vocabulary of honour, using the terminology of dignity, privilege, merit, and obligation etc. – a vocabulary which is more moral than political and least of all juridical – which is constantly and abundantly quoted in everything that is said on questions of nationality and naturalisation.
>
> (Sayad 1987: 135)

The interpenetration of the juridical and the 'moral'/symbolic sides to nationality again gives the lie to a simplistic dichotomy between two models of the nation. As we have already seen, the law (and therefore the enjoyment of rights) is not exempt from the influence of non-juridical (including racialised) factors. Yet if this has always been the case in the formation of the nation-state, it is the nature of the post-colonial order which has driven a wedge through that unstable relationship between the law and ideas of culture. To appreciate this more fully we need to look in more detail at the proposals to modify the Code and the debate which ensued.

The background to the proposal to change the Code in 1986 has already been discussed in Chapter 2. It will be remembered that the cornerstone of the New Right's discourse of opposition to non-European immigration had been the theme of 'national preference' (Le Gallou 1985) and French identity (Le Club de l'Horloge 1985). From the time of the municipal elections of 1983, with the increased electoral support for the FN, these ideas had a growing influence on all political parties. The manifesto for the right-wing coalition (UDF-RPR) which won the general election of 16 March 1986 contained a section setting out a vague commitment to establish 'a national community more certain of its identity'. After the election, the new Prime Minister, Jacques

Chirac, spoke of the necessity 'to preserve the identity of our national community' (quoted in Perotti 1986: 2). We have also seen that the new government's emphasis on national community and national identity was linked to a preoccupation with issues of security and public order concerning especially North African 'immigrants'. This orientation was quickly translated into tough anti-immigrant measures, principally under the auspices of the Minister of the Interior Charles Pasqua (the law of September 1986 on entry and residence, extension of visa regulations in the same month, the doubling of numbers of deportations and so on). The policies implemented by the Chirac government between 1986–8 certainly owed a great deal to the programme of 'national preference' set by the FN.

In his discussion of who 'merited' French nationality, Le Gallou wrote 'a quarter of a century after decolonisation we must end the last sequels of empire' (1985: 87). This remark (and others in the same text) not only makes abundantly clear who does not belong to the nation but also calls for the necessary legal changes to put this readjustment into practice. By suggesting the broad principle that French nationality for children born in France of foreign parents should no longer be an automatic right but a voluntary request, the proposal to change the Code of Nationality was a significant step in this direction. By putting in jeopardy the principle of the 'jus soli' ('loi du sol'), this measure aimed to delegitimise, in the main, those of North African parents.

This is clear if we consider the specific articles of the Code that were under threat in the proposal. The French Code of Nationality is a complex piece of legislation; foreigners in France are affected in different ways according to the diverse historical relations (especially colonial relations) between France and the emigrant's country of origin. For example, those from Algeria and French ex-colonies in sub-Saharan West Africa are subject to different regulations than are other foreigners because of their different former colonial status. Article 23 of the Nationality Code stipulates that the child born of foreign parents at least one of whom was born in France is French at birth (known as 'the double jus soli'). This article therefore covers those whose parents are from Algeria or French West Africa and who were born in their country of origin before independence (that is, when these countries were French territory). The proposed change to the Code would have meant that these children would have lost their automatic right to French nationality at birth. This would have affected about 23–24,000 children each year, of whom 16–17,000 have Algerian parents and about 7500 are from West Africa. For those other countries not made part of French territory under colonial rule, article 44 of the Code stipulates that any child born in France of foreign parents born abroad acquires French nationality automatically at the age of majority, providing their country of residence for at least five years prior to the age of majority has been France. The proposed change to article 44 would have affected about 17,000 children of whom a large proportion have either Moroccan or Tunisian parents. (For a detailed breakdown of the Code of Nationality, see GISTI 1989 or Commission de la Nationalité 1988, Tome 1.)

The government dropped the idea of changing article 23 fairly early on, thus removing the threat to those of Algerian parents (see *Le Monde*, 17 March 1987, and *Le Monde*, 20 June 1987). However, such are the intricacies of the Code (as is evident from the previous description) and such was the intensity of the debate that there seems to have been a certain confusion over who would be affected by the proposal, even amongst experts (see for example the statements by the historian Pierre Chaunu and the demographer Hervé Le Bras in *L'Express*, 31 October 1986). In fact, the issue of the Algerians did not simply disappear, for the decision to rule out a change to the 'double jus soli' was not popular with a sizeable number of right-wing deputies who thought that the change should cover the children of Algerians as well as other North Africans (*L'Express*, 31 October 1986).

This attitude is probably more significant than the decision to drop the change to article 23 (which was due more to political and pragmatic reasons than ideological ones).[9] The true spirit of the proposal lies in its initial motivation and raison d'être: namely, that these people are different (culturally) from previous immigrants, they do not assimilate in the 'normal' way and therefore they warrant different treatment. They cannot be accepted as legitimate French nationals; they must entreat for nationality. The 'jus soli' became the major site of struggle because, as with legal immigrant status, it is no guarantee of (cultural/ethnic) legitimacy. In other words, at the heart of the proposal is the idea that the link between the juridical and the cultural in the definition of nationality should be reformed so as to institutionalise more firmly the contemporary 'Europeanised' framework for considerations of French national identity.

The proposal to change the Code of Nationality therefore springs from the same structures of contemporary racialisation as those described previously. As with the discourses on the 'bidon-villes', the 'seuil de tolérance', the ghettos, the 'permanent installation' of immigrants and the 'clandestins', the proposal reveals the same ambivalence over the question of *place*. Like those other discourses, it is profoundly determined by the post-colonial reversal of the colonial structures of distance and proximity. And, like them, it is indicative of what Balibar locates as the fundamental paradox of this situation: the less a population designated as 'immigrant' is in fact foreign, the more it is denounced as 'a foreign body' (Balibar and Wallerstein 1988: 297).

The problem of place and its links with the contemporary debate on nationality make no sense outside the framework of French colonialism. It is the logic of colonialism coming home to roost, not simply in terms of the equivocal question of similarity and difference but also in terms of the question of equality. In this respect, the case of the Algerians is the classic model for the problem as a whole. We have already noted that, although Algeria was French territory during colonial rule, the status of the 'in-digènes' (as they were termed) was not that of French citizens. French nationality, in its colonial context, was divided into two categories, that of the full citizen and that of the subject. French Muslims were, for the most part, subjects. We have also noted that even those who managed to acquire the privileges of French citizenship did not, by that act, become equal to French citizens born and bred, for they then received the label of 'évolué' or 'développé', terms which implicitly suggest the passage from a lower to a higher order of existence (cf. Balibar 1984; Bruschi 1987: 42).

In the post-colonial context of migration to and settlement in the former 'metropole', the colonial distinction between the subject and the citizen is under threat. The 'double jus soli' means that these people have French nationality (and therefore French citizenship) from birth – but only because of the colonial incorporation of Algeria into French territory. In the new 'mixed' context of post-colonialism it is precisely the prospect of non-differentiation and *equality* which is of deep worry: that is, the problem of accepting as equals those who were previously inferiors, the problem of accepting as part of the universal those who were previously defined according to their religion, the problem of accepting as citizens those who were previously subjects. It is the moment when those previously defined ethnically/religiously *and* as inferiors (in the colonial context) come to resemble 'the French' culturally and socially (in the post-colonial context) that they pose a problem and must be differentiated (especially culturally). The post-colonial situation therefore strips away the mythology of universalism to reveal the racism ever-present within it.

Although there was much opposition to the proposal by the Chirac government to modify the Code, there was a far wider consensus on the need to change the Code in some way. This is indicative of the way in which the contemporary construction of 'the problem of immigration' had become legitimised as 'common sense'. It was generally accepted that the present Code (last modified in 1973) was ill-suited to define nationality in the modern age. The report of the Commission established in June 1987 to consider the whole question of nationality was clear that a reform was necessary 'if only to revise those articles which go back to the former colonial empire' (*Le Monde*, 11 September 1987). In its analysis of the changes which had taken place over the previous twenty or so years which would have to be considered in any modification of the Code, the report mentions the following: there have been significant changes in the origins and character of the foreign population in France, that is, it is now 'predominantly non-European', from cultures further and further away ('an immigration less sensitive to the European influence', 1988, Tome 2: 50), more settled ('sédentaire'), younger and including more women; there are greater difficulties of integration due in part to the above but also to the breakdown in the traditional institutions which facilitated assimilation in the past (Church, trade unions, army, etc.); the relations between France and the former colonies have changed in favour of considerations of European integration and free movement in Europe (1988, Tome 2).

In the main, the terms of this analysis are those of the standard definition of the 'problem of immigration' discussed previously. Through a number of dichotomies, they constitute the retrospective reconstruction of assimilation: temporary/permanent, European/non-European, close/distant cultures and the consequent problems of integration or assimilation. This apparent 'common-sense' description of recent developments legitimises the need for a change to the Code according to the new conjuncture. As far as France is concerned this necessitates (in very general terms) a) tying up the troublesome loose ends of decolonisation, and b) situating the question of nationality within the new reality of Europe. It is true that the report had far more to say about nationality than this. Yet the broad lines of the analysis of the 'problem' and the framework for a consideration of the 'solution' would appear to be very much in keeping with the contemporary racialisation of Europe (even if the propositions of the report were more liberal than those of the original proposal by the government).

The fact that the report agreed with the idea that nationality should be subject to a voluntary request rather than an automatic right and that this was welcomed by many on the Left, including a number of anti-racist organisations, seems to show how the broad lines of the construction of the 'problem' and the 'solution' traverse the political spectrum, and racism and anti-racism.[10] This demonstrates some of the problems for the Left and for anti-racism. Those on the Left and in anti-racist organisations who welcomed the report were (in one sense) implicitly legitimising the need to reinforce the link between a cultural/symbolic concept of the nation and the juridical category of nationality, a link which many of the same people and movements had been struggling to dismantle. Once again anti-racism was caught in the 'trap' of nationality. The limitations of the claims for cultural difference, pluralism and the ideas of being French 'differently' were also exposed. 'Identity' politics only goes so far in challenging complex structural and discursive practices (including especially the national framing of rights). The link between culture and the law has certainly been highlighted and rendered problematic; but at the same time, a new Europeanised racialisation of nationality threatens to reoccupy that contested space.

A further problem for the Left lay in the argument over the 'jus soli'. Once the threat had been posed to the 'jus soli' it is difficult to see how else anti-racists could have responded other than through a full-blooded defence of it. However, an exaggerated defence of the 'jus soli' ran the risk of reinforcing an idealised national past and effacing the complex links between juridical and non-juridical (especially cultural/moral) categories in the development of the Code. The suggestion that the right of the 'jus soli' signified a liberal and open approach to nationality (Costa-Lascoux 1987b: 85, 95; 1990a: 16) fails to problematise the historical development of the Code, and reproduces the myth of the contractual/assimilationist model of the French nation. For example, if access to French nationality was made easier at certain times (the law of 1889), this was more for demographic and economic reasons than for any idealistic concerns about liberty, equality and commitment to the land of asylum (Lochak 1988: 79–80). The laws of 1851 and 1889 which reorientated the Code towards the 'jus soli' (after the Napoleonic Code of 1804 had privileged the 'jus sanguinis') should be seen in the context of the industrialisation and nationalisation of society and state and colonial expansion during the second half of the nineteenth century. Neither should one forget the measures of the 1930s, when, in a climate of hostility towards foreigners, the enjoyment of political rights for those naturalised was set at five years after the decision of naturalisation. Naturalisation was more difficult for some than for others between the wars (Galissot 1985b). This is hardly evidence of an open approach to the acquisition of nationality for foreigners, and is a counterbalance to the idea that the 'jus soli' is another element in the (unproblematic) assimilationist/universalist development of the French republic.

An historical perspective on the development of the Code of Nationality shows how rights and identities were relentlessly nationalised in the second half of the nineteenth century, whilst the immigrant was removed progressively from the domain of the law and the nation (cf. Noiriel 1988a). The great era of the nation-state thus created an 'imagined community' which tied identity firmly to the juridical structures of the nation. However, today the context is very different from that of the early history of the Code. The institutional, juridical and administrative apparatus for defining identity and the frontiers between 'the French' and 'the immigrants' are in a state of flux. Today internationalisation and multiple migrations of people and products have unsettled the dividing lines between 'here' and 'there', and have cut across the idea of the sovereignty of the nation. The major problem for the demand for a new citizenship in France therefore lies in extricating rights from that historical baggage and bringing them into line with a new world order.

## RIGHTS AT THE CROSSROADS

Unfortunately, the 'new world order' is not at all clear and more often appears to be a new world disorder. As regards a new citizenship, it is perhaps possible for diverse groups to agree on a limited range of broad issues for fundamental rights. So, for example, throughout the 1980s the demand for the right to vote in municipal elections (which, as we have seen, was promised by Mitterrand in his 110-point programme as presidential candidate in May 1981 but which has never been implemented) was for many a symbolic demand for equal rights based on residence ('le droit de cité') rather than nationality (see for example the text signed by about 130 associations on a model of citizenship founded on residence rather than nationality, published in *Le Monde*, 9 February 1990). Similarly, the mass marches for equality of 1983 and 1984 helped to focus on this and other inequalities in French society (such as in housing and employment), thus providing a sharper focus on *systematic* exclusion built into the nation-state.

However, on a wider level there is confusion over language and action, just as there is elsewhere in Europe. The crisis in the language of universalism and the individual has left new social movements trapped within the contradictory claims of universalism and particularism, the individual and the collectivity. Conflicting claims from different organisations (and often from within the same organisations, as was the case for SOS Racisme in the headscarf affair or during the Gulf War) have meant that there is no clear common agreement over what would be a sound basis for a new citizenship. Many fear the splintering of common 'universalist' principles into a myriad of particularisms (Finkielkraut 1987) – not without reason, for down this road lies the possible rise of new 'fundamentalists' (cultural, religious, class-based, gender-based, ethnic-based and so on) who might usurp the new power vacuums and claim to speak politically for 'the group'. Who would define how the group is constituted, what are its common features and who are its spokespeople? Would it be the religious elders (normally patriarchs to a man), the middle classes amongst them, the cultural extremists? Certainly these are genuine problems in Britain: especially the political significance resulting from the way in which particular cultural signifiers become dominant in defining the group, and how ethnic groups are thus constituted in relation to the state. Peering across the Channel and the Atlantic, France is continually wary of allowing the state to be a prey to such 'multiculturalist' demands.

On the other hand, there are considerable problems down the universalist 'fundamentalist' road, not the least of which is the failure to recognise differences which have a concrete reality in people's lives and on the basis of which certain people suffer exclusion from the resources of the state and racist abuse and attack. To pretend that ethnic categories have not, do not and should not play a part in the French nation-state but are part of an undesirable alien tradition is a dangerous misreading of history and misunderstanding of the present.

A major problem therefore lies in thinking of rights 'between' the individual and the collectivity; that is, in a way that denies the fixed, unified and homogeneous character of each, and posits instead the multi-dimensionality of identity and the possibility of contradictory identifications. Yet if the language to characterise this new hybridity is in its infancy, the ability to translate it into a progressive political and social project has been barely conceived. The theoretical concepts underpinning new identities do not necessarily result practically in progressive political movements. (This has sometimes been the experience with British multiculturalism where reactionary and possibly sexist religious or cultural projects are condoned and patronised – by the Left as much as, if not more than, the Right – under the guise of cultural difference.) As Nira Yuval-Davies has pointed out, a new concept of citizenship:

> should develop a notion of difference which would retain the multiplexity and multi-dimensionality of identities within contemporary society, but without losing sight of the differential power dimension of different collectivities and groupings within the society and the variety of relationships of domination/subordination between them.
>
> (Yuval-Davies 1991: 66–7)

The 'differential power dimension' mentioned by Yuval-Davies is crucial to any effective reformulation of citizenship, for only then might citizenship be conceived across differences of class, gender, 'race' and sexuality instead of in favour of one at the expense of all others. This must therefore include some idea of access to and control by the state. The relationship between the nation-state and civil society has been another crucial element in the recent debate on citizenship in France. One of the problems with this discussion has been the tendency to see the nation-state and civil society in terms of a dichotomy (see, for example, the round table discussion at the end of Wihtol de Wenden 1988b, especially the contributions of Cordeiro and Sayad): either the national state is a determinant of social relations in civil society or individual and collective action has opened up new spaces for citizenship *beyond the reaches* of the national state.

We cannot here explore all the arguments around the contemporary relationship between the state and civil society. However, the following general points are relevant to the present discussion. Rather than being separate spheres, the state and civil society are part of a far more complex structuring of relations in contemporary societies. It is not possible to judge precisely where the functions of the state end, where civil society begins and which are the cut-off points of the market (Taylor 1989). Today, both 'spheres' have been, at one and the same time, internationalised and localised and privatised. Civil society is multicultural and international, on the one hand, but also subject to a greater degree of diversification and local action (for example, the scope of the movement of associations in France since 1981). Similarly, the uniformity of the state (if it ever existed) is undercut by multinationalism, internationalism, privatisation and diversification. Internationalisation and localisation have both contributed to challenging the monopoly of regulation by and identification with the national state. This is why the institutions of the state (especially the school) and parliamentary democracy – formed at a time of unification and 'uniformisation' of the public sphere – are in crisis today. These processes cut across the state and civil society. They pose questions for the structures and concepts of the nation-state, but they certainly have not effaced them. A reconstructed national racism is also prevalent and this too cuts across the state and civil society.

This perspective on the social complex casts a critical shadow over ideas of a new citizenship forged at a local level *outside* the net of the national state, and over theories of new social movements in general. On the one hand, the focus on the similarities rather than the differences between 'second-generation' and French youth and their collective social action is a welcome break from seeing 'immigrants' simply as victims ('misérabilisme') or simply according to 'their' differences (Lapeyronnie 1987). Yet this focus can tend to establish a new dichotomy between victim and actor, with an idealised view of the latter and a utopian view of social movements in general. The belief that the social/cultural similarities of French youth and 'second-generation youth' efface differences between them (Lapeyronnie 1989: 321) fails to address the wider institutionalisation of those differences in the social formation. Similarly, the belief that new forms of collective action can flourish outside the framework of the nation-state and create a new social order (Cordeiro 1988: 7; also Cordeiro in Wihtol de Wenden 1988b: 332–3) is perhaps more wishful thinking than an accurate reflection of the potential of new social movements.[11] Furthermore, oppositional movements are not necessarily politically progressive. And, just as cultural diversity and pluralism are not necessarily the guarantors of equality, neither is there any guarantee that new social politics divorced from proper consideration of their own political constitution and aspirations will result in progressive movements.

The problem with thinking of a new citizenship *outside* or *in opposition to* wider constraints (economic, institutional, etc.) is that it posits a free space of contestation. This idea resituates the question of rights within the old liberal concept of citizenship based on 'free' individuals. As we have seen, the idea of a pre-social subject whose natural rights are protected in law is a myth which dislocates the individual from society (especially if that individual happens to be an Algerian in France). The individual is always *already* situated socially. New social movements which are simply oppositional to exclusionary practices can fail to call into question how the 'differential power dimension' traverses their own space as well as the wider social complex. The interrelationships within the social formation which cut across the state and civil society do not allow the existence of a pure space of opposition *outside* this complex.

A redefinition of citizenship must consider the complex process of inclusion and exclusion in the modern state. As Said Bouâmama, the President of the association 'Mémoire Fertile', has argued, by enshrining the abstract principle of equal rights in law, inequalities in the economic domain were left untouched; the dissociation of citizenship from nationality must therefore go beyond the political and legal domains to redefine the citizen within the total social complex (see 1989a and 1989b; also Etienne Balibar and Yves Benot, 'Suffrage universel', *Le Monde*, 4 May 1983).

This chapter has therefore contextualised rights within the national social formation (and the legacy of colonialism) because this is still the fundamental framework within which rights for 'immigrants' are situated in France, despite the fact that these structures are in crisis today. As Balibar has remarked: 'If there is a crisis of citizenship in France today – comparable to the crisis which affects other countries, but with its own specific characteristics too – it is a crisis of this historical complex' (1988: 230).

Citizenship preceded nationality; only later did citizenship become nationalised (Galissot 1986: 10; Lochak 1988: 81). Any reformulation of citizenship must therefore take account of the historical construction of rights and the citizen in order to unravel the process by which they have been hijacked by the nation-state. In this way, the problem is tackled from within rather than from outside. The historicising and 'de-naturalising' of this process do not necessarily provide the answers to the thorny questions concerning what language and action are appropriate for a new citizenship. However, by demonstrating the way in which rights, the state and the nation became tightly articulated only at a particular period of industrial growth and are not therefore inherently bound to be constructed in a common formation, this approach can open the way to a dissociation and reappraisal of each. In other words, it becomes possible to think of them 'differently' – which is precisely the task of the new citizenship.

However, all the above questions are subject to different stakes when they are considered in the context of the Single European Act signed in 1986 and due to be fully implemented by 1 January 1993. The final chapter therefore discusses issues of migration, racism and citizenship within the framework of the 'New Europe'.

# Chapter 6

# France and the 'New Europe'

According to the OECD, the two major phases of immigration to the richest countries in Europe in the contemporary period have been the economic migration of single men in the 1950s and 1960s and the family immigration of the 1970s and the 1980s (OCDE 1987). What will be the future pattern of immigration in Europe, or is there a future at all for immigration in the 1990s and beyond, and what will the Europe of the 1990s actually look like? The implementation of the Single European Act for 1993, the changes in Eastern Europe (which have prompted fears of a massive migration from the East as well as the South to EC countries) and possibly the approach of the new millennium have led to much recent speculation: a sort of futurology of migration. Scenarios go from an end of contemporary immigration to a new explosion, from a multicultural Europe to a fortress Europe along racialised lines.

At present the shape of the new Europe – particularly as far as ethnic minorities, immigrants and non-EC nationals are concerned – is still unclear, although in recent years there have been significant moves towards harmonising policy on a number of levels amongst EC member states. The European Commission suggested on 7 December 1988 that the member states should coordinate their policies with regard to visas, right of asylum and the status of third country nationals. By 1991 the disappearance of internal frontiers, the creation of common external frontiers, a common policy on visas for non-EC nationals and free movement of EC nationals within the Community were already becoming a reality. The first report of the French Council for Integration (February 1991) emphasised the importance of harmonising national immigration policy within a common European policy, especially with regard to Eastern Europe.

However, as Jean-Pierre Garson at the OECD has pointed out, there are still problems. Member states are still keen to maintain some of their sovereignty in ways of dealing with immigration (*Espace Social Européen*, 8 March 1991). Different geographical factors and the fact that countries are at different stages of the cycle of contemporary immigration (immigration in Italy is a more recent phenomenon than in Britain, France or Holland) can lead to different priorities and approaches by member states. For example, there are still considerable differences over a policy on the crossing of external frontiers (*Le Figaro*, 17 January 1991) and a reluctance by some EC member states (especially Britain) to abolish internal border controls (*The Guardian*, 10 January 1991).

France plays a major role in the discussions over harmonising controls but is also at the forefront of the debate around rights, equality and a new citizenship in Europe. Yet rights for immigrants and minorities are also extremely diverse from one country to another (Mestiri 1990: 104–5). This again depends on the fact that member states are at different stages of the cycle of contemporary immigration, but is also due to different national and colonial histories. This chapter considers recent developments in the harmonisation of controls and rights in Europe. With regard to rights, I will consider some of the general problems faced by anti-racist movements when it is a question of mobilising across national frontiers rather than simply within them.

## REFUGEES, IMMIGRATION AND CONTROLS

One point is already clear: the third 'phase' of immigration to Europe, according to some, is refugees, on the one hand, and illegal immigration on the other. At least that is the present fear of western governments who have determined that the free movement of EC nationals between the countries of the Community depends on the ability to ensure that unwanted aliens are kept out. In France, fears were already being expressed in the early 1980s that many of those seeking asylum were really economic migrants rather than genuine refugees (cf. Gomane 1983: 3). This formed part of the wider debate on illegal immigration which was already a major preoccupation in the first half of the 1980s, as is clear from the discussion at the second conference of European ministers responsible for questions of migration in Rome, 25–7 October 1983 (see Costa-Lascoux 1986).

Yet it was in the second half of the 1980s that governments significantly tightened controls on entry into the country. As Margaret Thatcher stated in 1988, tougher frontier controls were essential to combat 'the problem of transnational criminals, drug smugglers, terrorists and illegal immigrants' (quoted in *The Guardian*, 27 December 1988).[1] A model equivalent to that of 'integration and control' is in the process of being established at the European level with all the repercussions that have accompanied that formula at the national level. This is particularly evident if we consider the way in which refugee status has been progressively delegitimised so that refugees, economic migrants, terrorists, drug traffickers and criminals can be placed in a single category of 'undesirable aliens'.

Applications for asylum rose considerably during the 1980s. However, the number accepted as refugees has not risen in proportion to applications. Stricter criteria for the assessment of applications for asylum are being used throughout Europe. The Geneva Convention of 1951 states that asylum should be accorded to all those who have a 'well-founded fear of being persecuted for reasons such as race, religion, nationality, membership of a particular social group or political opinion'. Many countries now require proof of persecution and often even this is no guarantee of being granted refugee status, for governments are claiming that asylum-seekers are not refugees at all but 'economic migrants'.[2]

Throughout Europe the term 'refugee' is being redefined in the context of increased control of non-EC nationals; that is, refugee and 'economic migrant' status are becoming a single reality for new political expediency. In France this process became particularly evident towards the end of the 1980s. Figures released in 1989 showed that the number seeking asylum tripled between 1980 and 1989, with the most significant increase being from 27,000 in 1987 to 60,000 in 1989. At least 80 per cent of these requests would be rejected on the grounds that claims of persecution could not be substantiated (see *Le Quotidien*, 6 January 1990). The government interpreted this large increase in applications for asylum as a new way to gain entry into France at a time when the severe controls on immigration ruled out the possibility of official entry for immigrants on most other grounds (apart from family reunification which, as we have seen, is itself subject to severe restrictions by the authorities). The Minister of Health Claude Evin echoed the views of a number of ministers (including the Minister of the Interior, Pierre Joxe, and the Prime Minister, Michel Rocard) when he expressed worries about 'the drift from the right of political asylum to the right of economic asylum' (quoted in *Le Point*, 4 December 1989). The view that political asylum was therefore being abused led the government to attempt to close the loop-hole. Asylum-seekers could wait for up to three years to have their case processed by l'OFPRA (the office which deals with claims for political asylum), during which time they are automatically entitled to a provisional residence permit. The government announced that the budget of OFPRA would be doubled in 1990 so that cases could be processed with no longer than a three- or four-month delay. This acceleration of the process of dealing with 'the stock' led in 1990 to an increased number of refusals of applications for asylum; at the end of the year OFPRA estimated that only about 13,000 of the 90,000 dossiers treated would be accepted (*Le Monde*, 27 December 1990). According to Gérard Noiriel, France has never rejected as many refugees as today (interview in *Le Quotidien* 26 March 1991; also Noiriel 1991).

The ministers mentioned above made it clear that it was essential to distinguish between political and economic refugees in order to safeguard the right of asylum and to control immigration. This was the view expressed by Bernard Kouchner, the Secretary of State with responsibility for humanitarian action, who said that France must accept only *genuine* refugees (*Le Monde*, 16 January 1990). In other words 'France remains a country of asylum' (François Mitterrand, quoted in *Le Quotidien*, 6 January 1990) whilst at the same time 'France is no longer and can no longer be a country of immigration. We cannot welcome all the world's poor' (Michel Rocard, 7 January 1990, quoted in *Le Figaro*, 8 January 1990). According to these statements, it is the abuse of the system of asylum which threatens both these objectives.[3]

However, to suggest that it is the applicants for asylum who are abusing the system is equivalent to blaming the 'problems of immigration' onto the immigrants. The rise in the applications for political asylum in the 1980s needs to be considered in the context of the North-South divide, the events in Eastern Europe, mounting political instability on a world scale and the rise in the number of victims of persecution (see Jean-Michel Belorgey in *Le Nouvel Observateur*, 23-9 November 1989). The principal applicants for asylum in France are not from the poorest countries in the world but from those where either brutal victimisation of opponents of the government is well-documented or where war and civil unrest are rife (Turkey, Angola, Sri Lanka, Zaire). This is also the case in Britain where the largest numbers of asylum-seekers come from Sri Lanka, Somalia, Ethiopia, Uganda, Turkey and Iraq. Furthermore, official statements referring to a 'massive influx' of asylum-seekers (for example, SOPEMI 1990: 2) are vastly exaggerated when figures are viewed in the context of the global refugee problem, the bulk of which falls on the shoulders of the developing countries (*Education Guardian*, 20 November 1990).

The real abuse of political asylum in the 1980s was the way in which the authorities elided asylum and immigration (already outlawed for certain categories of people), and refugees and illegal entrants (*Espace Social Européen*, 8 March 1991). The struggle against illegal immigration and the struggle against bogus demands for asylum became part of the same justification for controls. This was clearly the case when the package of controls announced in December 1989 by the newly created Inter-ministerial Committee for Integration bracketed together tighter measures on asylum, illegal immigration and deportation of illegal immigrants (*Le Monde*, 21 December 1989). (The fact that a committee on 'integration' should be interested primarily in tighter controls appears contradictory only when viewed outside the contemporary logic of 'integration and control'.)

As with the eliding of legal and illegal immigrants (discussed in the previous chapter), the new elision between immigrants and refugees was accompanied by the same rhetoric: the necessity to distinguish between the 'genuine' ('les vrais') and the 'false' claimants ('les faux'). In an interview in *L'Express*, the Secretary General of the Inter-ministerial Committee on Integration, Hubert Prévot, unequivocally stated that his first priority was to treat the problem of asylum-seekers. When asked why this was the top priority he replied: 'Because they are essentially seeking economic survival and their large numbers prevent us from carrying out our mission with regard to the authentic refugees' (9 February 1990). (It was only in the second half of the interview that he talked of social problems in France.) As we have already seen with regard to immigration, this logic is symptomatic of the delegitimisation and illegalising of political asylum. Henceforward, every immigrant (or every person who 'looks like an immigrant') *and* every refugee could be suspected of being a wolf in sheep's clothing. At the end of the 1980s, the coupling of 'immigration', political asylum, illegality and foreign invasion became such a standard element in the reporting of these issues (and in political discourse) that the sheep and the wolf were no longer distinguishable (cf. *Le Point*, 4 December 1989).

This process must be considered in the context of harmonisation of controls of non-EC nationals and the free movement of EC nationals within the Community. Questions that have for long been decided on the national level (regulation of the population, controls and so on) are now a very important part of 'European integration' (Claude-Valentin Marie in Marie and Wihtol de Wenden 1989: 14). However, these questions of policing and control are being discussed outside the institutional framework of the EC and 'thus contribute to the EC's "democratic deficit" – the term now given to the inability of parliaments to hold decision-makers to account' (*The Guardian*, 19 October 1990). Since the mid-1970s, the twelve interior and justice ministers have been meeting regularly in the Trevi group to discuss matters of police cooperation and exchange of information. According to Douglas Hurd when he was the British Home Secretary and speaking in a debate in parliament of the meetings of the Trevi ministers, 'our programme of work has become formidable' (Hansard, 4 May 1989). In the 1980s, the main priorities of this 'programme' were ways of combating drug trafficking, crime, terrorism, illegal immigration and questions of public order at an EC level. However, the discussions were rarely made public and much secrecy still surrounds the detail (see the debate in the British parliament on 'Intra-Community Frontiers (Control)', Hansard, 4 May 1989; also *The Guardian*, 19 October 1990). Today there are still differences of approach to policing activities, given the diverse criminal justice procedures of the member states, the diverse frontier control procedures based on geographical differences, questions of extradition and so on. Nevertheless, according to Alan Eastwood, Chairman of the British Police Federation, policing is far more internationalist than it has ever been before and harmonisation is becoming a reality (Eastwood 1989).

The evidence of harmonisation of controls – worked out in meetings that were even more secret than those of the Trevi group – were the discussions that took place between 1985–90 in the Schengen group, prior to the signing of a convention between the signatories on 19 June 1990 concerning concrete implementation of the Schengen agreement of 1985. These discussions were between only five of the twelve member states of the EC – France, West Germany and the three Benelux countries (although Italy has more recently become a sixth signatory to the accord). They met to work more specifically towards a suppression of controls on all common frontiers between the five states (articles 2–8) and the harmonisation of entry and visa regulations (articles 9–18). One of the main objectives of the Schengen agreement was to create a uniform policy to put an end to the abuse of requests for political asylum. The agreement introduces a computerised information system on undesirable aliens (the 'Schengen Information System' or SIS) (articles 92–119) and has provision for a frontier control system whereby a rejected application for asylum in one state could be valid for the other five states (articles 28–38). Given that more than half of those applying for asylum in France now come via another EC state, the introduction of a common control system around the countries who are signatories to the agreement would filter out many asylum-seekers before they ever get to France.[4]

These developments have, understandably, worried human rights groups and associations acting for refugees. The secretive nature of the discussions is disturbing. But more disturbing is the way in which requests for political asylum are being considered purely from the policing and controlling angle rather than from the perspective of human rights. A European conference on the right of asylum (Geneva, October 1989) denounced the priority given to the policing perspective on asylum-seekers. In fact, the harmonising of the control procedure for requests for asylum would break the Geneva Convention of 1951, which states that applicants can make requests to any number of European countries (see *Le Nouvel Observateur*, 23–9 November 1989). Furthermore, by making decisions of this nature purely a policing matter, treated at the frontier, political asylum will be removed from the rule of law and from juridical protection and placed in the hands of administrators, border control officers and the police. Indeed, this is already taking place. To safeguard against arbitrary decisions and a 'situation of non-law' at French frontiers, and to inform foreigners of their rights, a number of associations (including CIMADE, France-Terre d'asile and Amnesty International) founded in January 1988 the National Association of Assistance for Foreigners at the Frontiers (ANAFE) (*Le Monde*, 21 December

1989). If the Schengen agreement is adopted as the model for the EC as a whole then the worst fears of a 'fortress Europe' aimed at keeping out certain 'undesirables' would be realised.

The European dimension to controls has not been constructed in the full glare of the political and public arena. Yet it is a matter of great political and human importance, and has a profound bearing on the question of rights and citizenship in Europe. On the one hand, the 'ring fence' around Europe seems at present to have adopted the lowest common denominators to keep out 'undesirable aliens' (visa restrictions, arbitrary refusals of entry at borders beyond the jurisdiction of the law, racism, European-wide information system and so on). On the other hand, within Europe itself there is a movement towards the creation of two distinct legal categories: EC nationals with freedom of movement, access to employment, welfare rights and so on; and non-EC nationals with no freedom of movement and no absolute right to welfare and employment rights (Wrench 1990a; Escaffit 1990). There are between eight and ten million non-EC nationals residing in EC countries. The rights they enjoy at present in a number of these countries, often acquired through long struggle, are as yet not guaranteed in the new Europe.[5]

In the light of the possible construction of a 'two-tier' Europe (depending on whether one is or is not an EC national), the link between citizenship and nationality takes on a very distinctive perspective. It ties the knot tighter than ever. In this sense we are witnessing a Europeanisation of rights and the attempt to break with the diverse statutes that have emerged from different colonial histories (phasing out Commonwealth connections in Britain, attempting to remove the vestiges of colonialism in France and so on). The report of the commission on nationality in France (1988) indicates the attempt to replace agreements and rights based on former colonial relations with a new Europeanised framework for nationality.

However, the model of a two-tier Europe is not adequate to describe the possible future of citizenship in Europe. We have already said that nationality is essential for the acquisition of certain rights when citizenship is linked to nationality. Yet it does not guarantee legitimacy and is not necessarily a protection against racism, especially when national identity is defined by racialised criteria. Not only all legal immigrants but also all those who 'look like immigrants' risk suffering the controls and checks supposedly reserved only for drug traffickers, terrorists and illegal immigrants ('contrôles au faciès'). As one French commentator has remarked, 'how do you recognise a non-EC national if not by the colour of his skin?' (Escaffit 1990). If Schengen becomes a reality for the whole of the Community then, as Robert Solé has written in *Le Monde*, 'a Europe in which the juridical distinction [exists] between nationals and foreigners will give way to a visual distinction between Europeans and non-Europeans' (16 June 1989).

In order to combat this and other forms of exclusion, the struggle for equal rights clearly extends beyond the domain of nationality. It is not a question of European citizenship (that is, a citizenship for Europeans) but of citizenship in Europe (a citizenship for all those living in Europe). However, the major problem facing anti-racist and human rights movements and associations with the approach of the realisation of the Single European Act on 1 January 1993 is how to achieve a harmonised focus on rights when discussions at an official level have been predominantly about harmonised controls.

## WHICH MODEL FOR RIGHTS?

'European integration' has encountered problems at almost every level of harmonisation, from the question of monetary union to that of agriculture, from political union to a social charter. Many of these problems have not been resolved and perhaps never will be resolved. Given the differences in historical development, institutional structures and so on of the member states, this is of little surprise.

Questions of anti-racism and rights for minorities are also subject to the same problems. These too have developed largely within the framework of each individual nation-state and have grown out of the particular historical and structural circumstances (especially colonial) of that country. France has had a model of nationality whereby immigration can, in theory, lead to eventual naturalisation (based largely on the 'jus soli'); Germany's system for immigrants (whether categorised by the earlier term 'Gastarbeiter' or the more recent term 'Ausländer') has never envisaged that immigrants will become naturalised Germans (acquisition of nationality depending on the 'jus sanguinis').[6] In France only French nationals have full citizenship; in Britain citizenship is not determined simply by nationality. The right to vote for immigrants in local elections has already been granted in Denmark (1981), Ireland (1983) and the Netherlands (1983) (as well as in three other non-EC countries, Norway, Sweden and certain cantons in Switzerland); other EC countries have not yet followed suit (though in the UK Commonwealth citizens can vote in all elections). In France, though much debated since the end of the 1970s, the right to vote for immigrants in local elections has not been granted. However, there have been a number of local consultative experiments – at Mons-en-Baroeul (introduced in 1985), Amiens (1987) and Cerizay (1989). Foreigners have been allowed to vote to elect representatives to assist at municipal council meetings, although these representatives do not have the right to vote (Wihtol de Wenden 1989: 16).

Different rules govern access to social rights in the member states (see Wihtol de Wenden 1989: 11), to schooling and training and so on. I do not intend to consider all the differences in rights for immigrants and minorities that exist in the EC. It is clear that problems of harmonisation exist on a number of levels. The idea of a citizenship based on residence rather than nationality is a general demand which can mobilise support, especially when the right to vote in local elections will be granted to EC nationals living in another EC state but not to non-EC nationals who might have been resident in that country for a far longer period of time.[7] There have been a number of initiatives to establish a common platform for a new citizenship in Europe. For example, at a European conference in December 1988 SOS Racisme launched a Charter of Equality for Citizens which included rights to asylum, to nationality after five years residence, to guaranteed residence and to vote and stand in elections after five years.

However, beyond general principles there are also awkward problems. Because these issues have been framed largely within the nation-state, there are problems of awareness, misunderstanding and misinterpretation of the situation in neighbouring countries. For example, in Britain it seems to be a fairly commonly held view that legislation on equal opportunities for minorities and on racial discrimination is far in advance of measures adopted elsewhere. This is not necessarily the case. But more importantly, it is not comparing like with like. As we have seen, France has not institutionalised special provision for minorities in the same way as Britain; yet this does not necessarily mean that rights are less well protected in law. On the other hand, we have also seen that

French commentators have frequently perceived the British system as leading to the separation and segregation of ethnic groups and the creation of ghettos, and it is consequently seen as the antithesis of a model based on individual equal rights irrespective of 'race', religion or origin.

These are problems of language and conceptual framework, themselves profoundly informed by national characteristics. The word 'black' to describe a specific minority group does not necessarily translate to other countries where those groups are defined and define themselves differently, and where racism is perhaps not largely colour-based in the same way as it is in contemporary Britain. Similarly 'anti-Arab' sentiment in Britain is not equivalent to 'anti-Arab' racism in France, where colonial relations with the Maghreb have given very specific connotations to the term 'Arab' and to Islam. The term 'immigration' itself signifies differently in different countries, and is dependent on national and colonial histories. As we have already seen, strange misconceptions can arise when experts look across the Channel. The demographer Hervé Le Bras (1988b) has described immigration into 'England' and 'English' nationality in the following terms:

> The English, for example, have no experience of immigration. One cannot compare this question in England and in France. They have had to manufacture a concept of nationality in order to confront immigration from Pakistan. But for a long time we have been confronted with this problem, we have considered it and have provided our answers.

On the other hand, John Wrench has stated:

> in moving from the UK a black worker will be moving from the only member country which offers 'protection' – weak though it is – in the form of the Race Relations Act. No other member state offers legislative protection against racial discrimination, and there is no equivalent at EC level.
>
> (1990a: 286)[8]

In fact, France first introduced legislation against racial discrimination twenty years ago, in what Jacqueline Costa-Lascoux has described, in a report for the Council of Europe (1990b), as 'the trail-blazing French law of 1 July 1972', and Germany, Belgium and the Netherlands all have different legislation on racial discrimination (for an outline of different anti-racist legislation in Europe, see *Libération*, 5–6 May 1990).

In her report for the Council of Europe, Costa-Lascoux raised a fundamental problem concerning the choice of model for rights:

> There is a conflict between two institutional systems: – a system based on equal treatment and anti-discrimination legislation, with no institutional recognition of minorities;– a policy for the representation and emancipation of minorities combining positive discrimination[9] with the fight against racism. Is there not a risk that any specific reference to origin or group membership in the institutional context, even if it is inspired by a laudable concern to iron out *de facto* inequalities, will further stigmatise minorities? The question has to be raised, with a view to preventing the accentuation of socio-cultural differences, the establishment of minority 'lobbies' and intolerant reflexes on the part of the host society. The inconsistency of advocating equal rights while supporting claims for collective identity which discriminate between people on the grounds of origin or group membership and justify religious, ethnic or sex discrimination cannot fail to have an impact in terms of the stigmatisation of differences. Policies for the emancipation of minorities, involving reliance on exceptions to the general law, could backfire because of the perverse effects of measures focused on 'special categories' of the population and 'anti-racist' legislation sometimes encourages more subtle forms of discrimination. These various problems require not just technical solutions, but great insight into the new forms of discrimination, a discussion of the foundations and standards of citizenships, a political evaluation as Europe prepares for 1993.
>
> (1990b: 26–7)

Whether the problems raised here can be resolved dispassionately or whether national preferences will blur judgement on these issues remains to be seen. Certain misconceptions will no doubt have to be challenged, not the least of which concern the posing of the problem itself in the above terms. Costa-Lascoux discusses only the problems with the 'ethnic minority' approach here, not those of the 'individualist' approach. Earlier comments in the report on the 'ethnic minority' approach reinforce the sense that this assessment of rights is situated very firmly within the French universalist and individualist tradition:

> The danger of racialising or ethnicising social and intercultural relations is obvious here. The commentator, accustomed to the rationale of individual citizen equality irrespective of origin, appearance, affiliation or conviction, and aware of the minimal scientific worth of the concept of race or ethnic group, is compelled to think of the 'institutional discrimination' so strikingly analysed by Ann Dummet in the nationality and immigration legislation.
>
> (1990b: 26)

The fears expressed about institutionalising and naturalising socially constructed differences are valid ones which have been raised on numerous occasions within the debate on 'race' in the UK. The British model of equal opportunities linked with ethnic monitoring is considered sceptically not only by researchers and commentators in France but also by anti-racist organisations who fear that such measures would increase resentment by others who are socially and economically disadvantaged in France. As we have seen, the ideology of equality and individualism (counterposed to that of 'special pleading' and minorities) is profoundly ingrained in the French national consciousness.

However, we have also considered the problems with not recognising socially constructed differences and inequalities when they have been an integral part of the development of the nation-state and are today an everyday fact of life in a racialised society. The *de facto* inequalities referred to above are clear signs that ideology is not illusory but has a material effect on the structuring of social relations. Without wishing to pursue the wider debate on ideology, we might simply restate Colette Guillaumin's argument (1984a: 218) that ideologically constructed differences do not vanish simply by being proved to be of minimal scientific value: 'race' might not exist but racism does.

With regard to a sound assessment of the potential for international cooperation on rights, equality and non-discrimination, the most important criticism of the above presentation concerns once again the dichotomy between the two models. Throughout this book I have argued that 'the rationale of individual citizen equality irrespective of origin, appearance, affiliation or conviction' is an inadequate description of the French tradition; it obscures the ambivalence of individualism and equality, and effaces the presence of racialised categories in the history of the French republic. In order to avoid the 'either/or' scenario consisting of a choice between integration on an individual basis or 'the spectre of the ghetto' (see Le Bras 1989), perhaps a harder look at the ways in which racism is institutionalised within the structures of nation-states is necessary to appreciate the real problems for redefining rights. Though the 'two model' theory is valid on a general level, perhaps on a deeper level it obscures more than it reveals. The reappraisal of this dichotomy does not necessarily provide a solution to the question of a strategy for rights. Yet, by demythologising traditions, it might help to open up a way towards a strategy.

## ALTERITY AND CITIZENSHIP IN EUROPE

One of the most pressing problems seems to be no longer how to efface alterity, but rather how to deal with it. As Zygmunt Bauman has argued so forcefully, the rhetoric of the dissolution of alterity belongs to the age of modernity: 'The part of the world that adopted modern civilization as its structural principle and con-stitutional value was bent on dominating the rest of the world by dissolving its alterity and assimilating the product of dissolution' (1991: 232). This process was a perpetual struggle to 'manage' contingency, to remove it from the 'garden' of civilised society. Yet, of necessity, it established differences and hierarchies which always threatened a vision of unity and uniformity.

Today that tension (or ambivalence) at the heart of modern civilisation can no longer be suppressed; it is everywhere apparent. The common denominators of modernity have given way to the pluralism of post-modernity, and the discourse of universalism is under siege. Yet that too is a great source of anxiety. New imagined communities and new tribalisms do contain the risks and dangers against which French universalist republicans warn us, not the least of which is the threat of the European national racism (dressed up as cultural differentialism) of the New Right. The power of the message of the New Right comes from being situated firmly within the post-colonial and post-modern logic of difference and pluralism. It opposes proselytising universalism and assimi-lation; it attacks the 'levelling off' approach of republican egalitarianism; it preaches separate development for 'European civilisation' *and* the 'Third World' as the only way to guarantee the survival of both against the global expansionism of the West ('Europe and the Third World united against the West', de Benoist 1986: 19); it exploits an absolutist differentialism to protect 'the relative ethno-cultural homogeneity of European people' (Faye 1985: 17).[10]

The New Right's absolutist version of alterity is a prescription for exclusion and expulsion. It is a fundamental ingredient in the national racism of the FN. Le Pen has put it like this: 'I adore North Africans. But their place is in the Maghreb...I am not racist but national. ...For a nation to be harmonious it must have a certain ethnic and spiritual homogeneity' (*Arabies*, no. 9, September 1987: 36). This touches the core of contemporary racism in France (but also elsewhere in Europe). It is based on a specific conception of cultures and their roots within nations, and on the separateness, uniqueness and purity of European and non-European civilisations. It mobilises not around the concept of 'race' but around that of 'immigration'. As we have already seen, 'immigration' has become racialised through the discourse of cultural differentialism and new nationalism, not through the overt discourse of 'race'. According to Etienne Balibar, '"immigration" has become the name *par excellence* of the race.... "Immigrants" is the prime characteristic allowing the classification of individuals in a racist typology' (Balibar and Wallerstein 1988: 296); it is a 'racism without races' (Balibar and Wallerstein 1988: 32–3).

However, we have seen that the contemporary discourse on immigration and the reformulation of otherness in terms of the naturalisation of differences between Europe and the 'Third World' are not simply the ideas of ideologues of the New Right; contemporary 'Europeanism' is a far wider process in which the construction of the 'problem of immigration' and a retrospective assimilation are essential elements. The Left as well as the Right has produced this consensus. The problem for the Left has been to reify and oppose the evil of racism when, in reality, the Left is part of the very consensus which gives it life.

A further problem for the Left concerns its response to the racist cultural differentialism of the extreme Right and the New Right. This form of differentialism is bound to be rejected by anti-racists. Yet to equate *all* attempts to mobilise categories of difference with the racist separatism of the extreme Right rests on the illusory belief in a non-differentialist (universalist) discourse of opposition. The rejection of 'the right to (absolutist) difference' should not necessarily mean embracing 'the right to resemblance' (Marie 1988: 133), as has so often been the case in France. As I have argued here, differentialism and universalism are not opposites but part of the same process.

Certainly, there are problems with the 'ethnic minority' approach; yet there are also problems with the universalist approach. As François de Closets has remarked, 'It is true that the notion of alterity is loaded with danger but it is also heavy with reality. Banishing it does not lead to its disappearance; it deprives one of effective means to combat its dangers' (*L'Evénement du Jeudi*, 3–9 January 1991). De Closets points out that the conceptual/linguistic crisis of 'democracy' leaves the door open for Le Pen to exploit that territory which resembles reality for many people.[11] So that when New Right and extreme Right ideologues and politicians 'say things as they are' and address the 'real' problems of immigration (cf. Griotteray 1984) through an explicitly differentialist discourse, they are not peddling 'false' ideology (ideology is never 'false'); they are defining social relations in ways which 'make sense' in a society which is not simply racialised but fragmented through numerous other differentialist discourses as well.

The problem for anti-racist movements and movements for new citizenship caught in this dilemma is how to formulate ideas of equality and rights in the fragmented space of contemporary western societies; how to match a system of rights with a recognition of alterity. As Claude-Valentin Marie has remarked:

> The real challenge for the democracy of tomorrow is therefore that of the affirmation of the rights of the citizen, such that a 'difference', real or imagined, might never be the excuse for a denial (even partial) of the rights of common law.
>
> (1988: 133)

The 'race relations' perspective and multicultural approach is highly problematic in many areas (multiculturalism in schools, same-'race' adoption in social services and so on) which are increasingly debated by researchers and practitioners in the UK. Yet to think of identities and solidarities, on the one hand, and power relations, on the other, *across* the splintered lines of class, gender, 'race' and sexuality is a challenge to which, as yet, the Left has no organised response.

For immigrants and ethnic minorities in Europe, certain *common* (dare one say 'universal'?) criteria are surely necessary for a harmonisation of rights. The dissociation of rights from nationality and cultural conformity is fundamental. This has already been achieved (in statute) in a number of the member states of the EC with regard to employment, training and so on. It needs to be extended to cover political rights throughout the EC. Only then will European countries avoid the scandal of having in their midst people living, working and paying dues for ten, fifteen, twenty years and more with no access to political participation and representation (perhaps the slogan 'No taxation without representation' needs to be dusted down and put to use again! – cf. Layton-Henry ed. 1990). Residence (of at least five years) should be the criterion for the acquisition of political rights. In these areas, French movements for a new citizenship play a major role in setting an agenda for rights in Europe.

However, the effective dissociation of rights from nationality and cultural conformity goes beyond the law and the statute book. As I have argued here, a wider perspective on citizenship must inevitably consider the ways in which racism is located within the institutional/ideological structures of nation-states and shapes social relations. Whether the 'new Europe' is a chance to destabilise the national/racial complex of modern states or whether it is an opportunity to construct new forms of exclusion remains to be seen.

In conclusion it seems that the major contradiction today facing any new citizenship is between an individualist and a group perspective on identity and rights. Modernity's cults of the individual and equality before the law irrespective of 'race', religion and origin have belied the parallel development of a Eurocentric racialised discourse. The repressed tension between individualism and origins/communities has returned to haunt post-modernity. The confusion of anti-racist slogans – caught between the individual and the community – is indicative of this crisis in the naming and understanding of social relations today. It is a consequence of the unravelling of the tension and ambivalence of modern universalist assimilation. It is therefore useless to 'demonise' racism or mythologise the Enlightenment when the real crisis is located in the modern order upon which nation-states are founded. The suggestion that racism is an integral part of the development of modern 'egalitarian' society only seems to be a paradox if one accepts the opposition between universalism and racism, between civilisation and barbarity, between science and ideology and between the individual and the community. It is not a paradox if these are seen not as oppositions but as part of a wider and more complex unity.

# Notes

## INTRODUCTION

1 Cf. the reflection by the sociologist Abdelmalek Sayad: 'In France the nation appears in its most complete form. But what is a nation? It is almost a French invention' (Sayad 1983: 37).

2 Many of the French works dealing with this information will also be referred to during the course of the book. Recent general texts include Perotti 1985, Le Moigne 1986, Richer 1986, Fuchs 1987, Voisard and Ducastelle 1988, Milza 1988, Wihtol de Wenden 1988a, Costa-Lascoux 1989, Dubet 1989a and Mestiri 1990. There are no books in English which give the same comprehensive coverage of statistics, laws, policies and rights. However, for aspects of these, see Schain 1985, Hargreaves 1987, Ogden and White 1989, Silverman 1989 and (ed.) 1991, Lloyd and Waters 1991, *Ethnic and Racial Studies* 1991.

3 In France there has not been the same level of class analysis of immigration and 'race' as in Britain. For example, despite their diversity in approach, the analyses developed by Castles and Kosack 1973, Hall *et al.* 1978, Rex and Tomlinson 1979, Miles 1982 and 1984, Sivanandan 1982 and others during the 1970s and the 1980s considered the articulation between 'race' and class in a way which was significantly lacking in France during the same period.

## 1 IMMIGRATION AND THE NATION-STATE

1 Although Braudel emphasises the diversity of France, he nevertheless maintains the idea that immigrants assimilated easily into the French cultural landscape in the past, in contrast with what he sees as the breakdown in assimilation accompanying the new immigration of contemporary France. The problems with this approach will be discussed in Chapters 3 and 4.

2 It should be mentioned that Noiriel's discussion of the 'two models' is more nuanced than this. His aim is to show that, although historiography of the nation has frequently been presented in terms of an opposition between the assimilationist and differentialist tendencies, they are nevertheless closer than one thinks (see Noiriel 1988a).

3  In fact, rather than recover their former meanings, both the words 'patrie' and 'citoyen' were completely reworked in the eighteenth century.

4  Although the nation has frequently been discussed in terms of the two models, some commentators have recognised the less than clear-cut line between universalism and particularism. For example, although Hobsbawm collapses too quickly Renan's idea of the daily plebiscite into 'the French concept of the "nation"' and describes how 'French nationality was French citizenship: ethnicity, history, the language or patois spoken at home, were irrelevant to the definition of "the nation"' (Hobsbawm 1990: 88), he nevertheless achnowledges the racist element in French nationalism (1990: 93). Julia Kristeva also places the mystical, 'volksgeist' theory of the nation in opposition to 'the French national idea, inspired by the Enlightenment and embodied in the Republic in the form of the juridical and political pact of equal and free individuals' (*Le Monde*, 29 March 1991). Yet she too acknowledges that the 'contractual' character of the French idea of the nation does not efface its particularisms.

5  Finkielkraut's view that the eventual rehabilitation of Dreyfus was a clear indication that France 'prefers *in extremis* the contractual definition of society to the idea of the collective spirit' (1987: 62) seems to be a remarkable misreading of the continued power of the absolutist cultural concept of the nation in the twentieth century. One only has to consider Vichy to realise this.

6  Clearly it is impossible to put a date on the origins of the nation. The nation does not appear overnight but is the product of a number of disconnected developments which converge over time (see, for example, Anderson 1983 or Balibar 1990). For the present purposes, I will be considering developments in the nineteenth century. This is not to suggest that the nation sprang into existence at the time of the Revolution, or even that it was then that it came of age. It is simply because, as I shall argue, it was then that the development of modern immigration and the nationalisation of society by means of the state took place.

7  According to Weber (1976) even by the end of the century 25 per cent of the population did not speak French and another 25 per cent spoke it very poorly.

8  Alfred Sauvy, the most famous of all French demographers of the twentieth century, said 'all organised or tolerated migration risks opposing economists and demographers' (1948: 22).

9  The first census in France, in 1851, recorded 378,561 foreigners. The largest foreign population was from Belgium (128,103), followed by Italy (63,307) and Germany and Austria (57,000). Subsequent censuses showed a rise in the foreign population to 635,495 (1866), 723,507 (1872) and 801,000 (1876) (Wihtol de Wenden 1988a: 19–20; see also Ogden 1989).

10  It is interesting to note that the law on 'vagabondage' – which related to a moving and 'dangerous' population – was suppressed in 1890, at the very time of the institutionalisation of measures of control for

foreigners (the new moving and 'dangerous' population) with the decree of 1888 and the law of 1893 (see Bruschi 1989: 254–5).

11 It was only in 1880 that 14 July was instituted as a national holiday (see Nora 1984).

12 Article 39 of the French Code of Nationality states that the government can use the concept of 'insufficient assimilation' ('défaut d'assimilation') to block the acquisition of nationality by marriage. Article 69 of the Code states that applicants can be refused naturalisation if they cannot prove a sufficient assimilation into the French community, particularly if they do not have an adequate knowledge of the French language (Bruschi 1985: 62).

## 2   POST-WAR IMMIGRATION IN FRANCE

1 The case of the Harkis (of whom there are about 400,000 in France) is a classic example of French nationals who are invariably treated as immigrants in France. A young Harki explains: 'We are not Algerians but neither are we considered to be French.... Whenever we go out in a group we are always stopped by the police who ask to see our residence permits. But we don't have them; our papers are either our identity card or a French passport' (quoted in *Le Quotidien*, 5 January 1990).

2 For example, a recent poll published in the centre-Left weekly *Le Nouvel Observateur* (13–19 September 1990) contained this question: 'According to the census, there are now four million immigrants living in France. Would you say that their proportion in relation to the French population is too small, too large or that it is not a problem?' Respondents were also asked the following question: 'To guarantee a better distribution of immigrants in France, would you be for or against a policy of housing immigrant families in your neighbourhood?' The headline encapsulating the results of this survey was 'The worrying facts'.

3 Wihtol de Wenden has noted (1988a: 116): 'Following the "procedural arrangement" on immigration signed on 16 July 1956 with Spain, the communist group in the National Assembly declared its opposition to the arrival in France of thousands of foreign workers. It considered that the introduction of new workers was not in keeping with "the interest of our country".' A frequent analysis of the Left and trade unions was that immigration was responsible for the persistence of outdated economic practices and was therefore a bulwark against the modernisation of the French economy. Although the argument was used to criticise employers who exploited foreign workers, nevertheless the principal idea underlying the analysis perpetuated a dangerous myth surrounding the presence and role of the foreign worker in France (see Cordeiro 1984: 32–5).

4 The number of Algerians rose from 471,000 to 710,000 between the censuses of 1968 and 1975. This was not simply as a result of entries

of new primary immigrants but also due to family immigration and births in France.

5  The Fontanet circular was 'humanized' (Freeman 1979: 94) by the new Minister of Labour, Georges Gorse (circulars of 12 July 1973). The Marcellin-Fontanet circulars were subsequently annulled by the Conseil d'Etat in June 1974 which ruled that it was improper to define the conditions for entry and residence in the country by means of ministerial circulars (Costa-Lascoux 1989: 22–3).

6  This was not the first time that the Algerian government had expressed concern at the treatment of its citizens in France and at their chances of getting a fair hearing before French law. An outbreak of anti-Algerian racism led to nine deaths between March and May 1971. In twenty-five cases of violence the police did not proceed with investigations. On three occasions, they even refused to register the complaint. On 3 June 1971 the Algerian President, Houari Boumedienne, complained of racist attacks 'that the French government could stop... and which present an image which is completely contrary to the great tradition of hospitality of the French people' (quoted in Mangin 1982: 17).

7  In fact of the many circulars and decrees relating to immigration between 1975–80, seven were judged illegal by the Conseil d'Etat (see Mangin 1982: 49).

8  Yet, even before Stoléru's scheme, the three meetings of the Council of Ministers during Dijoud's term of office which defined immigration policy (9 October 1974, 21 May and 9 December 1975) all referred to the question of repatriation. Dijoud himself presided over a first scheme, introduced in 1975, which offered retraining to those who wished to return to their country of origin ('formation-retour').

9  In fact the census figure had to be rectified when it was discovered that 238,000 young people were declared wrongly as Algerian when they were in fact French at birth (according to article 23 of the Code of Nationality). After this correction the foreign population stood at 3,442,100 (Lebon 1988: 34).

10  The vote for the FN rose to just under 11 per cent in the European elections of 1984. Since then the FN has regularly polled around 10 per cent of the vote in different elections, but in certain areas (for example Marseilles) the percentage has been around 25 per cent in local elections.

11  For an analysis of how Islam was being used by workers, see Wihtol de Wenden 1985 and Mouriaux and Wihtol de Wenden 1988.

12  Founded in 1949, the MRAP has concerned itself particularly with racist attacks and a more effective protection in law against racial violence and discrimination. It played an important role both in the introduction of the law against discrimination in 1972 and its extension in 1990.

13  The term 'beur' is Parisian back-slang for 'Arab'. It originated in the early 1980s as part of the rejection by 'second-generation' youths of imposed terms like 'immigrant' and as an expression of new identity. However, it was seen by many 'second-generation' youths outside

Paris (and in Paris) as a term associated with a Parisian clique. Furthermore, it was quickly appropriated by the media and has therefore lost much of its original sense as a marker of identity.

14  This policy was not very successful at the time of the parliamentary elections of 1986. Most parties were reluctant to place 'beurs' in prominent positions on their lists and many 'beurs' did not exercise their right to vote.

15  The meeting of 10 May 1990 returned to the discussion of illegal immigration and deportations, which was apparently more newsworthy than the social concerns also under discussion (see *Le Monde*, 12 May 1990).

16  Just one example of the 'common-sense' link between integration and control can be seen in the two circulars sent to prefects within a few days of each other by the Minister of the Interior, Philippe Marchand; one concerned the struggle against illegal immigration on the frontiers, the other was on the question of the struggle against racism within the frontiers (*La Croix*, 10 April 1991).

17  The decline in housing conditions for foreigners and the difficulties of getting placed in council housing had been serious problems throughout the 1980s; see Barou 1980; de Rudder 1983; Marie 1989; Dubet 1989a: 44–5, 72.

18  This split was indicative of a general split amongst Left intellectuals over the war. See, for example, the different signatories to the pro-war and anti-war texts published in *Libération*, 21 February 1991 (Alain Finkielkraut, Elisabeth de Fontenay, Jean-François Lyotard, Pierre-André Taguieff and Alain Touraine in the first group, Etienne Balibar, Tahar Ben Jelloun and Pierre Bourdieu in the second).

19  Some of the problems of SOS Racisme at the time of its national congress of 28–30 April 1990 were a) that it had become part of the political landscape and too closely allied to the Socialist Party. Harlem Désir had recommended a vote for Mitterrand in the presidential elections of 1988. By the end of the 1980s a number of the original founders of the movement had moved into posts within the Socialist Party (Julien Dray became a deputy); b) that it was suffering from competition with France Plus which had itself made use of similar publicity techniques and had cultivated important links in political circles; c) that it had opted for the slogan of 'integration' when not only France Plus and the government were using the same term, but so too were politicians whose ideas on 'immigration' closely resembled those of Le Pen (for example, the former President Giscard d'Estaing and the former Minister of the Interior under Jacques Chirac in 1986, Charles Pasqua) (*Le Monde*, 28 April 1990).

20  Smaller associations had also criticised the media orientation of anti-racism and its failure to engage with the real causes of discrimination. Mémoire Fertile (founded in May 1988) sought to dissociate citizenship from nationality and to redefine citizens' rights and the national apparatus of the state (see Bouâmama, President of 'Mémoire Fertile', 1989a and 1989b). The feminist group Expression Maghrébines au Féminin (created in 1985) also deplored the media presentation and

distortion of the issue of rights. However, like the group Nanas Beurs, they have found themselves caught within the same paradoxes of a discourse of 'integration' (see for example their positions over the headscarf affair in *Libération*, 1 November 1989, and *L'Evénement du Jeudi*, 9–15 November 1989, and the wider discussion of these paradoxes in Chapter 4).

21  A 'democratic forum' was launched by SOS Racisme on 28 January 1990 in order to reappraise anti-racism within the context of democracy and rights. The forum included a number of prominent intellectuals: Marek Halter, Bernard-Henri Lévy, Pierre-André Taguieff, Julia Kristeva and Alain Touraine.

## 3  THE 'PROBLEM' OF IMMIGRATION

1  In terms of the switch from an economic to a more social perspective on immigration, the contribution of the Ministry of Social Affairs in the reformulation of immigration policy was considerable (see Calame and Calame 1972: 17–18).

2  It is interesting to note how this historiography of contemporary immigration frequently refers to the 'visibility' of today's immigrants (constituted as the 'problem') compared to the 'invisibility' of those in the past (constituted as 'easily assimilated'), as if visibility was a natural phenomenon rather than a social construct. Hubert Prévot, Secrétaire Général à l'Intégration in 1990, reproduced this classic version of recent history: 'We went from an immigration of men, living together in hostels, to a more turbulent family immigration which presented a greater degree of social "visibility"' (quoted in *La Croix*, 11 May 1990). For a similar official perspective, see also the section entitled 'D'une immigration de main-d'oeuvre à une immigration sédentarisée' in Commissariat Général du Plan 1988: 23–48.

3  For an appraisal of the significance of the views of Michel Massenet in the reformulation of immigration policy at this time, see Calame and Calame 1972, Tapinos 1975 and Freeman 1979.

4  The idea of the spontaneous assimilation of immigrants was invoked much earlier by Georges Mauco in his discussion of immigration between the wars. He writes: 'Just as a plant transplanted into good soil quickly takes root, so the emigrant in France, finding in general living conditions superior to those he had to leave, adapts and assimilates quickly' (1932: 555).

5  We noted in the previous chapter how, in the early 1960s, Massenet praised Algerians for their youth, their mobility, their status as unqualified workers and, consequently, their willingness to perform tasks that French workers refused to perform (see especially Massenet 1962: 18). It is interesting to compare these comments with his discussion of the problems of assimilation and adaptability of North Africans in 1970.

6  The sixth economic plan also concluded that immigration should be reorientated according to the criterion of 'assimilability': 'But, with

regard to these new emigrants who are both geographically and 'socio-culturally' more distant, can we expect to practise the same policy of settlement, integration and assimilation which was so successful in the past with Polish, Italian or Spanish immigrants?... The commissions preparing the sixth plan approached this question prudently, but their conclusion on this point was, more or less explicitly, that the definitive integration of non-European workers and their families in the national community cannot be considered as a general objective, even if the possibility of pursuing this approach must be safeguarded in specific instances' (*Hommes et Migrations. Etudes* 1971: 10–11). For an example of the use of the same ethnic, assimilationist criteria in political discussion of immigration at the time, see the Senate debate on work permits (19 December 1970) reported in Galissot 1978.

7  The importance of ethnic considerations in a sound immigration policy were emphasised by Louis Chevalier. He maintained that immigration was necessary but 'it is destined to continue the French nation and not to create a country which would perhaps be France economically and politically but not on a human level' (cited in Tapinos 1975: 18). The conclusion that immigrants should come from neighbouring countries was also shared by Sauvy and Debray.

8  Pompidou's optimistic view of French attitudes was not borne out by a survey carried out in April 1975. Of those questioned, 55 per cent thought that racism was widespread in France and 33 per cent thought that it was rare (sondage SOFRES-Midi Libre, 'Les Français et le problème des travailleurs immigrés', *Le Midi Libre*, 22 April 1975, quoted in Girard 1977: 226).

9  The growing debate in the 1970s around cultural difference, pluralism and the relationship between minorities and the state informs much of the debate of the 1980s. See, for example, Verbunt (ed.) 1984, Clanet (ed.) 1985 and AFA 1987. Paul Dijoud anticipated some of the problems ahead when he said: 'immigration policy, caught between the danger of egalitarianism at any cost and segregation, discovers its fundamental ambiguity: should it aim for equality or should it respect differences?' (Dijoud 1976: sp. 4). See also Hessel 1976.

10  As regards the costs/benefits debate on immigration, another report, written at about the same time as that of Le Pors and which started from exactly the same premises, came to directly opposite conclusions. The report produced by Fernand Icart, entitled *Le Coût Social des Travailleurs Etrangers en France* (Assemblée Nationale 1976) took as 'costs' the very things which Le Pors' study discussed as 'benefits' (see Sayad 1979: 18). For further discussion of the debate around the costs and benefits of immigration and the links between immigration, employment and repatriation, see Wihtol de Wenden 1988a: 204–8, Cordeiro 1984: 91–3, and Sayad 1979: 5–6 and 17–19.

## 4 ASSIMILATION AND DIFFERENCE

1 However, Mitterrand had already made the following statement during a visit to Vénissieux in Lyons on 10 October 1983: 'Certain communes should not have an excessive number of immigrants whilst others, which have the same housing conditions, the same geographical situation, and the same worries about unemployment, remain free from such problems' (quoted in Ben Jelloun 1984: 140). Although Mitterrand's remark on the threshold in 1989 was embarrassing for many socialists, it was welcomed by the 'Socialism and Republic' group within the party whose major spokesperson was the Minister of Defence, Jean-Pierre Chevènement. This group had been arguing since 1985 for an integration of immigrants based on a clear conception of national identity. Reacting to Mitterrand's statement, Jean-Marie Bockel, the deputy mayor of Mulhouse and close associate of Chevènement, declared: 'basically, the President's statement pleased me because it recognises a real problem. Even if the vocabulary used is debatable, it is nevertheless certain that in any case there is the phenomenon of the threshold whenever the concentration of immigrants in the same town is too great' (quoted in *Libération*, 22 January 1990). (For an exposition of the nationalist republicanism of this brand of French socialism, see for example Chevènement 1979.)

2 Barou cites the example of the euphemistic language of one mayor (at Tremblay-les-Gonesses) whose justification for her refusal to re-house an immigrant family in her municipality was not on the grounds of the 'seuil de tolérance' but according to 'the defence of the interests of citizens of long-standing' (Barou 1984: 116).

3 On 8 December 1832, in an article on workers' riots in Lyons, the *Journal des Débats* stated that 'the barbarians threatening society are not in the Caucasus or the Steps of Tartar; they are in the suburbs of our manufacturing towns' (quoted in Charlot 1989: 149). The theme of the 'alien wedge' and the 'enemy within' developed in Britain in the 1970s and 1980s (see Hall *et al.* 1978; CCCS 1982) – in which the target groups can be striking workers or ethnic minorities – is a contemporary reworking of the same flexible marginalisation. Balibar's analysis of the racialisation of the work-force instituting a 'racism of class' attempts to locate the origins of ethnic stigmatisation of designated groups in the modern period (Balibar and Wallerstein 1988; also Balibar 1991).

4 Mauco asked 'are there not already certain communes and certain districts which are thoroughly Italian, Polish or Spanish by the simple rule of the majority?' (1932: 559).

5 The contradiction between the theory of invisibility and the practice of visibility was heightened by the policy of decentralisation pursued by the socialist government in the early 1980s. The power to decide urban policy was handed over to mayors who frequently used it to exclude new immigrants in their communes and allow the deterioration of housing conditions of those who were already there (Barou

1984: 122). The effects of this approach have been felt more recently in the crises in the suburbs of large towns.

6 It is interesting to note that the refusal of the acquisition of nationality on the grounds of inadequate assimilation ('défaut d'assimilation') was introduced at this time through the ordonnance of 19 October 1945. There is no mention of it in the nationality laws of 1889 or 1927. According to Christian Bruschi, 'it is largely inspired by the procedure of accession to citizenship in the colonies where French subjects could become citizens only on condition of proof that they conformed to French morals and customs' (Bruschi 1989: 268).

7 Another composite term which denotes this immigration as external and alien to French traditions is 'immigration sauvage'. As already mentioned, this was employed in the late 1960s and early 1970s to refer to 'uncontrolled immigration'. However, as Colette Guillaumin has shown, the word 'sauvage' does not simply signify 'uncontrolled', it also means 'of savages' (Guillaumin 1984b, also 1991). Like the 'bidonvilles', they belong to an underdeveloped and uncivilised world.

8 Noiriel tends to underestimate the capacity for self-mobilisation of groups themselves. In his analysis of the 'second generation', he suggests that the major reason for the 'visibility' of the 'second generation' today (compared to their 'invisibility' in the inter-war period) is primarily because of the prolific state sector of social welfare, which has constructed this group institutionally and socially (1989: 217–18). Yet, although his analysis highlights the discursive mechanisms at work in the construction of a 'problem' group and the social construction of the notion of 'visibility', it tends to ignore the ways in which the vocabulary of ethnicity can serve the cause of anti-racism as well as racism.

9 Jean-Pierre Dupuy writes: 'How can we not see that what inspires fear is undifferentiation, and that is because undifferentiation is always the sign and the product of social disintegration – since the unity of the whole presupposes its differential or hierarchical structure. ... People fear Sameness, and that is the source of racism' (1985: 43; also Dumont 1983; de Rudder 1983: 87; Lorreyte 1985: 542; Jacquard and Pontalis 1984). Balibar has suggested that contemporary differentialist racism is in a way like 'a generalised anti-semitism' (Balibar and Wallerstein 1988: 37).

10 The use of 'ethnic' terms to describe workers from Algeria in the social institutions established in the 1950s (SONACOTRA and the FAS) once again reveals the myth of the uniform classification of French nationals according to the sole criterion of individualism.

11 It is rather ironic that, throughout the debate generated by the headscarf affair, the name of Jules Ferry should have been so frequently enlisted by anti-racists. For, although Ferry was a major proponent of a secular (i.e. non-Catholic) education system, he was also attacked vigorously by radicals during his periods of office in the 1880s for his racist colonial policy.

12 These debates around housing and education visibly converge at this

time over the application by some mayors of the 'seuil de tolérance' in schools. For example, the mayors of Montfermeil and Beaucaire – Pierre Bernard and Jean-Michel André respectively – refused to allow the registration of children from 'immigrant' families in nursery schools, arguing that the numbers of immigrant children were already too high. André Deschamps, the communist mayor of Clichy-sous-Bois, a neighbouring municipality to Montfermeil, said that he 'understood' his colleague in Montfermeil: 'it's no longer a question of talking about integration. Not with the level of immigrants that we've got' (*Le Monde*, 4 November 1989). These are extreme signs of the ambivalence of assimilation: it is founded on racialised criteria.

13  References to the 'Anglo-Saxon' model are normally in the form of 'what the French should avoid'. Another fascinating insight into the 'English' approach appeared at the same time as Rocard's statement in an article entitled 'What secularism?' by Paul Thibaut: 'Because they have a state religion, a monarchy, and pre-democratic institutions, the English can practise a relaxed segregationism (with a riot from time to time), a policy of ghettos whose destabilising effects would be much worse in France' (*L'Express*, 8 December 1989).

14  In response to statements like 'In Man, race doesn't exist' (Jacques Ruffié in his inaugural lecture at the Collège de France, quoted in Hannoun 1987: 37), Guillaumin has consistently responded in the following fashion: 'Whether or not race is a "fact of nature" or a "mental fact", it is today, in the twentieth century, a juridical and political reality, historically inscribed in concrete facts, playing a genuine role in certain societies' (1986: 64); or 'to say that race does not exist does not abolish racism' (1984a: 218).

15  Georges Mauco talks of France 'digesting' new immigrants over a period of time (1932: 558). Bernard Lorreyte has remarked on the biological and medical connotations of the 'seuil de tolérance' which, he says, is 'a notion...which defines French society as a pure and homogeneous body contaminated by a sort of virus or microbe: immigrants' (1988: 6). For the digestive and sexual connotations of the term 'assimilation', see also Sayad 1988: 171, note 8.

16  Cf. Nair's equation between racism and leprosy, 'this sickness ... which ravages the spirit' (1984: 14).

17  For (attempted) definitions of the terms assimilation, integration and 'insertion', see, for example, Gaspard and Servan-Schreiber 1985: 183–5, Costa-Lascoux 1989: 9–12 and Commissariat Général du Plan 1988: 215–18. For a discussion of assimilation and its euphemisms, see Sayad 1985: 29. The discussion of the definitions of these terms itself indicates the profound uncertainty in contemporary France about the nature of individualism and the collectivity and inclusion and exclusion.

18  According to Taguieff, one of the major problems with the slogan 'equality in difference' is that 'difference' is implicitly the primary definer and equality is of secondary importance in relation to it (1987: 172).

19  France Plus has consistently described differentialism as consigning

people to the ghetto according to cultural and phenotypical characteristics and establishing an apartheid in terms of rights (see for example *La Croix*, 15 September 1990, and *Le Quotidien*, 17 September 1990). Mouloud Aounit, the Secretary General of MRAP, maintains that integration in society can be accomplished only on an individual basis (interview in *L'Humanité*, 20 March 1991).

## 5 NATIONALITY AND CITIZENSHIP

1 Even these strikes were substantially different from previous ones. One aspect of this evolution was the use of Islam as a means of negotiation in the work-place (see Mouriaux and Wihtol de Wenden 1988).

2 In fact the debate around the right to vote in municipal elections dated from about 1977. In 1979 Jacques Chirac was in favour of the idea of giving the vote to foreigners who had been resident in France for at least five years. Chirac's position quickly changed in the 1980s. At the end of the decade he was calling for a referendum on the issue to prevent the socialist government of Michel Rocard from bringing it back onto the political agenda.

3 The contemporary discussion on citizenship in France dates from the early 1980s (see, for example, Leca 1983, 1985; also Wihtol de Wenden 1984). It is closely linked to questions of immigration and the nation (see Wihtol de Wenden 1988b). In Britain, by contrast, the discussion on citizenship has concerned primarily constitutional, political and social questions around rights and obligations but has touched only peripherally on the national question.

4 However, between 1981-6 there were sixteen laws relating to immigration (and 79 decrees, 62 'arrêtés' and 215 circulars and 'instructions'). This is indicative of the marked politicisation of immigration in the 1980s.

5 With regard to the Fontanet circular of February 1972, Tapinos notes that it did not even appear in the Journal Officiel (the official record of all legislative and executive measures). It was published instead in the 'Bulletin' of the Ministry of State for Social Affairs and was distributed only in non-official circles. Tapinos concludes that the fact that the Marcellin-Fontanet circulars were eventually suppressed by a ruling of the Conseil d'Etat (13 January 1975) – thus simplifying what was a complex juridical decision – suggests that the Conseil d'Etat in effect called into question the use of the circular for such a ruling (1975: 92).

6 In 1979, there was the case of a prefect of police in the Bouches-du-Rhône who took it upon himself to order the expulsion of immigrants with false papers at a time when this was not an offence punishable by this treatment in law. He had pre-empted the law (the Bonnet Law of 1980) that was about to facilitate expulsion of 'irregulars' in this way.

7   This familiar logic of racism was expressed at the end of the nine-
    teenth century by Georges Vacher de Lapouge in the following terms:

> We can easily understand how absurd even the idea of naturalisa-
> tion is. It is a biological nonsense and runs counter to political
> common sense. To fabricate a Frenchman by decree or an artificial
> Englishman or a false German is one of the finest aberrations of the
> law.... A foreigner can acquire the rights of a Frenchman, and if he
> is of a certain character he will be able to use them like a French
> national, but that will *never make him into a Frenchman*'
> (*L'Aryen. Son Rôle Social*, Paris: Albert Fontemoing,
> 1899, p. 368, quoted in Taguieff 1985: 172)

The influence of this view of naturalisation (particularly strong between the wars) on early studies of immigration can be seen in Georges
Mauco's warning of the possible drawbacks to a smooth assimilation of
foreigners:

> We might wonder whether this relatively rapid assimilation of
> foreigners is achieved only on the material and official levels;
> whether the 'francisation' is merely superficial and exterior, and
> whether there is really a 'francisation' of the soul alongside that of
> customs and life-styles. Without going so far as to say that those who
> are naturalised are merely 'paper Frenchmen', might one not fear
> that the new Frenchmen are sufficiently different from French
> nationals as to modify the homogeneity and spirit of the country?
> Do not the French race and culture risk being affected by this influx,
> this pacific invasion?
> (1932: 555–6)

It will be remembered that Georges Mauco was one of the team who,
in 1945, suggested an ethnic quota system for the new post-war
immigration policy.

8   Michel Rocard's statements on the acceleration of the process of
    naturalisation of immigrants (*L'Express*, 11 April 1991) therefore
    remain firmly entrenched within the 'assimilationist' tradition in
    which full rights are acquired only through the acquisition of nation-
    ality. This position rests on the assumption that naturalisation is the
    ultimate point in what is classified as a 'successful' immigration or
    completed assimilation (see Sayad 1988: 158). Naturalisation is per-
    ceived as a passage of progress and emancipation, from the 'ethnic'
    particularist domain of the non-national to the 'natural' universal
    state of the national (cf. Galissot 1985a: 53).

9   The danger for Chirac was to have the emotive issues of immigration
    and nationality at the centre of political attention in the run-up to the
    presidential elections of 1988. His problem was how to play the
    nationalist and anti-immigrant card to his own political and electoral
    advantage rather than that of Le Pen. The fact that the outcome of
    such a tactic was always likely to be uncertain was one of the major
    reasons why the government eventually shelved the proposal to
    change the Code and established a commission instead.

10 Arezki Dahmani, the President of France Plus, judged the report 'positive on the whole' and the MRAP welcomed its 'positive orientation'. On the other hand, Harlem Désir condemned it as a backward step. SOS Racisme's main objection was precisely to the report's recommendation that young foreigners born in France should be obliged to opt for nationality from the age of sixteen rather than receive it automatically at the age of eighteen. SOS Racisme claimed that this recommendation merely confirmed the attack on the principle of the 'jus soli' contained in the initial project (see *Libération*, 9 January 1988).

11 Cordeiro describes this social action beyond the reaches of the state as a paradoxical phenomenon: 'By an apparent paradox, groups who are *administered* and over-controlled develop an action which functions outside the domain of the state controlled by the actors themselves. But it is also a *collective* action which operates beyond the schema of the NATION-STATE' (1988: 7).

## 6   FRANCE AND THE 'NEW EUROPE'

1 This article also quotes the former Belgian interior minister, Joseph Michel, who in 1987 was more explicit in defining who these 'undesirables' really are: 'We run the risk of becoming like the Roman people, invaded by barbarian peoples such as Arabs, Moroccans, Yugoslavs and Turks, people who come from far afield and have nothing in common with our civilisation' (*The Guardian*, 27 December 1988).

2 In January 1990 Belgium announced that it was refusing to accept any more refugees. According to a report in France, this measure seemed to rouse little passion in Belgium, despite its illegality (*L'Evénement du Jeudi*, 18–24 January 1990).

3 In Britain, exactly the same reasons have been given to justify stricter procedures for processing the applications of asylum-seekers: namely, that many of those seeking asylum are not genuine refugees but economic migrants. Britain is one of the strictest of all EC countries in its procedures for vetting applications for asylum. The proportion of successful applicants fell from 60 per cent in the early 1980s to about 13 per cent at the end of the 1980s (*The Independent*, 14 December 1988; *The Guardian*, 27 December 1988). In a report published in November 1990 Amnesty International claimed that the government 'was failing to honour its obligations under the 1951 UN convention' (reported in *The Guardian*, 1 November 1990). The report accused the government of 'exposing Tamils to the threat of arrest and torture by deporting them' (*Education Guardian*, 20 November 1990). The Amnesty report did not deter the immigration minister, Peter Lloyd, from announcing a further cut in the number of asylum-seekers allowed to remain in Britain (*The Guardian*, 31 October 1990). The British government also placed the onus of keeping out 'undesirables' on the airlines by fining them £1000 for every passenger they carry

without valid entry documents, so that many genuine cases never even get the chance of a fair hearing.

4  For a description of the activities of the Trevi group, the Schengen agreement and the 'Ad Hoc group on Immigration' (established to combat 'abuses of the asylum process'), see Bunyan 1991.

5  This prompted a joint initiative in October 1990 by the National Council of Civil Liberties, the Joint Council for the Welfare of Immigrants and Charter 88 to set up a British civil liberties lobby in Brussels.

6  In one decade, West Germany granted nationality to 50,000 foreigners; the same number get French nationality every six months (Mestiri 1990: 104–5).

7  The incongruity and injustice of this state of affairs is captured in the following statement by a young socialist member of the European Parliament born in France of Algerian parents (and therefore eligible to vote and stand for election): 'Do you think that it is normal that someone from Portugal who has been living in France for five years has more of a right to vote in local elections than an Algerian who has toiled for France for forty-five years?' (Nora Mebrak-Zaidi quoted in Escaffit 1990). Preferential treatment for EC nationals was enhanced in a proposal by the French government to extend the right to certain jobs in the civil service to non-French EC nationals (*Le Monde*, 21 March 1991).

8  This statement was corrected in a subsequent article (Wrench 1990b: 577). Nevertheless, it is indicative of the problems involved in any consideration of rights for minorities in Europe. Misunderstandings, dubious self-congratulations and the problems of international co-operation have been discussed by Ann Dummet in an unpublished paper entitled 'The problems of international cooperation in anti-racist approaches within the European Community' given at a seminar on 1992 at the CRER, Warwick University, May 1990 and by Cathie Lloyd in an unpublished paper on 'Race relations in Britain and France: problems of interpretation', given at a conference on 'Migration and racism in Europe', September 1990, Hamburg.

9  In fact, 'positive discrimination' is not part of the legal armoury against racial discrimination in the UK; 'positive action' is, but this is not the same thing.

10  The term 'New Right' is an umbrella term to encompass a diverse range of neo-racist ideologues of the 1970s and 1980s. It has been used since 1978 to refer to GRECE (Group for research and study in European civilisation) which itself was founded in 1968. For detailed studies of the histories, ideologies and discourses of the different tendencies within GRECE, see especially Taguieff 1985, 1988a, 1988b, 1988c and *Mots* 1986.

11  Given that de Closets' criticisms of anti-racism (especially SOS Racisme; see *L'Evénement du Jeudi*, 3–9 May 1990) are founded, in part, on its conceptual/linguistic deficit and its naive faith in the disappearance of alterity, it is strange that he should favour the approach of France Plus (see *L'Express*, 8 June 1990). Of all the anti-racist

organisations, France Plus is by far the most integrationist/universalist and has been vociferous in its condemnation of any form of community-based, separatist and 'ghettoising' approach.

# Bibliography

AFA (1987) *Vers des Sociétés Pluriculturelles: Etudes Comparatives et Situation en France*, Paris: Editions de l'ORSTOM.

Allen, S. and Macey, M. (1990) 'Race and ethnicity in the European context', *British Journal of Sociology* 41, 3: 375–93.

Anderson, B. (1983) *Imagined Communities*, London: Verso.

Balibar, E. (1984) 'Sujets ou citoyens', *Les Temps Modernes* 'L'immigration maghrébine en France. Les faits et les mythes' 452–3–4: 1726–53.

—— (1988) 'Propositions sur la citoyenneté', in C. Wihtol de Wenden (coordonné par) *La Citoyenneté*, Paris: Edilig/Fondation Diderot.

—— (1989) 'Le racisme: encore un universalisme', *Mots* 18: 7–19.

—— (1990) 'The nation form: history and ideology', *Review. Fernand Braudel Center* XIII, 3: 329–61.

—— (1991) 'Race, nation and class' (translated by Clare Hughes) in M. Silverman (ed.) *Race, Discourse and Power in France*, Aldershot: Avebury.

Balibar, E. and Wallerstein, I. (1988) *Race Nation Classe: les Identités Ambiguës*, Paris: La Découverte.

Banton, M. (1967) *Race Relations*, London: Tavistock.

Barker, M. (1981) *The New Racism*, London: Junction Books.

Barou, J. (1980) 'Immigration et enjeux urbains', *Pluriel* 24: 3–20.

—— (1984) 'L'espace immigré ou comment les rendre invisibles', *Politique Aujourd'hui* 4: 115–23.

Bauman, Z. (1991) *Modernity and Ambivalence*, Cambridge: Polity Press.

Belorgey, J. -M. (1987) 'Le droit de la nationalité: évolution historique et enjeux', in S. Laacher (sous la direction de) *Questions de Nationalité: Histoire et Enjeux d'un Code*, Paris: CIEMI/L'Harmattan.

Ben Jelloun, T. (1984) *Hospitalité Française*, Paris: Seuil.

de Benoist, A. (1986) *Europe, Tiers Monde, Même Combat*, Paris: R. Laffont.

Benot, Y. (1989) 'De l'égalité des droits', *Différences* March: 40–1.

Berque, J. (1985) *L'Immigration à l'Ecole de la République* (report to the Ministre de l'Education Nationale), Paris: La Documentation Française.

Bideberry, P. (1969) 'Immigration et techniques de recrutement', *Economie et Humanisme* 189: 19–28.

Bouâmama, S. (1989a) 'Au-delà du droit de vote. La nouvelle citoyenneté', *Hommes et Migrations* 1118: 13–16.

—— (1989b) 'Du droit naturel à la démocratie', *Différences* March: 42.

Bourdieu, P. (1987) 'Communication', *Hommes et Migrations*, January.

Braudel, F. (1986) *L'Identité de la France*, 'Espace et Histoire', 1, Paris: Arthaud.

Bruschi, C. (1985) 'Le droit et l'insertion des immigrés', *Esprit* 102: 49–63.

—— (1987) 'Droit de la nationalité et égalité des droits de 1789 à la fin du XIXe siècle', in S. Laacher (sous la direction de) *Questions de Nationalité: Histoire et Enjeux d'un Code*, Paris: CIEMI/L'Harmattan.

—— (1989) 'La place du droit dans le processus d'intégration des jeunes d'origine immigrée', in B. Lorreyte (sous la direction de) *Les Politiques d'Intégration des Jeunes Issus de l'Immigration*, Paris: CIEMI/L'Harmattan.

Bruschi, C. and Bruschi, M. (1984) 'Le pouvoir des guichets', *Les Temps Modernes* 'L'immigration maghrébine en France. Les faits et les mythes' 452-3-4: 2019–30.

Bulletin GIP (1971).

Bunyan, T. (1991) 'Towards an authoritarian European state', *Race and Class* 32, 3: 19–27.

Calame, P. and Calame, P. (1972) *Les Travailleurs Etrangers en France*, Paris: Editions Ouvrières.

Calvez, C. (1969) 'Extraits du Rapport de Corentin Calvez sur le problème des travailleurs étrangers', *Hommes et Migrations* 768: 1–13.

Castles, S. and Kosack, G. (1973) *Immigrant Workers and Class Structure in Western Europe*, 2nd edn, Oxford: Oxford University Press, 1985.

Centre for Contemporary Cultural Studies (CCCS) (1982) *The Empire Strikes Back: Race and Racism in 70s Britain*, London: Hutchinson.

Centre d'Information sur le Développement (1972) 'Les idées reçues concernant les travailleurs immigrés', *CCFD-CIMAD*, October.

Charlot, B. (1989) 'L'intégration scolaire des jeunes d'origine immigrée', in B. Lorreyte (sous la direction de) *Les Politiques d'Intégration des Jeunes Issus de l'Immigration*, Paris: CIEMI/L'Harmattan.

Chevènement, J.-P. (1979) *Etre Socialiste Aujourd'hui*, Paris: Cana.

Citron, S. (1985) 'Interculturel et crise d'identité nationale: vers une laïcité ouverte à la dimension pluriculturelle', in C. Clanet (préparé par) *L'Interculturel en Education et en Sciences Humaines*, tome 2, Toulouse: Université de Toulouse-le-Mirail.

—— (1988) 'Mémoire nationale, mémoire plurielle', *Hommes et Migrations* 1114: 17–24.

—— (1990) 'Retours d'un refoulé?', *Hommes et Migrations* 1129–30: 65–8.

Clanet, C. (préparé par) (1985) *L'Interculturel en Education et en Sciences Humaines* (2 tomes), Toulouse: Université de Toulouse-le-Mirail.

Clavairolle, F. (1987) *Inventaire et Bilan Critique. Population Immigrée et Société d'Accueil Française 1970–1985*, Paris: AFA.

Colonna, F. (1975) *Instituteurs Algériens: 1883–1939*, Paris: Presses de la Fondation Nationale des Sciences Politiques.

Commissariat Général du Plan (1988) *Immigrations: le Devoir d'Insertion* (2 tomes), Paris: La Documentation Française.

Commission de la Nationalité (1988) *Etre Français Aujourd'hui et Demain* (2 tomes), Paris: La Documentation Française.

Commission Nationale Consultative des Droits de l'Homme (1991) *La*

*Lutte Contre le Racisme et la Xénophobie*, Paris: La Documentation Française.

Conseil Economique et Social (1969) 'Avis adopté par le Conseil Economique et Social au cours de sa séance du 26 février 1969 sur le problème des travailleurs étrangers', *Hommes et Migrations* 767: 3–10.

—— (1983) *Le Travail Clandestin*, Paris: Journal Officiel.

Cordeiro, A. (1984) *L'Immigration*, Paris: La Découverte.

—— (1988) 'Pour la nouvelle citoyenneté: l'effet ha(l)logène', contribution aux 'Etats généraux de l'immigration: vers la nouvelle citoyenneté', St. Denis, 27–9 May.

Costa-Lascoux, J. (1985) 'Droits des immigrés, droits de l'Homme et politique de l'immigration', *Regards sur l'Actualité*, 113: 20–33.

—— (1986) 'Europe: les limites des politiques migratoires', *Actuel Développement* 70: 38–41.

—— (1987a) 'Discrimination et processus de différenciations identitaires: la part du droit', in AFA *Vers des Sociétés Pluriculturelles: Etudes Comparatives et Situation en France*, Paris: Editions de l'ORSTOM.

—— (1987b) 'L'acquisition de la nationalité française, une condition d'intégration?', in S. Laacher (sous la direction de) *Questions de Nationalité: Histoire et Enjeux d'un Code*, Paris: CIEMI/L'Harmattan.

—— (1989) *De L'Immigré au Citoyen*, Notes et Etudes Documentaires 4886, Paris: La Documentation Française.

—— (1990a) 'Perspectives "93"', *Accueillir* 165: 14–16.

—— (1990b) 'Equality and non-discrimination: ethnic minorities and racial discrimination', report for the Council of Europe, Strasbourg.

Coulon, C. (1979) 'Idéologie jacobine. Etat et ethnocide', *Pluriel* 17: 3–20.

*Différences* (1983) 26: September.

Dijoud, P. (1976) 'La politique de l'immigration', *Droit Social* 5: 3–5.

Dubet, F. (1989a) *Immigrations: qu'en Savons-nous? Un Bilan des Connaissances*, Notes et Etudes Documentaires 4887, Paris: La Documentation Française.

—— (1989b) 'Trois processus migratoires', *Revue Française des Affaires Sociales* 'L'insertion des immigrés', 3: 7–28.

Dumont, L. (1983) *Essais sur l'Individualisme*, Paris: Seuil.

Dupuy, J.-P. (1985) 'Egalité, science et racisme', *Le Débat* 37.

Eastwood, A. (1989) 'The need for a public debate', *Police* July.

Escaffit, J.-C. (1990) 'Immigrés: un défi pour l'Europe', *La Vie*, 1 February.

Espace 89 (1985) *L'Identité Française*, Paris: Editions Tierce.

*Ethnic and Racial Studies* (1991) 14, 3.

Etienne, B. (1989) *La France et l'Islam*, Paris: Hachette.

Fanon, F. (1952) *Peau Noire, Masques Blancs*, Paris: Seuil.

Faye, G. (1985) *Les Nouveaux Enjeux Idéologiques*, Paris: Le Labyrinthe.

Finkielkraut, A. (1987) *La Défaite de la Pensée*, Paris: Gallimard.

Freeman, G. (1979) *Immigrant Labor and Racial Conflict in Industrial Societies. The French and British Experience 1945–1975*, Princeton: Princeton University Press.

Fuchs, G. (1987) *Ils Resteront. Le Défi de l'Immigration*, Paris: Editions Syros.

Gaboriau, S. (1984) 'Entretien', *Les Temps Modernes* 'L'immigration maghrébine en France. Les faits et les mythes' 452-3-4: 2003-18.

Galissot, R. (1978) 'Le seuil d'intolérance', *Pluriel* 14: 73-9.

—— (1984a) 'Nationalisme français et racisme: à l'encontre d'idées reçues', *Politique Aujourd'hui* 'La France Plurielle' 4: 58-65.

—— (1984b) 'Le mixte Franco-Algérien', *Les Temps Modernes* 'L'immigration maghrébine en France. Les faits et les mythes', 452-3-4: 1707-25.

—— (1985a) *Misère de l'Antiracisme*, Paris: Arcantère.

—— (1985b) 'Un regard sur l'histoire: les générations de l'entre-deux-guerres', *Revue Européenne des Migrations Internationales* 1, 2: 55-65.

—— (1986) 'Nationalité et citoyenneté. Aperçus sur cette contradiction à travers l'évolution du nationalisme français', *Après-Demain* 286: 8-15.

—— (1987) 'Sous l'identité, le procès d'identification', *L'Homme et la Société* 'La mode des identités', 83: 12-27.

Gaspard, F. and Servan-Schreiber, C. (1985) *La Fin des Immigrés*, Paris: Seuil.

Gellner, E. (1983) *Nations and Nationalism*, Oxford: Blackwell.

*Le Genre Humain* (1986) 'La Science Face au Racisme' 1, Bruxelles: Editions Complexe.

Gilroy, P. (1987) *There Ain't no Black in the Union Jack*, London: Hutchinson.

Girard, A. (1977) 'Opinion publique, immigration et immigrés', *Ethnologie Française* (7) 3: 219-28.

Girard, A. and Stoetzel, J. (1953) *Français et Immigrés*, Paris: Presses Universitaires de France.

GISTI (1989) *La Nationalité Française. Comment l'Acquérir? Comment la Perdre?*, supplément au no. 8 de 'Plein Droit', October.

Gollot, A. P. (1990) 'Droits acquis et manqués à combler', *Accueillir* 165: 13.

Gomane, J.-P. (1983) 'Avant-propos', in 'Les réfugiés dans le monde', *Problèmes Politiques et Sociaux* 455: 3-5.

Grillo, R. (1991) 'Les chargeurs sont dans la rue!: racism and trade unions in Lyons', in M. Silverman (ed.) *Race, Discourse and Power in France*, Aldershot: Avebury.

Griotteray, A. (1984) *Les Immigrés: le Choc*, Paris: Plon.

Guillaumin, C. (1972) 'Caractères spécifiques de l'idéologie raciste', *Cahiers Internationaux de Sociologie* LIII: 247-74.

—— (1984a) 'Avec ou sans race', in 'La Société Face au Racisme', *Le Genre Humain* 11, Bruxelles: Editions Complexe.

—— (1984b) 'Immigrationsauvage', *Mots* 'L'Autre, l'Etranger. Présence et Exclusion dans le Discours', 8: 43-51.

—— (1986) '"Je sais bien mais quand même" ou les avatars de la notion "race"', in 'La Science Face au Racisme', *Le Genre Humain* 1, Bruxelles: Editions Complexe.

—— (1991) '"Race" and discourse', in M. Silverman (ed.) *Race, Discourse and Power in France*, Aldershot: Avebury.

Guiral, M. (1977) 'Vue d'ensemble sur l'idée de race et la gauche française', in P. Guiral and E. Temime (présenté par) *L'idée de Race dans la Pensée Politique Française Contemporaine*, Paris: Éditions du CNRS.

Hall, S., Critcher, C., Jefferson, T., Clarke, J. and Roberts, B. (1978) *Policing the Crisis: Mugging, the State and Law and Order*, London: Macmillan.

Hannoun, M. (1987) *L'Homme est l'Espérance de l'Homme*, report on racism and discrimination in France to the Secrétaire d'Etat auprès du Premier Ministre chargé des Droits de l'Homme, Paris: La Documentation Française.

Hargreaves, A. G. (1987) *Immigration in Post-War France. A Documentary Anthology*, London: Methuen.

Haut Conseil à l'Intégration (1991) *Premier Rapport*.

Henry-Lorcerie, F. (1989a) 'L'intégration scolaire des jeunes d'origine immigrée en France', in B. Lorreyte (sous la direction de) *Les Politiques d'Intégration des Jeunes Issus de l'Immigration*, Paris: CIEMI/L'Harmattan.

—— (1989b) 'L'universalisme en cause? Les équivoques d'une circulaire sur la scolarisation des enfants immigrés', *Mots* 18, 38–56.

Hessel, S. (1976) 'Une politique culturelle avec les immigrés', *Droit Social* 5: 178–180.

Hobsbawm, E. J. (1990) *Nations and Nationalism since 1780*, Cambridge: Cambridge University Press.

*Hommes et Migrations*. *Etudes* (1971) 'Les travailleurs étrangers dans les diverses commissions du VIe Plan', 118.

Icart, F. (1976) *Le Coût Social des Travailleurs Etrangers en France: Note de Synthèse*, Paris: Assemblée nationale.

INSEE (1983) *Les Etrangers en France: Contours et Caractères*, Paris: La Documentation Française.

Jacquard, A. and Pontalis, J.-B. (1984) 'Entretien: une tête qui ne revient pas', in 'La Société Face au Racisme', *Le Genre Humain* 11, Bruxelles: Editions Complexe.

Kennedy-Brenner, C. (1979) *Les Travailleurs Etrangers et les Politiques d'Immigration: Le Cas de la France*, Paris: Centre de Développement, OCDE.

Krulik, J. (1988) 'Nos mythes fondateurs sous une autre lumière', *Projet* 210: 67–73.

Kundera, M. (1983) 'Afterword: a talk with the author by Philip Roth', in *The Book of Laughter and Forgetting*, Harmondsworth: Penguin.

Lapeyronnie, D. (1987) 'Assimilation, mobilisation et action collective chez les jeunes de la seconde génération de l'immigration maghrébine', *Revue Française de Sociologie* XXVIII: 287–318.

—— (1989) 'Les jeunes d'origine immigrée, acteurs de leur intégration', in B. Lorreyte (sous la direction de) *Les Politiques d'Intégration des Jeunes Issus de l'Immigration*, Paris: CIEMI/L'Harmattan.

Layton-Henry, Z. (ed.) (1990) *The Political Rights of Migrant Workers in Western Europe*, London: Sage.

Lebon, A. (1988) 'La présence étrangère en Europe occidentale. Dénombrement et méthode', *Revue Française d'Administration Publique*, 'Immigration' 47: 27–35.

—— (1989) *Immigrés et Etrangers en France: Tendances 1988/mi–1989*,

Ministère de la Solidarité, de la Santé et de la Protection Sociale, Paris: La Documentation Française.

Le Bras, H. (1988a) 'Les projections démographiques relatives aux étrangers', reprinted in Commissariat Général du Plan (1988) *Immigrations: le Devoir d'Insertion*, 1 'Synthèse', Paris: La Documentation Française.

—— (1988b) 'Le peuplement de la France et son identité', *CIMADE Information*, 2 February: 15–17.

—— (1989) 'Le spectre des ghettos', in Documents Observateur *L'Europe Multiraciale* 4: 161–4.

Le Bras, H. and Todd, E. (1981) *L'Invention de la France*, Paris: Hachette-Pluriel.

Leca, J. (1983) 'Questions sur la citoyenneté', *Projet* 'Ces Etrangers qui Sont Aussi la France' 171–2: 113–25.

—— (1985) 'Une capacité d'intégration défaillante' (interview with Jean-Louis Schlegel), *Esprit* 'Français/Immigrés' 102: 9–23.

Le Club de l'Horloge (1985) *L'Identité de la France*, Paris: Albin Michel.

Le Gallou, J.-Y. (1985) *La Préférence Nationale: Réponse à l'Immigration*, Paris: Albin Michel.

Le Moigne, G. (1986) *L'Immigration en France*, Paris: Presses Universitaires de France.

Le Pors, A. (1976) *Immigration et Développement Economique et Social*, Paris: La Documentation Française.

*Lettre* (1973) 'Travailleurs immigrés en lutte contre les circulaires Fontanet et Marcellin' 117, March.

Lloyd, C. (1981) 'What is the French CP up to?', *Race and Class* 22, 4: 403–7.

Lloyd, C. and Waters, H. (1991) 'France: one culture, one people?', *Race and Class* 32, 3: 49–65.

Lochak, D. (1976) 'Observations sur un infra-droit', *Droit Social* 5: 43–9.

—— (1987) 'Immigration: glissements du discours et pratiques à la dérive', *GISTI* June, 1–41.

—— (1988) 'Etrangers et citoyens au regard du droit', in C. Wihtol de Wenden (coordonné par) *La Citoyenneté*, Paris: Edilig/Fondation Diderot.

Lorreyte, B. (1985) 'Identité et altérité. Une approche de l'hétérophobe', in C. Clanet (préparée par) *L'Interculturel en Education et en Sciences Humaines* (2 tomes), Toulouse: Université de Toulouse-Le-Mirail.

—— (1988) 'Français et immigrés: des miroirs ambigus', *Presse et Immigrés en France* 165–6.

MacMaster, N. (1991) 'The "seuil de tolérance": the uses of a "scientific" racist concept', in M. Silverman (ed.) *Race, Discourse and Power in France*, Aldershot: Avebury.

Malewska-Peyre, H. (1982) *Crise d'Identité et Déviance Chez les Jeunes Immigrés* (report to the Ministère de la Justice), Paris: La Documentation Française.

Mangin, S. (1982) *Travailleurs Immigrés. Le Bilan*, Paris: CIEM.

Marangé, J. and Lebon, A. (1982) *L'Insertion des Jeunes d'Origine Etrangère dans la Société Française* (report to the Ministre du Travail), Paris: La Documentation Française.

Marie, C.-V. (1988) 'La fonction idéologique de la notion de "clandestin"', *Hommes et Migrations* 1114: 133–8.

—— (1989) 'Le logement des étrangers', *Hommes et Migrations* 1127: 43–52.

—— (1990) 'Le prétexte clandestin', *Différences* September: 16–19.

Marie, C.-V. and Wihtol de Wenden, C. (1989) 'Droits civiques et action politique', *Migrations Société* 1, 1: 5–14.

Massenet, M. (1962) 'L'apport de la main-d'oeuvre d'origine algérienne au développement économique français', *Documents Nord-Africains* 471: 1–19.

—— (1968) 'Discours prononcé par M. Michel Massenet à la réunion du "Comité Lyautey" au Cercle Républicain le 30 novembre 1968', *Hommes et Migrations* (1969) 761: 1–10.

—— (1970) 'Les travailleurs étrangers en France. Un renfort nécessaire ou une source de conflits?', *Hommes et Migrations* 793: 19–25.

Mauco, G. (1932) *Les Etrangers en France*, Paris: A. Colin.

Memmi, A. (1982) *Le Racisme*, Paris: Gallimard.

—— (1985) *Portrait du Colonisé*, Paris: Gallimard.

Mestiri, E. (1990) *L'Immigration*, Paris: La Découverte.

*Migrations Société* (1989a) 'Dossiers Europe/1: Droits civiques et action politique' 1, 1.

*Migrations Société* (1989b) 'Dossiers Europe/2: Les politiques migratoires' 1, 2.

Miles, R. (1982) *Racism and Migrant Labour*, London: Routledge & Kegan Paul.

—— (1984) 'Marxism versus the sociology of "race relations"', *Ethnic and Racial Studies* 7, 2: 217–37.

—— (1987a) 'Racism and nationalism in Britain', in C. Husband (ed.) *'Race' in Britain: Continuity and Change*, London: Hutchinson.

—— (1987b) 'Recent Marxist theories of nationalism and the issue of racism', *British Journal of Sociology* 38, 1: 24–43.

—— (1989) *Racism*, London: Routledge.

Milza, O. (1988) *Les Français Devant l'Immigration*, Bruxelles: Editions Complexe.

Ministère des Affaires Sociales et de la Solidarité Nationale (1983) *Immigration Clandestine: la Régularisation des travailleurs 'sans papiers' (1981–1982)*, Bulletin Mensuel des Statistiques du Travail, supplément no. 106.

—— (1986) *1981–1986: Une Nouvelle Politique de l'Immigration*, Documents Affaires Sociales, Paris: La Documentation Française.

Ministère du Travail/Secrétariat d'Etat aux Travailleurs Immigrés (1977) *Immigration et 7e Plan*, 'Migrations et Sociétés', Paris: La Documentation Française.

Mission de Liaison Interministérielle pour la Lutte contre les Trafics de Main-d'oeuvre (1983) *Bilan de la Lutte Contre les Trafics de Main-d'oeuvre*, report to the Ministère des Affaires Sociales et de la Solidarité Nationale, Paris: La Documentation Française.

*Mots* (1986) 'Droite, nouvelle droite, extrême droite. Discours et idéologie en France et en Italie' 12.

—— (1989) 'Racisme et antiracisme: frontières et recouvrements' 18.

Mouriaux, R. and Wihtol de Wenden, C. (1988) 'Syndicalisme français et Islam', in G. Kepel and R. Leveau (sous la direction de) *Les Musulmans dans la Société Française*, Paris: Presses de la Fondation Nationale des Sciences Politiques.

Nair, S. (1984) 'Marseille: chronique des années de lèpre', *Les Temps Modernes* 'L'immigration maghrébine en France. Les faits et les mythes' 452-3-4: 1591–1615.

—— (1988) 'L'Immigration maghrébine: quelle intégration? quelle citoyenneté?', in C. Wihtol de Wenden (coordonné par) *La Citoyenneté*, Paris: Edilig/Fondation Diderot.

Nairn, T. (1977) *The Break-up of Britain: Crisis and Neo-nationalism*, London: New Left Books.

Noiriel, G. (1988a) *Le Creuset Français. Histoire de l'Immigration XIXe-XXe Siècles*, Paris: Seuil.

—— (1988b) 'Enseigner l'histoire de l'immigration', *Expression Français-Immigrés* 56: 4–7.

—— (1989) 'Les jeunes "d'origine immigrée" n'existent pas', in B. Lorreyte (sous la direction de) *Les Politiques d'Intégration des Jeunes Issus de l'Immigration*, Paris: CIEMI/L'Harmattan.

—— (1990) 'L'Héritage révolutionnaire', *Accueillir* 165: 6–10.

—— (1991) *La Tyrannie du National. Le Droit d'Asile en Europe 1973-1993*, Paris: Calmann-Lévy.

Nora, P. (1984) 'Entre mémoire et histoire', introduction to P. Nora (sous la direction de) *Les Lieux de Mémoire*, vol. 1, 'La République', Paris: Gallimard.

Nordman, D. (1986) 'Des limites d'Etat aux frontières nationales', in P. Nora (sous la direction de) *Les Lieux de Mémoire*, vol. 2, 'La Nation'.

OCDE (1987) *L'Avenir des Migrations*, Paris: OCDE.

Ogden, P. (1989) 'International migration in the nineteenth and twentieth centuries', in P. Ogden and P. E. White (eds) *Migrants in Modern France*, London: Unwin Hyman.

Ogden, P. and White, P. E. (eds) (1989) *Migrants in Modern France*, London: Unwin Hyman.

Oriol, M., Sayad, A. and Vieille, P. (1985) 'Inverser le regard sur l'émigration-immigration', *Peuples Méditerranéens* 31-2: 5–21.

Perotti, A. (1985) *L'Immigration en France depuis 1900*, Paris: CIEMI.

—— (1986) 'Plaidoyer pour le droit du sol', *Presse et Immigrés en France* 139–40.

—— (1988) 'L'Immigration en France: son histoire, ses nouvelles réalités, ses nouveaux enjeux', in C. Wihtol de Wenden (coordonné par) *La Citoyenneté*, Paris: Edilig/Fondation Diderot.

Perotti, A. and Thepaut, F. (1983) 'A propos du discours institutionnel sur les clandestins: une politique "otage" d'une opinion publique désinformée', *Presse et Immigrés en France* 110: 1–6.

Perrot, M. (1989) 'Jeunesse et société en France (XVIIIe-XXe siècle)', in

B. Lorreyte (sous la direction de) *Les Politiques d'Intégration des Jeunes Issus de l'Immigration*, Paris: CIEMI/L'Harmattan.

Poliakov, L. (1977) 'Racisme et antisémitisme: bilan provisoire de discussions et essai de description', in P. Guiral and E. Temime (présenté par) *L'idée de Race dans la Pensée Politique Française Contemporaine*, Paris: Editions du CNRS.

Ponty, J. (1985) 'Une intégration difficile, les Polonais en France dans le premier vingtième siècle', *Vingtième Siècle* 7: 51–70.

Renan, E. (1990) 'What is a nation?' (translation of 'Qu'est qu'une nation?' by Martin Thom) in H. K. Bhabha (ed.) *Nation and Narration*, London: Routledge.

Rex, J. (1983) *Race Relations in Sociological Theory*, London: Routledge & Kegan Paul.

Rex, J. and Tomlinson, S. (1979) *Colonial Immigrants in a British City: A Class Analysis*, London: Routledge & Kegan Paul.

Richer, L. (1986) *Le Droit de l'Immigration*, Paris: Presses Universitaires de France.

de Rudder, V. (1980) 'La tolérance s'arrête au seuil', *Pluriel* 21: 3–13.

—— (1982) 'Vivent les ghettos?', *GRECO 13* 'Recherches sur les migrations internationales' 4–5: 52–67.

—— (1983) 'L'exclusion n'est pas le ghetto. Les immigrés dans les HLM', *Projet* 'Ces étrangers qui sont aussi la France' 171–2: 80–91.

Said, E. (1981) *Covering Islam*, London: Routledge & Kegan Paul.

Samuel, R. (ed.) (1989) *Patriotism: The Making and Unmaking of British National Identity*, London: Routledge.

Sauvy, A. (1948) 'Quelques aspects du problème des migrations', *Revue Internationale du Travail* LVIII, 1: 20–39.

Sayad, A. (1979) 'Qu'est-ce qu'un immigré?', *Peuples Méditerranéens* 7: 3–23.

—— (1983) 'Culture dominante, cultures dominées', *Projet* 'Ces étrangers qui sont aussi la France' 171–2: 34–49.

—— (1984a) 'Tendances et courants des publications en sciences sociales sur l'immigration en France depuis 1960', *Current Sociology* 32, 2: 219–304.

—— (1984b) 'Etat, nation et immigration: l'ordre national à l'épreuve de l'immigration', *Peuples Méditerranéens* 27–8: 187–205.

—— (1985) 'L'immigration algérienne en France, une immigration "exemplaire"', in J. Costa-Lascoux and E. Temime (eds) *Les Algériens en France: Genèse et Devenir d'une Migration*, Paris: Publisud.

—— (1986) '"Coûts" et "profits" de l'immigration. Les présupposés politiques d'un débat économique', *Actes de la Recherche en Sciences Sociales*, 61: 79–82.

—— (1987) 'Les immigrés algériens et la nationalité française', in S. Laacher (sous la direction de) *Questions de Nationalité: Histoire et Enjeux d'un Code*, Paris: CIEMI/L'Harmattan.

—— (1988) 'Immigration et naturalisation', in C. Wihtol de Wenden (coordonné par) *La Citoyenneté*, Paris: Edilig/Fondation Diderot.

Schain, M. (1985) 'Immigrants and politics in France', in J. S. Ambler (ed.)

*The French Socialist Experiment*, Philadelphia: Institute for the Study of Human Issues Press.

Schnapper, D. (1988) 'La nation comme communauté de culture', *Revue Française d'Administration Publique* 'Immigration' 47: 89–94.

—— (1991) *La France de l'Intégration. Sociologie de la Nation en 1990*, Paris: Gallimard.

Schor, R. (1985) *L'Opinion Française et les Etrangers en France 1919–1939*, Paris: Publications de la Sorbonne.

Schumann, M. (1969) 'La politique française d'immigration', *Revue de la Défense Nationale* 25: 933–40.

Secrétariat d'Etat aux Travailleurs Immigrés (1977) *La Nouvelle Politique de l'Immigration*, Paris: La Documentation Française.

Secrétariat d'Etat Chargé des Immigrés (1983) *Vivre Ensemble: les Immigrés Parmi Nous*, Paris: ONI.

Siblot, P. (1989) 'De l'anticolonialisme à l'antiracisme: de silences en contradictions', *Mots* 18: 57–73.

Silverman, M. (1988) 'Questions of nationality and citizenship in the 1980s', *Modern and Contemporary France* 34: 10–16.

—— (1989) '"Travailleurs immigrés" and international relations', in R. Aldrich and J. Connell (eds) *France in World Politics*, London: Routledge.

—— (1990a) 'The racialization of immigration: aspects of discourse from 1968–1981', *French Cultural Studies* 1, 2: 111–28.

—— (1990b) 'Peut-on être musulman et Français?', in M. Cornick (ed.) *Beliefs and Identity in Modern France*, Loughborough: Association for the Study of Modern and Contemporary France and European Research Centre.

—— (ed.) (1991) *Race, Discourse and Power in France*, Aldershot: Avebury.

—— (1991) 'Citizenship and the nation-state in France', *Ethnic and Racial Studies* 14, 3: 333–49.

Sivanandan, A. (1982) *A Different Hunger: Writings on Black Resistance*, London: Pluto Press.

*Sociologie du Sud-Est* (1975) 'Le "seuil de tolérance" aux étrangers', Colloque du CIRDOM, 5–6.

SOPEMI (1990) *Continuous Reporting System on Migration: 1989*, Paris: OECD.

Stasi, B. (1984) *L'Immigration, une Chance pour la France*, Paris: R. Laffont.

Sternhell, Z. (1977) 'Le déterminisme physiologique et racial à la base du nationalisme de Maurice Barrès et de Jules Soury', in P. Guiral and E. Temime (présenté par) *L'idée de Race dans la Pensée Politique Française Contemporaine*, Paris: Editions du CNRS.

—— (1983) *Ni Droite ni Gauche*, Paris: Seuil.

Taguieff, P.-A. (1985) 'L'identité française et ses ennemis. Le traitement de l'immigration dans le national-racisme français contemporain', *L'Homme et la Société* 77–8: 167–200.

—— (1987) 'Hétérophobie, hétérophilie. Note sur la difficulté de définir le racisme', in AFA (1987) *Vers des Sociétés Pluriculturelles: Etudes Comparatives et Situation en France*, Paris: Editions de l'ORSTOM.

—— (1988a) *La Force du Préjugé: Essai sur le Racisme et ses Doubles*, Paris: La Découverte.

—— (1988b) 'Les métamorphoses du racisme', *Hommes et Migrations* 1114: 114–28.

—— (1988c) 'De l'anti-socialisme au national-racisme. Deux aspects de la recomposition idéologique des droites en France', *Raison Présente* 88: 15–54.

—— (1989) 'Politisation de l'immigration et racisme: lectures', *Mots* 18: 97–103.

—— (1991) (sous la direction de) *Face au Racisme* (2 tomes), Paris: La Découverte.

Talha, L. (1985) 'Espace migratoire et espace national: opposition et convergence', in J. Costa-Lascoux and E. Temime (coordonnateurs) *Les Algériens en France: Genèse et Devenir d'une Migration*, Paris: Publisud.

Tapinos, G. (1975) *L'Immigration Etrangère en France (1946–1973)*, INED, Travaux et Documents 71.

Taylor, D. (1989) 'Citizenship and social power', *Critical Social Policy* 26, 9 (2): 19–31.

Thom, M. (1990) 'Tribes within nations: the ancient Germans and the history of modern France', in H. K. Bhabha (ed.) *Nation and Narration*, London: Routledge.

UNESCO (1983) *Vivre Dans Deux Cultures*, Paris: UNESCO.

Verbunt, G. (1973) 'Les immigrés contre les circulaires', *Projet* 76: 707–16.

—— (présenté par) (1984) *Diversité Culturelle, Société Industrielle, Etat National*, Paris: L'Harmattan.

*Vingtième Siècle* (1985) 'Etrangers, Immigrés, Français' 7.

Voisard, J. and Ducastelle, C. (1988) *La Question Immigrée dans la France d'Aujourd'hui*, Paris: Calmann-Lévy.

Weber, E. (1976) *Peasants into Frenchmen: the Modernization of Rural France 1870–1914*, Stanford: Stanford University Press.

Weil, P. (1990) 'La politique française d'immigration: au-delà du désordre', *Regards sur l'Actualité* 158: 3–22.

Wieviorka, M. (1991) *L'Espace du Racisme*, Paris: Seuil.

Wihtol de Wenden, C. (1978) 'Les immigrés et l'administration', *Hommes et Migrations Documents* 952: 4–18.

—— (1984) 'Questions sur la citoyenneté', *Les Temps Modernes* 'L'immigration maghrébine en France. Les faits et les mythes' 452-3-4: 1869–76.

—— (1985) 'L'émergence d'une force politique? Les conflits des immigrés musulmans dans l'entreprise', *Esprit* 'Français/Immigrés' 102: 222–31.

—— (1987) *Citoyenneté, Nationalité et Immigration*, Paris: Arcantère.

—— (1988a) *Les Immigrés et la Politique*, Paris: Presses de la Fondation Nationale des Sciences Politiques.

—— (coordonné par) (1988b) *La Citoyenneté*, Paris: Edilig/Fondation Diderot.

—— (1989) 'Les politiques d'immigration', *Migrations Société* 'Dossiers Europe/2: Les politiques migratoires' 1, 2: 9–17.

Wrench, J. (1990a) 'Employment and the labour market', *New Community* 16, 2: 275–87.

—— (1990b) 'Employment and the labour market', *New Community*, 16, 4: 575–83.

Yuval-Davies, N. (1991) 'The citizenship debate: women, the State and ethnic processes', *Feminist Review* 39: 58–68.

Zolberg, A. (1988) 'L'incidence des facteurs externes sur la condition des citoyens: approche comparative', in C. Wihtol de Wenden (coordonné par) *La Citoyenneté*, Paris: Edilig/Fondation Diderot.

# Index